The Treasure
of Grace

The Treasure of Grace

101 Nuggets of Truth About the Riches
of God's Grace for Consolation,
Meditative Reflection, Inspiration and
Instruction

by
Frank R. Shivers

LIGHTNING SOURCE
1246 Heil Quaker Blvd.
La Vergne, TN

Unless otherwise noted, Scripture quotations are from
The Holy Bible *King James Version*

Library of Congress Cataloging-in-Publication Data

Shivers, Frank R., 1949-
The Treasure of Grace / Frank Shivers
ISBN 978-1-878127-46-4

Library of Congress Control Number:
2021917849

Cover design by
Tim King

For Information:
Frank Shivers Evangelistic Association
P. O. Box 9991
Columbia, South Carolina 29290
www.frankshivers.com

Grace outweighs every thorn, tear, terror, threat and temptation.
     ~ Frank Shivers (2021)

Wonderful the matchless grace of Jesus,
   Deeper than the mighty rolling sea,
Higher than the mountain,
Sparkling like a fountain,
   All-sufficient grace for even me.
     ~ Haldor Lillenas (1918)

Publications by Frank R. Shivers

"We are not writing upon water but carving upon
imperishable material."[1] ~ C. H. Spurgeon

When the Rain Comes
The Treasure of Grace
Persecuted for Christ's Sake
Christian Basics 101
Grief Beyond Measure, but Not Beyond Grace
Grief Beyond Measure, but Not Beyond Grace (Funeral
    Home Version)
Growing Old, Honorably and Happily
The Wounded Spirit
The Wounded Spirit: Companion Workbook
Growing in Knowledge, Living by Faith
Marriage and Parenting Boosters
Caught Up to Heaven
Expositions of the Psalms (Three Volumes)
Life Principles from Proverbs
The Evangelism Apologetic Study Bible
Hot Buttons on Apologetics
Hot Buttons on Morality
Hot Buttons on Discipleship
The Pornography Trap
The Poison of Porn
Heavy Stuff
Heavy Stuff (Student Workbook)
Clear Talk to Students
Nuggets of Truth (Three Volumes)
Soulwinning 101
Spurs to Soulwinning
Evangelistic Preaching 101
Evangelistic Praying
The Evangelistic Invitation 101
The Minster and the Funeral
Revivals 101

Children's Sermons That Connect
Be Careful, Little Eyes
How to Preach Without Evangelistic Results (Pamphlet)
False Hopes of Heaven (Tract)
First Steps for New Believers (Tract)
The Goal Line Stand (Tract)
The Death Clock (Tract)

To

Paul Pender

In gratitude for his partnership in my ministry, abiding
friendship, and encouragement.

"I cannot navigate so huge a sea [grace]. My skiff is too small;
I can only coast along the shore. *But* we will swim in this sea
though we cannot fathom it, and feast at this table though we
cannot reckon up its costliness."[2]
~ C. H. Spurgeon

Jesus, I am resting, resting
          In the joy of what Thou art;
I am finding out the greatness
          Of Thy loving heart.
Thou hast bid me gaze upon Thee
          As Thy beauty fills my soul,
For by Thy transforming power,
          Thou hast made me whole.

Oh, how great Thy lovingkindness,
          Vaster, broader than the sea!
Oh, how marvelous Thy goodness
          Lavished all on me!
Yes, I rest in Thee, Beloved,
          Know what wealth of grace is Thine,
Know Thy certainty of promise
          And have made it mine.

Simply trusting Thee, Lord Jesus,
          I behold Thee as Thou art;
And Thy love, so pure, so changeless,
          Satisfies my heart;
Satisfies its deepest longings;
          Meets, supplies its ev'ry need;
Compasseth me round with blessings.
          Thine is love indeed.

Ever lift Thy face upon me
          As I work and wait for Thee;
Resting 'neath Thy smile, Lord Jesus,
          Earth's dark shadows flee.
Brightness of my Father's glory,
          Sunshine of my Father's face,
Keep me ever trusting, resting,
          Fill me with Thy grace.

~ Jean Sophia Pigott (1876)

Content

Preface

Alexander Maclaren spoke correctly in saying that "the word 'grace' has got to be worn threadbare and to mean next door to nothing in the ears and minds of a great many continual hearers of the Gospel."[3] It is a term that is used much, defined little, understood minimally and therefore robbed of much of its intrinsic value, meaning and magnificence to the believer. Andrew Murray explains, "Very frequently, the reason for this…is the limited meaning attached to the word *grace*. Just as we limit God Himself by our little or unbelieving thoughts of Him, so we limit His grace at the very moment we are delighting in terms like the 'riches of grace' and 'grace exceeding abundant.'"[4]

The Treasure of Grace is a comprehensive and concise theological handbook containing golden nuggets of grace extracted from the deep caverns of Holy Scripture, written to expand and enlarge the believers' understanding of the biblical doctrine of grace. Its format, relatively simple and short chapters highlighting the various facets of grace, make it an excellent meditative or devotional resource for edification ('growth in grace'—2 Peter 3:18), consolation (comfort and hope in sickness, sorrow and suffering), adoration (springboard to praise God for His marvelous grace) and instruction (teaching and mentoring manual). Various aspects of grace are repeated throughout for emphasis and clarity of understanding. Inspirational, theological and practical insight upon grace from the church's greatest conservative theologians and pastors is included (C. H. Spurgeon, J. C. Ryle, W. A. Criswell, John MacArthur, Warren Wiersbe, Charles Simeon, Alexander Maclaren, William Barclay, Albert Barnes, Adam Clarke, A. C. Dixon, A. W. Pink, G. Campbell Morgan, Robert Murray McCheyne, Oswald Chambers, and Matthew Henry).

May the Holy Spirit enhance the reader's understanding and application of God's amazing grace with the turn of each page. With Peter, my prayer for you is that "grace and peace [will] be multiplied unto you through the knowledge of God, and of Jesus our Lord" (2 Peter 1:2).

Help me, Savior, more each day
Gladly Thy sweet will obey,
More and more Thy love display;
Oh, help me grow in grace!

Purer, holier I would be,
From my sin completely free;
Draw me, Savior, nearer Thee
And help me grow in grace.

Out of dawning into light,
Out of groping into sight,
Out of weakness into might,
Oh, help me grow in grace!

Pressing on to win the prize,
Crown and throne before my eyes,
Let my soul's ambition rise;
And help me grow in grace. ~ E. S. Lorenz (1893)

1   Statement of Grace

J. Gresham Machen said, "The very center and core of the whole Bible is the doctrine of the grace of God."[5] "Even where the vocabulary of grace is absent, God's actions are suffused [permeated] with grace (Deuteronomy 7:6–9; Deuteronomy 32:10; Ezekiel 16:8; Isaiah 49:14–18)."[6] MacArthur states, "God's grace is older than history, reaching back before the creation of time itself. It is not merely poured out in the moment of salvation; it is evident throughout His eternal plan of redemption."[7] See Ephesians 1:4. One scholar writes, "Paul could not think of Christian truth and conduct apart from God's grace."[8] A summary of the whole of the Bible—Genesis to Revelation— is contained in its final verse: "The grace of our Lord Jesus Christ be with you all" (Revelation 22:21).

The Old Testament revealed God's grace and prepared man for its fuller revelation through Jesus Christ in the New Testament. It was manifested in the salvation of Noah's household through the Flood (Genesis 6:8), in granting Joseph strength to persevere (Genesis 50:20), in graciously guiding Moses amidst his doubting (Exodus 4:13), making Abraham righteous (Genesis 15:6), compassionately forgiving David though he committed adultery and murder (Psalm 32:1–2), granting pardon to the Israelites when they rebelled (Judges 10:16), and in provision of what was good to the upright and godly (Psalm 84:11).

Understanding the covenant or doctrine of grace is at the heart of the Christian faith. What is grace? Grace, although a much used word, is much misunderstood because it is much underdefined. Rick Warren says, "Grace is...the secret of Christian living."[9] Grace is the supernatural power of God enveloped in His lovingkindness, favor, blessing, and concern to supply man's need though it is undeserved and unmerited. Grace, distinctive of Christianity alone, "is the true grace of God" (1 Peter 5:12). Saith W. E. Vine about grace: "That which bestows or occasions pleasure, delight, or causes favorable regard; on the part of the bestower, the friendly disposition from which the kindly act proceeds, graciousness, lovingkindness, goodwill generally...especially with reference to the Divine favor or grace."[10] Grace is "a favor done without expectation of return; the absolutely free expression of the lovingkindness of God to men finding its only motive in the bounty and benevolence of the Giver; unearned and unmerited favor."[11] A historical document on the power of God's grace is the Westminster Confession of 1646. On the matter of grace, its authors write: "When God converts a sinner, and translates him into the state of grace, He frees him from his natural bondage under sin; and, by His grace alone, enables him freely to will and to do that which is spiritually good...."[12] Phillip Yancey says, "Grace is 'the last best word' that expresses the heart of the Gospel."[13]

Matthew Henry states, "Grace includes God's goodwill towards us and His good work upon us; and peace, all that inward comfort or outward prosperity which is really needful for us. They come from God the Father, as the Fountain, through Jesus Christ."[14] In an oft repeated sermon, G. Campbell Morgan said, "'My grace.' What is the meaning of this great word? Who shall answer that question? The word runs through the New Testament. We see it everywhere, first shining and flashing in revealed glory in the face of Jesus Christ....Grace is the fact of the heart of God."[15] "The Gospel is called the grace of God" (Acts 13:43).[16]

R. C. Sproul says, "The essence of grace is its voluntary free bestowal. As soon as it's a requirement, it's no longer grace."[17] Philip Yancey states, "Grace teaches us that God loves us because of who God is, not because of who we are. Categories of worthiness simply don't apply."[18] Grace is the active influence of the Holy Spirit in a person's life. Murray says, "Grace can actually give us strength every moment for whatever the Father wills us to be and do."[19] "Grace is God's favor," writes Warren Wiersbe, "to the undeserving. God in His mercy does not give us what we do deserve; God in His grace gives us what we don't deserve."[20] The means of grace is accessed by faith in the Lord Jesus Christ (Romans 5:2). Alexander Maclaren summarizes its meaning, stating, "The grace of God, in Paul's use of the words, which is the scriptural use of them generally, implies these two things which are connected as root and product—the active love of God, in exercise towards us low and sinful creatures, and the gifts with

2

which that love comes full charged to men. These two things, which at bottom are one, love and its gifts, are all, in the apostle's judgment, gathered up and stored, as in a great storehouse, in Jesus Christ Himself, and through Him are made accessible to us, and brought to bear upon us for the ennobling of our natures and the investing of us with graces and beauties of character, all strange to us apart from these."[21] Grace includes both the attitude and action of God toward sinful man (Numbers 6:25).

"The Lord may not give gold," says Spurgeon, "but He will give grace; He may not give gain, but He will give grace. He will certainly send us trial [or allow it], but He will give grace in proportion thereto. We may be called to labor and to suffer, but with the call there will come all the grace required."[22]

2   Spheres of Grace

The word *grace* is found in every New Testament book except: Matthew, Mark, 1 John and 3 John. It appears no less than 170 times in the Bible (131 times in the New Testament) and its five forms fall under three biblical spheres: the universal (all mankind), ungodly (sinner) and the godly (saint).

The universal sphere. Common grace is the indiscriminate benevolent acts of God toward *all* men (Acts 14:17 and Romans 2:4). God sends the rain upon the just and the unjust (Matthew 5:45). To all men God has "'not left himself without witness' anywhere; everywhere he has 'done good, and sent rain from heaven, and fruitful seasons, filling our hearts with food and gladness' (Acts 14:15–17), pouring out, with the lavish hand of Divine beneficence, beauty and plenty, love and joy, peaceful memories and inspiring hopes, onto the path and into the heart of man."[23] That's common grace (and evidence for God's existence that man often ignores). See Romans 1:20.

The ungodly sphere. Grace is provided to grant forgiveness of sin and reconciliation to God (Ephesians 2:7–10). Zodhiates says, "*Charis* (grace) is initially regeneration, the work of the Holy Spirit in which spiritual life is given to man and by which his nature is brought under the dominion of righteousness."[24] Lucado said, "Grace is the voice that calls us to change and then gives us the power to pull it off."[25] Bridges states, "Grace... expresses two complementary thoughts: God's unmerited favor to us through Christ, and God's divine assistance to us through the Holy Spirit."[26] Warfield says, "Grace is free sovereign favor to the ill-deserving."[27] It is grace that saves a person from all that's wrapped up in the word *sin:* meaninglessness, emptiness, separation and Hell. W. S. Plumer wrote, "Sin is slavery. Vice is bondage. Corruption loads us with fetters. Divine grace brings us out of prison, knocks off our chains, and sets us at large. The faculties of mind and heart and body never in so high a sense enjoy liberty as when renewed by God's Spirit."[28]

> Oh, the love that drew salvation's plan!
> Oh, the grace that brought it down to man!
> Oh, the mighty gulf that God did span
> At Calvary!
> ~ William Reed Newell (1868–1956)

There's an undocumented story told about C. S. Lewis attending a conference on comparative religions. The debate was regarding the uniqueness of Christianity. Numerous suggestions were voiced and rejected. Lewis then interjected, "What's unique about Christianity? Oh, that's easy. It's grace."[29] He is right. Grace distinguishes Christianity from all other religions in its condition (means) for rightness with God and forgiveness of sin. The faiths of the world say "do" this and that or "don't do" this or that to gain and keep salvation. Christianity says its "done" ("It is finished," John 19:30), come and freely receive. This free grace for reconciliation to God and justification from sin is unparalleled by other faiths (Ephesians 2:8–9).

The remaining facets of grace operate strictly in the *godly sphere*. "There is an element of sameness in all graces, just as water is water; but in many respects one kind of grace is not like another."[30] It will be these *differentials* of grace that primarily will be expounded upon in this volume. Preserving (keeping) grace secures the saved from sin's power and penalty (Romans

5:21); sanctifying grace sets the believer apart for God's purpose of holiness and enables growth in Christlikeness, holy conduct, spiritual disciplines and knowledge of the Word (Hebrews 10:14 and 1 Thessalonians 5:23); serving grace empowers the believers' use of their spiritual gifts (Hebrews 12:28; 1 Peter 4:10 and 1 Corinthians 12:4–31) to extend the kingdom of God (2 Corinthians 9:8 and Acts 14:3); and sustaining grace is the supernatural help of God given in times of need, hardship, suffering, sorrow, trouble, sickness (2 Corinthians 12:8–9). "Let us therefore come boldly unto the throne of grace, that we may obtain mercy, and find grace to help in time of need" (Hebrews 4:16). That is, as Vincent says, "Mercy for past sins; grace for future work, trial, and resistance to temptation."[31]

3   Source of Grace

One of God's great names is "the God of all grace" (1 Peter 5:10). Brown says, "It does not mean that God is gracious in His tendency or simply gracious by His nature, but that He Himself is the reservoir, the home, the source, the supply of grace in all its manifestations."[32] "The God of" means that He is the source of all grace. "All" refers to every kind of grace, the comprehensiveness of God's grace. That is, it is sufficient to help the believer at any time or place regardless of the need. Whatever the problem confronted, God has the remedy. See Ephesians 4:7 and John 1:14. Wuest states, "The phrase 'the God of all grace' speaks of God as the source of all spiritual comfort and help for every occasion."[33] See Exodus 34:6; Psalm 86:15; Psalm 103:8; Psalm 145:8 and Romans 5:15–17. And it also means "the God who loves us completely."[34]

> The phrase "the God of all grace" speaks of God as the source of all spiritual comfort and help for every occasion.
> K. S. Wuest

Spurgeon comments about grace: "No labor of man procures it; no effort of man can add to it. God is good from the simple necessity of His nature; God is love, simply because it is His essence to be so, and He pours forth His love in plenteous streams to undeserving, ill-deserving, Hell-deserving objects, simply because He 'will have mercy on whom He will have mercy, and He will have compassion on whom He will have compassion,' for it is not of him that willeth, nor of him that runneth, but of God that sheweth mercy. Do remember that this fountain of love has its spring in itself, not in you, nor in me, but only in the Father's own gracious, infinite heart of goodness."[35]

> It's all of grace, by Your sov'reign hand,
> Through His death which long before was planned,
> That we can come before Your throne
> And in Your presence stand.
> It's all of grace. ~ Isaac Watts (1674–1748)

Jesus possessed divine grace (lovingkindness, goodness, steadfast love) as an infant (Luke 2:40; John 1:14), grew in grace (Luke 2:52), spoke words of grace (Luke 4:22), and performed works of grace (Mark 2:1–12; Mark 7:31–37; Luke 13:10–17; Mark 1:40–45; Mark 5:25–26, Mark 6:34–44, John 8:2–11, etc.). Jesus exemplified and demonstrated grace from childhood to His death at Calvary (Galatians 1:4). "John testified [repeatedly] about Him and has cried out [testifying officially for the record, with validity and relevance], 'This was He of whom I said, "He who comes after me has a higher rank than I and has priority over me, for He existed before me."'" For out of His fullness [the superabundance of His grace and truth] we have all received grace upon grace [spiritual blessing upon spiritual blessing, favor upon favor, and gift heaped upon gift]" (John 1:15–16 AMP).

Jesus proclaimed Himself to be the *chief cornerstone*: "Because of God's grace to me, I have laid the foundation like an expert builder. Now others are building on it. But whoever is building on this foundation must be very careful. For no one can lay any foundation other than the one we already have—Jesus Christ" (1 Corinthians 3:10–11 NLT). Cornerstones often bear an inscription citing the occasion for the building's construction. The cornerstone of the church reads, "Christ also hath once suffered for sins, the just for the unjust, that he might bring us to

God, being put to death in the flesh, but quickened by the Spirit" (1 Peter 3:18).

> Christ is our cornerstone;
>> On him alone we build.
> With his true saints alone
>> The courts of Heaven are filled.
>
> On his great love
>> Our hopes we place
>> Of present grace
> And joys above.
>> ~ John Darwall (1837)

"All the grace," says Matthew Henry, "contained in [the Bible] is owing to Jesus Christ as our Lord and Savior; and, unless we consent to Him as our Lord, we cannot expect any benefit by Him as our Savior." "As grace is first from God, so it is continually from Him, as much as light is all day long from the sun, as well as at first dawn or at sunrising." So saith Jonathan Edwards.

Simeon states, "God is the only fountain of all grace. There is none in the creature which has not been derived from Him. But in him is 'all grace': converting, comforting, sanctifying, establishing grace. He is 'the God of' all grace; all kinds of it and all degrees are in Him. Whatever be the grace that we severally want, we shall find an inexhaustible fulness of it treasured up in Him. And if we ask of Him in terms of the most extensive import and then stretch our imaginations far beyond what it is in the power of language to express, it still will be true that 'he giveth more grace,' and giveth it freely too, according to His own sovereign will, even to the very chief of sinners."[36]

> Oh, the love that sought me!
> Oh, the blood that bought me!
> Oh, the grace that brought me to the flock,
> Wondrous grace that brought me to the flock!
>> ~ William Spencer Walton (1850–1906)

7

4   Site of Grace

In the Old Testament, the ark of the covenant was God's throne to Israel (Exodus 25:17–22); but it was not "a throne of grace," for it was concealed from the people (only the high priest could go beyond the veil on the Day of Atonement—Leviticus 16).[37] Warren Wiersbe says, "Grace does not veil itself from the people. Grace does not hide itself in a tent."[38] But to the "throne of grace" in Heaven, every believer is invited to enter boldly (through prayer) to make his needs known unto God. A. C. Dixon states, "A throne means power. Back of it stand the army and navy ready to support its claims. Back of it are all the wealth and prestige of the realm. Back of it is the life of every patriotic citizen. Back of it are all the alliances with friendly powers. The throne of grace means that GOD is now ruling in the power of His love and we have access to that power."[39]

The "throne of God" (Hebrews 4:16) is the place to obtain grace (the gracious help of God) in the time of need from any spot on earth (bedside, hospital, assisted living home, foxhole on a foreign field, prison, funeral home, ambulance, church). A throne is "the place from which authority or rule is exercised—'place of authority, place of ruling.'"[40] Lane says, "The 'throne of grace' is the place of God's presence, from which grace emanates to the people of God."[41] "It was at the throne of God," MacArthur states, "that Christ made atonement for sins, and it is there that grace is dispensed to believers for all the issues of life (2 Corinthians 4:15; 9:8; 12:9; Ephesians 1:7; 2:7)."[42] Matthew Henry says, "There [at the throne of God] grace reigns and acts with sovereign freedom, power, and bounty. It is our duty and interest to be often found before this throne of grace, waiting on the Lord in all the duties of His worship, private and public. It is good for us to be there."[43] Hebrews 8:1; 12:2. "Pleading our High Priest Jesus' meritorious death, we shall always find God on a throne of grace."[44]

Behold the throne of grace!
    The promise calls me near;
There Jesus shows a smiling face
    And waits to answer prayer.

That rich atoning blood,
  Which sprinkled round we see,
Provides for those who come to God
  An all-prevailing plea.

My soul, ask what thou wilt;
  Thou canst not be too bold.
Since His own blood for thee He spilt,
  What else can he withhold?

Beyond thy utmost wants
  His love and pow'r can bless;
To praying souls He always grants
  More than they can express.

~ John Newton (1779)

Coming to the throne of grace for help is a reflection and demonstration of the believers' trust in God's willingness and ability to meet their need, and a witness to the world of that confidence (Hebrews 11:6).

5 Superiority of Grace

Grace is superior to works. Matthew Henry says, "Man in his depraved state under the power of such corruption could never by any works of his own gain acceptance with God, but it must be resolved purely into the free grace of God given through Jesus Christ to all true believers that receive it as a free gift."[45] See Ephesians 2:8–9.

Grace is superior to the law. The purpose of the law (Ten Commandments) is to reveal sin, but it has no power to forgive it or reconcile the sinner to God (Romans 8:3–4). Grace alone enables man's trespass against God to be forgiven and enables him to be reconciled (made right) to Him (Romans 5:20).

The law demands a weighty debt,
And not a single mite will bate;
But Gospel sings of Jesus' blood
And says it made the payment good.

The law provokes men oft to ill,
And churlish hearts makes harder still;
But Gospel acts a kindly part
And melts a most obdurate heart.

"Run, John, and work," the law commands,
Yet finds me neither feet nor hands.
But sweeter news the Gospel brings;
It bids me fly and lends me wings.

Such needful wings, O Lord, impart,
To brace my feet and brace my heart;
Good wings of faith, and wings of love,
Will make the cripple sprightly move.

With these a lumpish soul may fly
And soar aloft and reach the sky,
Nor faint nor falter in the race,
But cheerly work and sing of grace.

~ John Berridge (1838)

Grace is superior to legalism. Legalism entangles man in bondage and fear with its insistence on conformity to rules, regulations and religious rituals to be acceptable to God, while grace brings freedom and liberty. Ferguson says, "Thus it's understanding God's grace—that is to say, understanding God Himself—that demolishes legalism. Grace highlights legalism's bankruptcy and shows that it's not only useless, it's pointless; its life breath is smothered out of it."[46] Don't live by a list of *do*s and *don't*s. All that man needs for reconciliation to God is provided at Calvary, not Sinai (Colossians 2:11–17).

Grace is superior to "religions," philosophies, and the help of man. Paul admonishes in Colossians 2:8, "Beware lest any man spoil [plunder, rob of the faith] you through philosophy [worldly speculation about God and the divine, mere human wisdom, counterfeit knowledge] and vain deceit [deceitful in its promises and premises], after the tradition of men [unauthorized teachings of Christ], after the rudiments of the world [the elementary 'principles or spirits,' which possibly refer to the demonic host who inspire such heresy, 2 Corinthians 4:3–4] and not after Christ [that is, Jesus' sinless life, blood atonement, and resurrection alone to secure man's salvation—grace]."[47] The text may be rendered, "Don't let anyone capture you with empty philosophies and high-sounding nonsense that come from human thinking and from the spiritual powers of this world, rather than from Christ" (NLT).

A story illustrates the superiority of grace over all things.

A man fell into a pit and couldn't get out. A SUBJECTIVE person came along and said, "I FEEL for you down there!" An OBJECTIVE person came along and said, "It's logical that someone would fall down there." A CHRISTIAN SCIENTIST came by and said, "You only think you are in the pit." A PHARISEE said, "Only bad people would fall into a pit. You deserve your pit." A MATHEMETICIAN calculated HOW he fell in the pit. A NEWS REPORTER wanted the exclusive story on his pit. CONFUCIOUS said, "If you would have listened to me, you would not have fallen into that pit." BUDDHA said, "Your pit is only a state of mind." A REALIST said, "That's a pit." A SCIENTIST calculated the pressure necessary (lbs./sq. in.) to get him out of the pit. A GEOLOGIST told him to appreciate the rock strata in the pit. AN EVOLUTIONIST said, "You are a rejected mutant destined to be removed from the evolutionary cycle. In other words, you are going to die in the pit, so you can't produce any pit-falling offspring." The COUNTY INSPECTOR asked if he had a permit to dig the pit. A PROFESSOR gave him a lecture on the elementary principles of the pit. An EVASIVE person came along and avoided the subject of pits all together. A SELF-PITYING person came along and said, "You haven't seen anything till you've seen *my* pit." A

SOUL WINNER, seeing the man, told him about Jesus who alone could deliver him from the pit. The man was saved, and now this man spends his time helping others out of their own pits.[48]

Only the grace of God can help the person in the pit of sin, despair, adversity and affliction. The psalmist testifies, "He brought me up also out of an horrible pit, out of the miry clay, and set my feet upon a rock, and established my goings" (Psalm 40:2). Whatever may be your present pit, grace is more than capable to grant relief and rescue. Hammond says, "That grace will carry us, if we do not willfully betray our succors [support], victoriously through all difficulties."[49]

> Through grace He lifted me.
> From sinking sand, He lifted me;
> With tender hand He lifted me.
> From shades of night to plains of light,
> Oh, praise His name, He lifted me!
>
> ~ Chas. H. Gabriel (1905)

"Divine grace is not a limp, shallow attribute, but one of glorious riches, deserving infinite praise."[50] See Ephesians 2:7.

6   Stages of Grace

Any work on the subject of grace would be amiss to exclude reference to John Newton's classic hymn "Amazing Grace," which was unveiled publicly to a rural church congregation on January 1, 1773 (published 1779).[51] Each stanza of the hymn pictures the operation of God's grace. Stanzas one and two, the past deliverance of grace (forgiveness and salvation). Stanzas three and four, the present deliverance of grace ("help in the hour of need" to cope with various temptations, troubles, trials and empowerment to live and serve victoriously). Stanzas five to seven, the future deliverance of grace (liberation from the body of decay and sin by replacing it with an incorruptible body [resurrection] similar to that of Christ's resurrected body and transition to the eternal abode of Heaven). That is, *justification* (salvation)—stanzas one and two; *sanctification* (holiness), *alleviation* (help), and *preservation* (security)—stanzas three and four; *glorification* (Heaven)—stanzas five to seven (Psalm 84:11).

Amazing grace! How sweet the sound
    That saved a wretch like me!
I once was lost, but now am found;
    Was blind, but now I see.

'Twas grace that taught my heart to fear,
    And grace my fears relieved.
How precious did that grace appear
    The hour I first believed!

Through many dangers, toils and snares
    I have already come;
'Tis grace hath brought me safe thus far,
    And grace will lead me home.

The Lord has promised good to me;
    His Word my hope secures.
He will my Shield and Portion be
    As long as life endures.

Yea, when this flesh and heart shall fail
    And mortal life shall cease,
I shall possess, within the veil,
    A life of joy and peace.

The earth shall soon dissolve like snow;
    The sun forbear to shine.
But God, Who called me here below,
    Will be forever mine.

When we've been there ten thousand years,
    Bright shining as the sun,
We've no less days to sing God's praise
    Than when we'd first begun.

~ John Newton (1779)

13

7   Scope of Grace

Grace, the loving-kindness and compassion of God that supernaturally works in man's behalf, is God's response to man's every sin, sorrow, trial, and need. It stands taller than the highest mountain, deeper than the deepest sea, and wider than the widest ocean. It is without limitation, deficiency, or inadequacy. Its boundaries are immeasurable (universally available) and supply inexhaustible. Asia is 5,000 miles wide, the Nile River exceeds 4,000 miles in length, Mount Everest is more than 29,000 feet high, and the Pacific Ocean is at one point about 7 miles deep. But the love and grace of God is wider than Asia, longer than the Nile River, taller than Mount Everest, and deeper than the Pacific Ocean. See Ephesians 3:18–19.

T. Dewitt Talmage writes, "Oh, this mercy of God! I am told that it is an ocean. Then I place four swift-sailing crafts with compass and charts and choice rigging and skilled navigators, and I tell them to launch away for me and discover the extent of this ocean. That craft puts out in one direction and sails to the north, this to the south, this to the east, and this to the west. They crowd on all their canvas and sail ten thousand years and one day come up the harbor of Heaven, and I shout to them from the beach, 'Have you found the shore?' They answer, 'No shore to God's mercy.' Swift angels dispatched from the throne attempt to go across it. For a million years they fly and fly, but they come back and fold their wings at the feet of the throne and cry, 'No shore! No shore to God's mercy.'"[52] Yancey said, "We can never sink so far that God's grace will not reach us. At the same time, grace does not leave us there. It raises us to new heights."[53] See Psalm 40:2–3.

> It is folly to think the Lord provides grace for every trouble but the one you are in today.
> C. H. Spurgeon

Spurgeon says, "It is folly to think the Lord provides grace for every trouble but the one you are in today."[54] Whatever the trouble, sin, pain or sickness, grace is Heaven's effectual source of rescue, remedy, coping or endurance. There has yet to be a need that divine grace has been unable to meet—nor shall there ever be.

> I walk today in the Christian way,
>> Though dangers I may see;
> I will not fear for the Lord is near,
>> And He will care for me.
>
> No matter what happens, He will care for me,
>> He will care for me, He will care for me;
> And His mighty hand will enable me to stand,
>> No matter what happens to me.
>
> No test I face but sufficient grace
>> Is ready for my need;
> When sorrows rise to obscure my skies,
>> He proves a friend indeed.
>
> He will not fail in the strongest gale
>> That stormy winds can blow,
> And in His grace is a hiding place
>> Unknown to any foe.
>
> I trust in Him though disasters grim
>> Before me seem to be;
> He calms my fears, and He dries my tears,
>> And faithful is to me.
>
> ~ Charles W. Naylor (1919)

8   Splendor of Grace

Paul calls the grace of God a 'glorious or wondrous grace' (Ephesians 1:6). Its splendor and magnificence are revealed in the treasure (the riches of God) it affords to the child of God (Ephesians 1:7). In 1 Corinthians 1:5–7 Paul states that the Corinthian saints in every way were *enriched* ("spiritual enrichment; cause to have an abundance"[55]) without any deficiency by His grace. A Spanish ambassador visiting the

15

French ambassador in the prosperous days of Spain, was shown the vast treasures of the King. With pride the repositories were displayed which were abundantly stored with earth's most precious and most costly wealth. "Could you show gems so rich," he asked of the Spanish ambassador, "or aught the like of this for magnificence of possessions in all the king's kingdom?" "Call your king rich?" replied the ambassador of Spain. "Why, my King's treasures have no bottom," alluding, of course, to the mines of Peru and Petrosa.[56]

The riches of God's grace in Christ Jesus to His children is a "mine" unfathomable in depth, undiminishable in content, and incalculable in value. Its best description or explanation falls short of its actuality.

"According to the riches of his grace" (Ephesians 1:7). "Riches denote superfluity, or what abounds, or which exceeds a man's present desires; and hence, the word in the New Testament is used to denote abundance, or what is very great and valuable."[57] That is, the treasure of grace greatly exceeds in value and benefit that which is man's need. Whatever the need, God, "according to His riches" ("in proportion to"), will make provision (regardless of the amount of grace needed). However heavy the need, grace always outweighs it. Note, Paul says, "according to his riches," not "out of his riches." The latter would be like a billionaire giving a hundred dollars to the church, as it would be "out of" his riches, whereas the former means to give "in proportion to" one's riches.

> However heavy the need, grace always outweighs it.

Well of water ever springing, Bread of Life so rich and free,
Untold wealth that never faileth, my Redeemer is to me.
~ Clara T. Williams (1875)

In Christ we have an infinite treasury of grace to meet every difficulty, challenge, crisis, heartache, sorrow, pain and failure, as well as needed wisdom, guidance, peace, discernment, strength and power. His grace is sufficient for our every trial and need. With greater knowledge of and intimacy with God comes enhanced understanding of His riches of grace and its appropriation and enjoyment. See 2 Peter 3:18. Spurgeon says, "Value every part of the work of divine grace because it came from God and leads to God. God's gifts are always worthy of the Giver. God gives not trinkets and counterfeits—His gifts are solid gold and lasting treasure. The gifts of divine grace have a quality of divinity about them—they are all God-like."[58]

The splendor and triumph of grace is seen in its bestowal of full and spontaneous forgiveness, removal of the oppressive burden of sin, granting of a peaceful conscience and assurance that all sins are once and for all forgiven.[59] Tozer said, "On the basis of grace as taught in the Word of God, when God forgives a man, He trusts him as though he had never sinned."[60]

Its splendor is also seen in its implantation of a new nature with new principles and disciplines for the governing of life, strength, consolation and perseverance in trial and service, and the inheritance which it grants in Heaven of rest from labor, tranquility after agitation, deliverance from temptation, pain, suffering and sorrow, elevation to the highest of all positions of honor and an unfading crown and the complete and glorious resurrection of the body made into the likeness of our Christ.[61]

> When through the deep waters I call you to go,
> The rivers of sorrow shall not overflow,
> For I will be with you, your troubles to bless,
> And sanctify to you the deepest distress.
>
> When through fiery trials your pathway shall lie,
> My grace, all sufficient, shall be your supply.
> The flames shall not hurt you. I only design
> Your dross to consume and your gold to refine.
>
> The soul that on Jesus doth lean for repose,
> I will not, I will not desert to its foes.
> That soul, though all Hell should endeavor to shake,
> I'll never, no, never, no, never forsake!
> ~ attributed to George Keith (1787)

9   Substance of Grace

The core of grace is the loving-kindness and care of God supernaturally dispatched to His children through the Holy Spirit to provide help in the hour of need (Romans 8:26). While grace is undivided, attached to its core are innumerable and varied tentacles. (As mentioned before, the foundational tentacle of grace is forgiveness of sin and reconciliation to God through Christ Jesus, but here I address specifically its assistance and enablement to the saints.)

The tentacle of consolation in grief and sorrow. "He healeth the broken in heart, and bindeth up their wounds" (Psalm 147:3). Spurgeon says, "Christian, remember the goodness of God in the frost of adversity." Rutherford said, "Grace grows best in winter."

The tentacle of boldness in fear. "I sought the LORD, and he heard me, and delivered me from all my fears" (Psalm 34:4). Grace makes the "righteous...bold as a lion" (Proverbs 28:1).

The tentacle of enablement in service. "But unto every one of us is given grace according to the measure of the gift of Christ" (Ephesians 4:7). Whatever the ministry task, grace is supplied to enable its accomplishment. Its measure is in proportion to the need. There is no demand placed upon the servant that is not also placed upon the Holy Spirit within him to provide the needed grace for successfully undertaking it.

The tentacle of endurance in suffering and illness. "But he said to me, 'My grace is enough for you. When you are weak, my power is made perfect in you'" (2 Corinthians 12: 9 NCV). Where healing is delayed or denied for God's divine purposes and our best good, persevering grace is dispensed. Grace lives not only in the pleasantries of life but also in its painful places. In hospital rooms, funeral parlors, doctors' offices, prisons, divorces, bitter suffering, sickness and disappointments, grace enables us to stand through the worst and hardest circumstances.

The tentacle of care in loneliness. "When my father and my mother forsake me [or my spouse is taken from me to Heaven], then the Lord will take me up" (Psalm 27:10). God's caring grace will encompass the widow, the abandoned child and forsaken parent, assuring His sovereign presence and their provision for every need. He is to them a sheltering presence that is safe and reliable (Psalm (27:9–10). "For I, the Lord your God, will hold your right hand, saying to you, 'Fear not, I will help you'" (Isaiah 41:13 NKJV). He that holds God's hand is never alone or without care. Spurgeon said, "O for grace to see our future glory amid present shame! Indeed, there is a present glory in our afflictions."[62] Grace sees to that.

The tentacle of guidance in loss of direction. Matthew Henry comments, "Sometimes those that are much in care to walk right are in doubt, and in the dark, which is the right way. Let them come boldly to the throne of grace and beg of God, by His word and Spirit and providence, to show them the way and prevent their missing it. A good man does not ask what is the way in which he must walk, or in which is the most pleasant walking, but what is the right way, the way in which he should walk."[63]

The tentacle of tranquility when anxious. "In the multitude of my thoughts [anxiety] within me thy comforts delight [soothe] my soul" (Psalm 94:19). Within the treasure chest of grace is grace sufficient to repel, and thereby grant relief from, the believers' anxiety, stress, and worry, granting a peace that surpasses all understanding (Philippians 4:6–7).

The tentacle of peace amidst the storm. God bestows calming and strengthening grace in trials and troubles (Job 35:10). Matthew Henry states, "He gives songs in the night; that is, when our condition is ever so dark and sad and melancholy, there is that in God, in His providence and promise, which is sufficient not only to support us, but to fill us with joy and consolation and enable us in everything to give thanks and even to rejoice in tribulation."[64]

The tentacle of strength in temptation. "The Lord knoweth how to deliver the godly out of temptations" (2 Peter 2:9). Through Christ, the believer is able to cast down every stronghold of the enemy and thwart his advances into their lives (Philippians 4:13).

The tentacle of deliverance from sin's captivity. Jesus said, "If the Son therefore shall make you free, ye shall be free indeed" (John 8:36). Grace can deliver from and keep the believer from bondage to any sin.

The tentacle of holy consolation in the hour of death. "Yea, though I walk through the valley of the shadow of death, I will fear no evil: for thou art with me; thy rod and thy staff they comfort me" (Psalm 23:4). We don't have to cross Jordan alone. G. Campbell Morgan reminds us, "He [God] is nigh when He seems absent. He is watching when He seems blind. He is active when He seems idle."[65]

> And when my task on earth is done,
> When, by Thy grace, the victory's won,
> E'en death's cold wave I will not flee,
> Since God through Jordan leadeth me.
> ~ Joseph H. Gilmore (1862)

F. B. Meyer says, "The soul in the dark valley becomes aware of another at its side."[66] "In that silent chamber of yours," says C. H. Spurgeon, "there sitteth by your side One whom thou hast not seen, but whom thou lovest. Thy friend sticks closely to thee. Thou canst not see Him, but thou mayest feel the pressure of His hands. Dost thou not hear His voice?"[67] W. S. Plumer remarks, "He who gives grace to His chosen to live to His glory will not deny them grace to die in His peace."[68]

> There's been grace for every trial.
> There's been grace for every mile.
> There's been grace sufficient from His vast supply.
> Grace to make my heart more tender,
> Grace to love and pray for sinners,
> But there'll be new grace when it's my time to die.
> ~ Tom Hayes

Space, but even more so knowledge, hinders inclusion of all the treasured tentacles of grace, for they are new every morning (Lamentations 3:23), continuously enlarged (James 4:6), and in part unknown until their hour of need (Ephesians 4:7).

10 Sufficiency of Grace

The apostle Paul besought the Lord three times for the removal of the 'thorn in his flesh" (2 Corinthians 12:7–8). Although Paul's prayer was not answered as desired, sufficient grace was given to support him. God told him, "My grace is sufficient for thee: for my strength is made perfect in weakness" (2 Corinthians 12:9). Paul was satisfied with that answer once he understood the thorn had a divine purpose. His experience provides four invaluable lessons relating to divine grace.

First, prayers (even the godliest) are not always literally answered. See 2 Samuel 12:16–20.

Second, when prayers are not answered as wished, sufficient grace (supernatural help of God) is supplied to manage, undergird, and comfort in the wailing tide. Isaiah says, "The Lord will guide you continually, and satisfy your soul in drought, and strengthen your bones; you shall be like a watered garden, and like a spring of water, whose waters do not fail" (Isaiah 58:11 NKJV).

Third, in times when the "thorn" is not removed, God will use it to the believer's benefit (2 Corinthians 12:7; Romans 8:28). Barnes says, "The grace that will be imparted if the calamity is not removed will be of greater value to the individual than would be the direct answer to his prayer. Such was the case with Paul [it humbled him]; so it was doubtless with David, and so it is often with Christians now. The removal of the calamity might be apparently a blessing, but it might also be attended with danger to our spiritual welfare; the grace imparted may be of permanent value and may be connected with the development of some of the loveliest traits of Christian character."[69] Billy Graham stated it thus: "The will of God will not take us where the grace of God cannot sustain us."[70]

Fourth, the Lord promises His constant love and favor and companionship through the entire ordeal so that in our 'weakness we are made strong' (2 Corinthians 12:9). Matthew Henry writes, "Though God accepts the prayer of faith, yet He does not always give what is asked for: as He sometimes grants in wrath, so He sometimes denies in love. When God does not take away our troubles and temptations, yet if He gives grace enough for us, we have no reason to complain. Grace signifies the good will of God toward us, and that is enough to enlighten and enliven us, sufficient to strengthen and comfort in all afflictions and distresses."[71]

G. Campbell Morgan said, "'My grace is sufficient for thee.' Upon that great word many a weary head has rested; many wounded hearts have been healed by it; discouraged souls have heard its infinite music and have set their lives to new endeavor until they have become victorious."[72]

> I'll sing of the wonderful promise
> That Jesus has given to me:
> "My strength is made perfect in weakness;
> My grace is sufficient for thee."
>
> His grace is sufficient to save me
> And cleanse me from guilt and from sin,
> Sufficient to sanctify wholly
> And give me His Spirit within.
>
> His grace is sufficient for trials,
> No matter how hard they may be;
> This promise stands over against them:
> "My grace is sufficient for thee."
>
> His grace is sufficient for sickness,
> Sustaining and making me whole;
> His grace is sufficient when sorrows
> Like billows roll over the soul.
>
> His grace is sufficient for service;
> It sets us from selfishness free
> And sends us to tell to the tried ones,
> "His grace is sufficient for thee."
>
> His grace is sufficient to live by,
> And should we be summoned to die,
> 'Twill light up the valley of shadows
> And bear us away to Him nigh.

Or when we shall stand in His vict'ry
　　And Christ in His glory shall see,
We'll fall at His footstool confessing,
　　"Thy grace was sufficient for me."

It is not our grace that's sufficient,
　　But His grace it ever must be.
Our graces are transient and changing;
　　His grace is unfailing as He.

And so I am ever repeating
　　His wonderful promise to me:
"My strength is made perfect in weakness,
　　My grace is sufficient for thee."
　　　　　　　~ Albert Benjamin Simpson (1843–1919)

"There is a fulness of blessings," states Spurgeon, "of every sort and shape: a fulness of grace to pardon, of grace to regenerate, of grace to sanctify, of grace to preserve, and of grace to perfect. There is a fulness at all times, a fulness of comfort in affliction, a fulness of guidance in prosperity. A fulness of every divine attribute: of wisdom, of power, of love; a fulness which it was impossible to survey, much less to explore. "It pleased the Father that in him should all fulness dwell."[73] See also Colossians 2:9. Thompson summarizes the all sufficiency of divine grace: "There is grace to blot out your trespasses, though they be 'red like crimson.' There is grace to purify your hearts, though they be full of all uncleanness. There is grace to subdue your enemies, though they 'come upon you as a flood.' There is grace to console you amidst all your sorrows, though they be great, and multiplied, and protracted. There is grace to guide you through life, to cheer you at death, and to carry you to Heaven."[74] There is no shortage of grace.

And should I die with mercy sought,
　　When I his grace have tried,
I sure should die—delightful thought!—
　　Where sinner never died![75]

11 Satisfaction of Grace

"Therefore, with joy shall ye draw water out of the wells of salvation" (Isaiah 12:3). Frederick North (Lord North) asked Rev. Fletcher of Madeley what he might do to help him. The minister requested but one thing, something that was not in the prime minister's power to give. The request was that he might be given more grace.[76] Fletcher treasured grace above the riches and powers of Great Britain! All who taste of God's grace will be of the same mind and disposition, for it satisfies and delights with inward peace and strength inexpressible, unimaginable, and unfathomable.

This is why, as Thomas Brooks wrote, "Souls that are rich in grace labor after greater measures of grace out of love to grace, and because of an excellency that they see in grace. Grace is a very sparkling jewel, and he who loves it and pursues after it for its own native beauty has much of it within him."[77] And M'Cheyne says, "It is a sure mark of grace to desire more." Upon tasting of grace, the believer will pine for more. See Psalm 34:8.

> The cross that He gave may be heavy,
>   But it ne'er outweighs His grace;
> The storm that I feared may surround me,
>   But it ne'er excludes His face.
>
> The thorns in my path are not sharper
>   Than composed His crown for me;
> The cup that I drink not more bitter
>   Than He drank in Gethsemane.
>
> The light of His love shineth brighter,
>   As it falls on paths of woe;
> The toil of my work groweth lighter,
>   As I stoop to raise the low.
>
> His will have I joy in fulfilling,
>   As I'm walking in His sight.
> My all to the blood I am bringing;
>   It alone can keep me right.

The cross is not greater than His grace;
The storm cannot hide His blessed face.
I am satisfied to know
That with Jesus here below,
I can conquer every foe.

~ Ballington Booth (1892)

Gore said, "If you will to be His disciple, He will enrich your life; He will purge it of its pollution; He will conquer your lusts; He will enlighten your mind; He will deepen in you all that is generous and rich and brotherly and true and just. He will make your life worth having—yea, increasingly worth having—as you gain in experience of His power and His love, even to the end. He will touch your sufferings and your labors with the glory of His sympathy; He will deepen your hopes for yourselves and others with the security of an eternal prospect. At the last He will purify and perfect and welcome you."[78] Matthew Henry states, "It is only the favor and grace of God that can give satisfaction to a soul, can suit its capacities, supply its needs and answer to its desires."[79] Spurgeon said, "*Satisfaction*—a rare word! It rings like a silver bell—*satisfaction*. The richest man in England [or the United States] has not found it. The greatest conqueror has never won it. The proudest emperor cannot command it. It is a spiritual blessing, a divine grace that comes from *the great satisfying God— the God who is Himself all sufficient to fill the human heart*."[80]

Before his conversion, Spurgeon wrestled with grave bitterness of soul through conviction of sin, hungering for the Lord. He said, "My heart was broken in pieces. I lived a miserable creature, finding no hope, no comfort."[81] Spurgeon sought guidance for forgiveness of sin through visiting various chapels all in vain. That which was preached failed to address the sinner's chief need. That is, until on a snowy day he visited a Primitive Methodist Chapel where a layman told all in attendance to look up to God to be saved (but Spurgeon felt the words were directed to him personally). Waiting to do fifty things to get right with God, he now understood that the only thing he had to do was to look up in faith and repentance. He said of that moment, "Oh! I looked until I could have almost looked my eyes away!"[82]

On the twenty-fifth anniversary of his conversion, Spurgeon wrote, "I have never been sorry for what I did then; no, not even once. The day I gave myself to the Lord to be His servant was the very best day in my life. Then I began to be safe and happy, then I found the secret of living and had a worthy object for my life's exertions and an unfailing comfort for life's troubles."[83] Grace never disappoints its recipient but does exceedingly beyond and above his fondest expectations, filling the soul with delight, peace, comfort and great joy.

12   Sum of Grace

The sum and total of the Christian experience (achievements, victories, comfort, strength, endurance in trials, etc.) from beginning to end is dependent upon grace (divine, supernatural enablement). Of this truth, Paul said, "By the grace of God I am what I am, and His grace toward me was not in vain" (1 Corinthians 15:10 ESV). See 1 Samuel 7:12. Henry Ward Beecher says, "This is, in other words, the doctrine of man's dependence upon God. That same hand that has taken care of you, that same power that has taken the obstacles out of your way or marvelously put them in your way, that same Providence that has conducted you thus far through life yet exists and rules over the affairs of men. By Thy grace, O God, in the past, I have been what I have been; and by Thy grace I desire, in the future, to be what Thou wilt have me to be. Glorify Thyself, and I shall be satisfied."[84] Matthew Henry states, "We are nothing but what God makes us, nothing in religion but what His grace makes us. All that is good in us is a stream from this fountain."[85]

Every devoted follower of Christ testifies to the same and joins John Newton in declaring, "I am not what I ought to be; I am not what I want to be; I am not what I hope to be in another world, but still I am not what I once used to be, and by the grace of God I am what I am."[86] Grace molds the believer into God's design, fits him for His divine assignment and provides whatever consolation and help is needed in the pilgrimage to Heaven. All saints testify that "grace is my story from salvation to glory."

26

Grace is the bookends to the story of the Christian's life. Are we careful to ascribe praise to Christ's grace for every good thought, word, benefit and deed? See James 1:17.

> Naught have I gotten but what I received;
> Grace hath bestowed it since I have believed.
> Boasting excluded, pride I abase;
> I'm only a sinner saved by grace!
> ~ James Martin Gray (1851–1935)

We are debtors to God's amazing grace, not to our flesh (own merit and efforts), for past and present deliverances, successes, protection, and preservation from the weaknesses of the flesh (Romans 8:12). Although grace has blessed and prospered us plenteously, it yet would have wrought a greater work had it not on occasion been blocked (squandered, neglected).

> Oh, to grace how great a debtor
>   Daily I'm constrained to be!
> Let that grace now, like a fetter,
>   Bind my yielded heart to Thee.
> ~ Robert Robinson (1758)

13   Seal of Grace

What is the believer's pledge (seal) that grace will be dispensed in the hour of need? What is its assuring mark or evidence that even you might attain it? Its confirming seal is threefold.

The seal is God's Work for you. The sparing not of His only Son at Calvary to make the provision of grace possible gives assurance that it will not be withheld from His children. Paul makes the argument for grace, saying, "He that spared not his own Son, but delivered him up for us all, how shall he not with him also freely give us all things?" (Romans 8:32). The purpose of Calvary (the atoning work of Christ) was to make saving grace possible upon which hang all graces.

The seal is God's Word to you. Hear, receive and believe the promise of grace: "'Though the mountains be shaken and the hills be removed, yet my unfailing love ("loving-kindness; steadfast love; *grace*; mercy; faithfulness; goodness"[87]) for you will not be shaken nor my covenant of peace be removed ("withdraw, give way, fail to be present"[88]),' says the LORD, who has compassion ('to behold with tenderest affection'[89]) on you" (Isaiah 54:10 NIV). God's Word is His pledge that grace will be always afforded to you, and He "is not a man, that he should lie; neither the son of man, that he should repent: hath he said, and shall he not do it? or hath he spoken, and shall he not make it good?" (Numbers 23:19). See Titus 1:2 and Hebrews 6:18. All that God hath promised shall happen. Dixon says Christ promises grace (strength, enablement) necessary to live a life of victory.[90] "What we have to do is take what He gives; and as we do, the victory will be sure. How can we take His grace? Well, ask for it, and receive it in accordance with Hebrews 4:16."[91]

The seal is God's Witness in you. The Holy Spirit resident within the believer gives attestation not only to the reality of saving grace (Romans 8:16) but to all other forms of grace. "The Holy Spirit," states C. H. Spurgeon, "is often pleased, in a most gracious manner, to witness with our spirits of the love of Jesus. He takes of the things of Christ and reveals them unto us. No voice is heard from the clouds, and no vision is seen in the night, but we have a testimony surer than either of these. If an angel should fly from Heaven and inform the saint personally of the Savior's love to him, the evidence would not be one whit more satisfactory than that which is borne in the heart by the Holy Ghost."[92]

14   Sap of Grace

Jesus gives the illustration of the Vine and its Branches in John 15 to underscore the necessity of the sap of the Holy Spirit provided by Christ's grace to infuse power into the believer to enable the victorious Christian life. Here is how Jesus explains it: "Take care to live in me, and let me live in you. For a branch can't produce fruit when severed from the vine. Nor can you be fruitful apart from me. Yes, I am the Vine; you are the branches. Whoever lives in me and I in him shall produce a large crop of fruit. For apart from me you can't do a thing" (John 15:4–5 TLB).

The Vine is Christ, believers are the branches, and the sap of the Vine is Christ's enabling power provided by grace to live the victorious Christian life and bear much fruit for His glory. To be the recipient of the sap, the believer must abide constantly in the Vine. To abide in Christ means to keep Him at the center of life, to obey Him without vacillating, to take cues from Him regarding decisions and conduct, and to steadfastly walk in intimacy with Him.

James McConkey says, "The believer receives life not as a gift apart from Christ, but by the gift of Christ [grace]. Jesus Christ does not so much *impart* life as He *inbrings* life."[93] "Do we desire power? We must look to Him for it each time it is needed. Do we desire anointing for service? We must look to Him renewedly, at each recurrence of such service. Do we need guidance, wisdom, tact, gentleness, longsuffering, peace, joy? We must look to Him for it all."[94] "For without me ye can do nothing" (John 15:5). These are all graces that Christ freely gives His children.

All of God's graces are linked to this key Christian discipline. Jesus says, "Take care to live in me, and let me live in you. For a branch can't produce fruit when severed from the vine. Nor can you be fruitful apart from me" (John 15: 4 TLB). Failure to abide in Him veils the manifestation of His presence and manifold grace. This truth the renown missionary to China, Hudson Taylor, learned from experience. Struggling with spells of anger, frustration and discouragement, he felt unqualified to be a spiritual leader as a Christian who was not victorious. That was until a letter arrived from a godly friend explaining the secret of the victorious Christian life (John 15:1–8). Upon learning that the victorious life was not hinged upon one's fleshly efforts but upon abiding in the Vine constantly, his life and ministry forever changed.

The "sap" grace provides by union with the Vine (Christ) not only supplies life-giving nutrients for spiritual growth, vitality, power and victory, but grants us accessibility to all of the graces of God as the need demands by faith. Paul says, "Therefore being justified by faith, we have peace with God through our Lord Jesus Christ: *By whom also we have access by faith into this grace* wherein we stand, and rejoice in hope of the glory of God" (Romans 5:1–2).

> I have learned the wondrous secret
> > Of abiding in the Lord.
> I have tasted life's pure fountain;
> > I am drinking of His Word.

> I have found the strength and sweetness
> > Of abiding 'neath the blood.
> I have lost myself in Jesus;
> > I am sinking into God.

> I'm abiding in the Lord
> And confiding in His Word;
> > I am hiding in the bosom of His love.
> Yes, abiding in the Lord
> And confiding in His Word,
> > I am hiding in the bosom of His love.

> I am crucified with Jesus,
> > And He lives and dwells with me.
> I have ceased from all my struggling;
> > 'Tis no longer I, but He.

> All my will is yielding to Him,
> > And His Spirit reigns within,
> And His precious blood each moment
> > Keeps me cleansed and free from sin.

> All my sicknesses I bring Him,
> > And He bears them all away.
> All my fears and griefs I tell Him,
> > All my cares from day to day.

All my strength I draw from Jesus;
  By His breath I live and move.
E'en His very mind He gives me,
  And His faith, and life, and love.

For my words I take His wisdom;
  For my works, His Spirit's power.
For my ways His ceaseless presence
  Guards and guides me every hour.

Of my heart, He is the portion;
  Of my joy, the boundless spring;
Savior, Sanctifier, Healer,
  Glorious Lord and coming King.

~ Albert Benjamin Simpson (1843–1919)

15 Sympathy of Grace

"For we have not an high priest [Mediator that stands between God and man, bridging the gap, and man's intercessor before the throne of God, the Lord Jesus Christ] which cannot be touched with the feeling of our infirmities" (Hebrews 4:15). See 1 Timothy 2:5. Wuest says, "The use of the word [touched] here means more than a knowledge of human infirmity."[95] That is, not only is Christ aware of our weaknesses (frailty, incapacity to handle something like sickness, grief, suffering, temptation), but He sympathizes (to "suffer with" another person, to experience the heartache of another[96]) with us in them. He is not impassive (heartless, crude, or cold or indifferent) but full of compassion and gentleness toward us in our hurts and hardships. The psalmist declared, "But thou, O Lord, art a God full of compassion, and gracious, longsuffering [patient], and plenteous [overflowing with] in mercy and truth" (Psalm 86:15).

The Great Physician now is near,
  The sympathizing Jesus;
He speaks the drooping heart to cheer.
  Oh, hear the voice of Jesus!

~ William Hunter (1859)

31

Pink states, "The Lord Jesus is filled with tender compassion and the most profound, lively, and comprehensive sympathy. We may come in to Him expecting full, tender, deep sympathy and compassion."[97] Wescott says, "The power of sympathy in our High Priest is made effective by the power of help."[98] That is, He not only sympathizes with us in our hurts but is able to provide the relief and solution needed. And that's the game-changer. Spurgeon summarizes, "Let us come to the throne, when we are sinful, to find mercy. Let us come to the throne, when we are weak, to find help. Let us come to the throne, when we are tempted, to find grace."[99]

> I must tell Jesus all of my troubles;
>   He is a kind, compassionate friend.
> If I but ask Him, He will deliver,
>   Make of my troubles quickly an end.
>   ~ E. A. Hoffman (1894)

16   Specificity of Grace

Make known the specific grace needed at the throne of God in prayer. There is but one grace, but there are various tentacles attached to its core (grace of comfort, mercy, preservation from temptation, deliverance, empowerment for service, strength, help, etc.) upon which the believer may draw for help. It may simply be a fresh supply of the grace experienced yesterday or a new grace to meet a new circumstance today. Grace of yesterday is not sufficient to supply the need of today. It is like the heavenly manna in Israel's wilderness wandering—it needs to be gathered each morning and immediately put to use. And it is plenteous, available, and easily accessible. But alas, "we are very slow," Chambers writes, "to draw on God's grace through prayer."[100] See Luke 18:1. Tozer explains the reason behind that sluggishness: "Sometimes when we get overwhelmed, we forget how big God is."[101]

The time to ask for grace is at the moment of its need. Don't delay and await a more "convenient time" or setting. "Therefore let us [with privilege] approach the throne of grace [that is, the throne of God's gracious favor] with confidence and without fear, so that we may receive mercy [for our failures] and find [His amazing] grace to help in time of need [an appropriate blessing, coming just at the right moment]" (Hebrews 4:16 AMP). Take the bow of faith in hand and shoot the arrow of request for the specific grace needed to the throne of God immediately (audibly or mentally). Millions of such arrows are shot to Heaven's throne daily from ambulances, emergency vehicles, police cars, hospital beds, surgical wards, emergency rooms, hospices, funeral homes, the impoverished, the persecuted and the imprisoned.

Be confident of God's ready response to your request. James says, "He giveth more grace [grace on top of grace]" (James 4:6). The psalmist said, "Let them shout for joy, and be glad, that favour my righteous cause: yea, let them say continually, Let the LORD be magnified, which hath pleasure in the prosperity of his servant" (Psalm 35:27). Jesus said, "Ask, and it shall be given you" (Matthew 7:7). Clarke says, "No help can be expected where there is no cry, and where there is no cry there is no felt necessity; for he that feels he is perishing will cry aloud for help, and to such a cry the compassionate High Priest will run."[102] Often the believer fails to receive the grace needed because of failure to ask (James 4:2), unbelief (Matthew 21:22), pride (James 4:6b) or confidence in man over God (Psalm 118:8 and Psalm 20:7).

Don't underestimate the expediency of grace in the hour of need (for others and yourself). It can make the difference between despair and delight, hope and giving up, victory and defeat, comfort and sorrow, joy and gloom, wise and foolish decisions, peace and distress, and at times sickness and recovery.

17 Supply of Grace

"Genuine Christians," states Pink, "themselves 'fail of the grace of God' by not improving that which God has already bestowed upon them. Faith has been imparted to them, but how little they exercise it. There is an infinite fullness in Christ for them, but how little do they draw upon it. Wondrous privileges are theirs, but how little do they use them. Light has been communicated to them, but how little do they walk in it."[103] Bountiful grace is readily available to supply every need for the believer, but how often he lives in 'lack of the grace of God' for failure to access it.

Grace is all-sufficient and inexhaustible. It is unstinted. Newton says, "Thou art coming to a King; large petitions with thee bring, for His grace and power are such, none can ever ask too much."[104] Trench describes the superabundance of God's grace: "The fountain of God's grace is not as a little scanty spring in the desert, round which thirsty travelers meet to strive and struggle, muddying the waters with their feet, pushing one another away, lest those waters be drawn dry by others before they come to partake of them themselves; but a mighty, inexhaustible river, on the banks of which all may stand, and of which none may grudge, lest, if others drink largely and freely, there will not remain enough for themselves."[105] Grace is always plenteous and procurable. No believer will be left destitute of it in the hour of need. Wesley says, "One of the greatest evidences of God's love to those that love Him is to send them afflictions, with grace to bear them."[106]

> Grace upon grace, like the waves on the shore,
>> Always enough, always more.
> Grace upon grace, like the waves on the shore,
>> All that we need is ours from the Lord.
>>>> ~ Gordon Jensen (1984)

An impoverished woman from the slums of London visited the shore of the ocean for the first time. As tears streamed down her face, someone asked her why she was crying. "Oh, it is so wonderful," she replied, "to see something that there is enough of!" Just so we can stand on the shore of the ocean of divine grace, and as we behold its grandeur and vastness, we may shed tears of rejoicing that at last we have found something there is enough of. Yea, even more than enough of!

> He giveth more grace as our burdens grow greater;
>> He sendeth more strength as our labors increase.
> To added afflictions He addeth His mercy;
>> To multiplied trials He multiplies peace.
>>>> ~ Annie Johnson Flint (1866–1932)

34

Spurgeon said, "Oh! how rich the grace which supplies us so continually and doth not refrain itself because of our ingratitude! The golden shower never ceases; the cloud of blessing tarries evermore above our habitation."[107] Chambers says, "All the great prevailing grace of God is ours for the drawing on, and it needs scarcely any drawing on. Take out the 'stopper,' and it comes out in torrents; yet we manage just to squeeze out enough grace for the day. The overflowing grace of God has no limits, and we have to set no limits to it, but 'grow in grace, and in the knowledge of our Lord and Savior Jesus Christ.'"[108]

Maclaren states, "'According to your faith be it unto you'; that statement lays down the practical limits of our present possession of the boundless gift [of grace]. We have as much as we desire; we have as much as we take; we have as much as we use; we have as much as we can hold. We are admitted into the treasure house, and all around us lie ingots of gold and vessels full of coins; we ourselves determine how much of the treasure should be ours, and if at any time we feel like empty-handed paupers rather than like possible millionaires, the reason lies in our own slowness to take that which is freely given to us of God. For so, on the one hand, should we be encouraged to expect great things from God, and, on the other hand, be humbled by the contrast between what we might be and what we are."[109]

18   Solicitation of Grace

Believers may come boldly (not rash brazenness but reverently with great freedom) to the throne of grace (Hebrews 4:16) to freely and frankly address (prayer) their need without trepidation. Wescott says *boldly* in the "primary sense here means, 'giving utterance to every thought and feeling and wish.'"[110] Biblical examples: Job insisted God tell him why he was suffering (Job 7:20); Habakkuk asked God why his prayers were unanswered (Habakkuk 1:2); Abraham bargained with God for the sparing of Sodom (Genesis 18:16–33); David frankly expressed his innermost feelings to God (Psalm 38:8–15);

Martha told Jesus that her brother would still be alive if He had only responded sooner (John 11:21).

This marvelous access and freedom to say what is on the heart is made possible through "the blood of Jesus" (Hebrews 10:19). Pink says, "'Finding grace' is active and signifies that we humbly, earnestly, and believingly seek it."[111] Therefore, "let us draw near [literally, 'continually draw near'] with a true heart in full assurance of faith" (Hebrews 10:22) unto Christ. "The grace thou hast will soon be less, if thou addest not more to it."[112] Whatever the shame or disgrace or desperation, the believer is not to draw back but "draw near" unto the Lord.

> In the holiest place, touch the throne of grace;
> Grace as a river shall flow.
> In the holiest place, touch the throne of grace;
> Grace as a river shall flow.

> Hallelujah! Hallelujah!
> Grace as a river shall flow.
> Hallelujah! Hallelujah!
> Grace as a river shall flow.
>
> ~ William J. Kirkpatrick (1838–1921)

19 Subversion of Grace

Paul debunked the belief that since grace covers all of our sin, we are free to sin all we want. In Romans 6:15 he said, "What then? shall we sin [deliberately sin], because we are not under the law [Mosaic law], but under grace [forgiveness of sin at the Cross]? God forbid" (Clarke says the Greek word means, "Let it not be, far from it, by no means."[113]). Paul is making clear that it is egregiously wrong to equate grace with liberty to sin; that is, grace is not a license to sin all you want. Christ died upon the Cross to forgive man of sin, not to enable him in it. In fact, the evidence that a man has experienced grace is manifested in his desire to avoid sin, not to seek it (1 John 3:4–10). The bottom line is that the Gospel (grace) does not allow man to sin any more than the statutes, commandments, and regulations of the Mosaic law did. Therefore, be careful to use grace rightfully and not abuse it through a heretical presumptuousness that sanctions a lifestyle of licentiousness and wantonness. See Hebrews 10:26.

R. M. Edgar says, "The liberty *grace* gives is totally distinct from license. License is liberty to please ourselves, to humor the flesh, to regard liberty as an end and not a means. But God in his Gospel gives no such liberty. His liberty is a means and not an end; it is liberty to live as He pleases, liberty to love Him and love men, liberty to serve one another by love. We must guard ourselves, then, from the confusion of mistaking license for liberty."[114]

Barnes says, "It is needful to guard the doctrine of grace [the freedom it renders] from abuse at all times. There has been a strong tendency, as the history of the church has shown, to abuse the doctrine of grace."[115] Christians have engaged in gross acts of immorality and other wicked indulgences due to a ludicrous and perverted view of gospel liberty. The Bible makes crystal clear that "Christ came to call sinners to repentance, not to licentiousness; to take His yoke upon them and yield their members instruments of righteousness unto holiness"[116] (Romans 6:13). Peter says similarly, "You are free from the law, but that doesn't mean you are free to do wrong. Live as those who are free to do only God's will at all times" (1 Peter 2:16 TLB). MacArthur explains "The freedom Christians have is not a base from which they can sin freely and without consequence."[117]

MacDonald agrees, saying, "The Christian's freedom is in Christ Jesus (Galatians 2:4), and this excludes any possible thought that it might ever mean freedom to sin."[118] Matthew Henry says, "The Gospel is a doctrine according to godliness (1 Timothy 6:3), and is so far from giving the least countenance to sin, that it lays us under the strongest obligation to avoid and subdue it."[119] See Romans 6:1–4. McGee states, "What does the Gospel of grace do for the believer? It is grace, not law, that frees us from doing wrong and allows us to do right. Grace does not set us free *to* sin, but it sets us free *from* sin."[120]

It is clear that the freedom that grace grants the believer is not purposed to allow the indulgence of sinful and corrupt passions but to enable a life of righteousness and holiness. But by what means is moral restraint to be bestowed? Not by the law, but by the indwelling and controlling ministry of the Holy Spirit (2 Thessalonians 2:7). "Walk in the Spirit, and ye shall not fulfil the lust of the flesh" (Galatians 5:16). See Galatians 2:21.

> Shall we go on to sin
> Because Thy grace abounds,
> Or crucify the Lord again
> And open all His wounds?
>
> Forbid it, mighty God!
> Nor let it e'er be said
> That we whose sins are crucified
> Should raise them from the dead.
>
> We will be slaves no more,
> Since Christ has made us free,
> Has nailed our tyrants to His cross
> And bought our liberty.
>
> ~ Isaac Watts (1674–1748)

MacArthur summarizes, "A true Christian does not see God's promise of forgiveness as a license to sin, a way to abuse His love and presume on His grace. Rather, he sees God's gracious forgiveness as the means to spiritual growth and sanctification. He continually thanks God for His great love and willingness to forgive."[121]

20 Summons of Grace

Grace invites its continual usage. Christ says, "Come [keep coming] to Me, all of you who work and have heavy loads [weary, troubled, burdened]. I will give you rest" (Matthew 11:28 NLV). Robertson says, "'Let us keep on coming to' our High Priest, this sympathizing and great High Priest. Instead of deserting Him, let us make daily use of Him."[122] You can never come too often, request too much, or stay too long at the throne of grace. The storehouse of grace is limitless and inexhaustible.

Thomas Brooks wrote, "'Come,' saith Christ, 'and I will give you rest.' I will not show you rest, nor barely tell you of rest, but I will *give* you rest. I am faithfulness itself and cannot lie; I will give you rest. I that have the greatest power to give it, the greatest will to give it, the greatest right to give it—come, laden sinners, and I will give you rest. Rest is the most desirable good, the most suitable good, and to you the greatest good. 'Come,' saith Christ—that is, believe in Me, and I will give you rest; I will give you peace with God and peace with conscience. I will turn your storm into an everlasting calm; I will give you such rest that the world can neither give to you nor take from you."[123]

A monument in Newport Church (Isle of Wight) erected by Queen Victoria portrays the manner in which Princess Elizabeth met with death. The princess from her youth had been imprisoned, separated from family and friends until she died. Upon her death she was found with her head reclining on a Bible opened to the Scripture that read, "Come unto me, all ye that labour and are heavy laden, and I will give you rest." What a sermon in stone that monument preaches, reminding all that ultimate rest is found not in status or possession but in the grace of the Lord Jesus Christ.[124]

Come, ye who from your hearts believe
    That Jesus answers prayer,
Come boldly to a throne of grace
    And claim His promise there,

That, if His love in us abide
    And we in Him are one,
Whatever in His Name we ask
    It surely will be done.

Come lovingly and trustingly;
    Take Jesus at His Word,
For He has said, "The prayer of faith
    Was never yet unheard."

~ Fanny Crosby (1889)

21 Surety of Grace

The summons of grace results in its being provided. Whyte says, "Grace, then, is grace—that is to say, it is sovereign, it is free, it is sure, it is unconditional, and it is everlasting."[125] Grace that is promised will be provided. Delay of grace is not its denial.

The Bible says, "And after you have suffered a little while, the God of all grace, who has called you to his eternal glory in Christ, will himself restore, confirm, strengthen, and establish you" (1 Peter 5:10 ESV). The believer will find (but not might acquire) grace to help in the hour of need.

Charles Simeon says, "If we want grace to sustain suffering, to fulfil duty, to transform the soul into the Divine image, 'Ask and have' is the Divine command; and our boldness in asking cannot be too great, provided it be of a right kind."[126] See Matthew 7:7–8. Pink comments, "He is ever ready to strengthen

> Doubt not His grace because of thy tribulation, but believe that He loveth thee as much in seasons of trouble as in times of happiness.
> C. H. Spurgeon

and comfort, to heal and restore. He is prepared to receive the poor, wounded, sin-stained believer; to dry the tears of Peter weeping bitterly; to say to Paul, oppressed with the thorn in the flesh, 'My grace is sufficient for thee.'"[127]

"There is One who careth for you. His eye is fixed on you," states Spurgeon. "His heart beats with pity for your woe, and His hand omnipotent shall yet bring you the needed help. The darkest cloud shall scatter itself in showers of mercy. The blackest gloom shall give place to the morning. He, if thou art one of His family, will bind up thy wounds and heal thy broken heart. Doubt not His grace because of thy tribulation, but believe that He loveth thee as much in seasons of trouble as in times of happiness."[128] "When I cannot *feel* the faith of assurance," says Matthew Henry, "I live by the *fact* of God's faithfulness."[129] "Not one thing hath failed or shall fail of all that the Lord hath spoken."[130]

Arise, my soul, arise;
   Shake off your guilty fears.
The bleeding Sacrifice
   In my behalf appears.
Before the throne my Surety stands;
Before the throne my Surety stands;
My name is written on his hands.

~ Charles Wesley (1742)

"If God makes heavy demands of His people, He supplies the grace to comply with the commands."[131] Ellsworth says, "The world would prove to be too strong for us if the Lord of grace did not grant us grace for living in it. If we humbly seek His grace, He will not fail to give it."[132] Chambers said, "Grace is the overflowing favor of God, and you can always count on it being available to draw upon as needed."[133] Luther states, "Faith is a living, daring confidence in God's grace, so sure and certain that a man would stake his life on it one thousand times. This confidence in God's grace and knowledge of it makes men glad and bold and happy in dealing with God and with all creatures, and this is the work of the Holy Ghost in faith."[134]

The well of Beer in the wilderness was a promised source of water to the Israelites. Of it Numbers 21:16 states, "That is the well whereof the LORD spake unto Moses, Gather the people together, and I will give them water." "The people needed water," writes Spurgeon, "and it was promised by their gracious God. We need fresh supplies of heavenly grace, and in the covenant the Lord has pledged Himself to give all we required."[135]

22 Speed of Grace

Note its timeliness. The very moment in which grace is requested it is dispensed. G. Campbell Morgan helpfully wrote, "I am never tired of pointing out that the Greek phrase translated 'in time of need' [Hebrews 4:16] is a colloquialism of which 'in the nick of time' is the exact equivalent. 'That we may receive mercy and find grace to help in the nick of time'—grace just when and where I need it. You are attacked by temptation. At the moment of assault, you look to Him, and the grace is there to help in the nick of time. There is no postponement of your petition until the evening hour of prayer. But there in the city street with the flaming temptation in front of you, turn to Christ with a cry for help, and the grace will be there in the nick of time."[136] See Psalm 143:7.

> But I unto my God will cry;
>> To Him for aid I flee.
> The Lord will help me speedily,
>> And He will succor me.
>
> ~ John Hopkins (1790)

23   Stipulation of Grace

To obtain saving grace (forgiveness for sin, reconciliation to God, transformation and, at life's end, Heaven) man must be repentant of sin (expression of godly sorrow over sin and willingness to turn from it) and through faith embrace Christ as Lord and Savior (Acts 20:21). Upon saving grace the convert becomes eligible for assisting and sustaining grace.

> Come boldly to the throne of grace,
>> Ye wretched sinners, come
> And lay your load at Jesus' feet
>> And plead what He has done.
>
> He makes the dead to hear His voice;
>> He makes the blind to see.
> The sinner lost He came to save
>> And set the prisoner free.
>
> ~ Fanny Crosby (1902)

Stipulations of sustaining and assisting grace for the believer are few and simple.

Acknowledgement of need. Many saints acknowledge grace theoretically but fail to request it out of ignorance, sense of its need, or just plain arrogance and pride.

Entreaty for it by faith. Express confidence that God is able to provide whatever act of kindness, mercy and love needed (Romans 5:15). The Bible implores, "Let us draw near to God with a sincere heart and with the full assurance that faith brings" (Hebrews 10:22 NIV). "We are not to be wavering in our minds when we draw nigh to God," states Simeon. "To doubt either His power or His willingness to help us is to disparage both the Father and the Son, and prayers offered with a doubtful mind will never bring with them an answer of peace."[137] See James 1:6–7.

Matthew Henry says that it is through faith and prayer that we fetch fresh supplies of grace.[138] Saith Spurgeon, "Scripture is a never-failing treasury filled with boundless stores of grace. It is the bank of Heaven; you may draw from it as much as you please, without let or hindrance. Come in faith and you are welcome to all covenant blessings. There is not a promise in the Word which shall be withheld."[139]

Expression of humility. James says, "But he giveth more grace. Wherefore he saith, God resisteth [opposes] the proud [arrogant, haughty, contemptuous], but giveth [generous] grace unto the humble" (James 4:6). See 1 Peter 5:5. "A humble person," says David Wilkerson, "is not one who thinks little of himself, hangs his head and says, 'I'm nothing.' Rather, he is one who depends wholly on the Lord for everything, in every circumstance."[140]

Andrew Murray said, "Humility is the displacement of self by the enthronement of God,"[141] and that it is "the disposition which prepares the soul for living on trust."[142]

It is the humble that acknowledge inability to cope with life's temptations, failures, pains, trials and challenges apart from God's help (grace) and who, therefore, seek it. In contrast, "The wicked in his proud countenance does not seek God; God is in none of his thoughts" (Psalm 10:4 NKJV). Spurgeon states, "Humility makes us ready to be blessed by the God of all grace."[143]

24 Season of Grace

Provisional grace (that which provides any and all good and beneficial things to us) is always operational (James 1:17). Everything good is a gift of grace. It may be evidenced in health, from special friends that love us, possessions, finances, interruption of plans or decisions that would be disastrous, and multitudinous other ways. The bottom line is that whatever good is received, from whatever source, can ultimately be traced back to God's hand (including those close escapes from auto accidents or other injuries). Regrettably, we often fail to connect all the good things that happen with grace. If every "gift" of grace was boxed in red wrapping and adorned with a beautiful bow, they would literally be seen everywhere in our homes, jobs, schools, hospitals, and battlegrounds. Spurgeon correctly says, "Between here and Heaven, every minute that the Christian lives will be a minute of grace."[144]

> When all thy mercies, O my God,
>   My rising soul surveys,
> Transported with the view, I'm lost
>   In wonder, love, and praise.
>
> Ten thousand thousand precious gifts
>   My daily thanks employ,
> Nor is the least a cheerful heart
>   That tastes those gifts with joy.
>
> ~ Joseph Addison (1712)

However, there are specific times when special grace is needed. The Bible says, "Let us therefore come boldly unto the throne of grace, that we may obtain mercy, and find grace to help in time of need" (Hebrews 4:16). "To help in time of need" literally means "seasonal help."[145] Jamieson, Fausset and Brown say, "A supply of grace is in store for believers against all exigencies, but they are only supplied with it according as the need arises."[146] Grace is bestowed in degrees and in response to need. Moody said, "A man can no more take in a supply of grace for the future than he can eat enough today to last him for the next six months, nor can he inhale sufficient air into his lungs with one breath to sustain life for a week to come. We are permitted to draw upon God's store of grace from day to day as we need it."[147] Bridges wrote, "Your worst days are never so bad that you are beyond the reach of God's grace. And your best days are never so good that you are beyond the need of God's grace."[148]

Each morning new grace awaits the believer (like manna in the wilderness) to be appropriated as its need demands. "They are new every morning: great is thy faithfulness" (Lamentations 3:23). Continuously, "he giveth more grace" (James 4:6). Whatever the specificity of the need and whenever it arises, bountiful grace awaits at the throne room of God to satisfy it.

Just when I need Him, Jesus is near;
Just when I falter, just when I fear;
Ready to help me, ready to cheer,
Just when I need Him most.

Just when I need Him most,
Just when I need Him most,
Jesus is near to comfort and cheer,
Just when I need Him most.

Just when I need Him, Jesus is true,
Never forsaking, all the way through;
Giving for burdens pleasures anew,
Just when I need Him most.

Just when I need Him, Jesus is strong,
Bearing my burdens all the day long;
For all my sorrow giving a song,
Just when I need Him most.

Just when I need Him, He is my all,
Answering when upon Him I call;
Tenderly watching lest I should fall,
Just when I need Him most.

~ William C. Poole (1907)

25 School of Grace

J. C. Ryle said, "The spiritual health and prosperity, the spiritual happiness and comfort of every true-hearted and holy Christian are intimately connected with the subject of spiritual growth."[149] A. W. Pink says, "Growing in grace is an increasing living outside of myself, living upon Christ. It is a looking to Him for the supply of every need. It is the apprehension of how much I need His precious blood to cleanse me, His righteousness to clothe me, His arm to support me, His advocacy to answer for me on High, His grace to deliver me from all my enemies both inward and outward. It is the Spirit revealing to me that there is in Christ everything that I need both for earth and Heaven, time and eternity."[150] Grace's growth absolutely has nothing to do with the believer's salvation (it cannot grow for he cannot become any more pardoned and redeemed than he was at the moment he believed) but with the spiritual graces bestowed to the believer by the Holy Spirit to enhance His Christian walk, character, and testimony (2 Peter 1:5–7). Spurgeon explains, "We are in the sea of God's grace. We cannot be in a deeper sea, but let us grow now that we are in it. We cannot be more in it than we are, or than we always have been. We are in God's grace; we are in the covenant; we are in the scheme of redemption; we are in union with Jesus. We cannot be more or less so, for we are eternally secure through the blood of our Savior. But while it cannot grow more, we can grow more in it, and so we shall 'grow in grace.'"[151]

Grace's growth is not always perceptible. It is not based on feelings. It is not determined by years of age or religious activity. It's not to be measured by another's. Without growth in grace, progress in holiness is impossible. Without growth in grace, effective witnessing is impeded. Without growth in grace, greater likeness to Christ will not occur. Without growth in grace, spiritual stagnation results. Without growth in grace, it is impossible to be of benefit to the Church and kingdom of God. And without growth in grace, strength to bear all things becomes stunted. Grace's growth ought to be used to extend beyond our personal benefit to that of others. Grace's growth brings satisfaction, peace, comfort, security, hope, and perseverance to the whole realm of life, including that of trial. Grace's growth always magnifies and pleases Christ (Colossians 1:10). Without growth in grace, God is not pleased or honored (1 Thessalonians 4:1; Hebrews 13:16).

The reality of the need to grow in grace is overtly apparent. Spurgeon frankly said, "There are many who are barely Christians and have scarcely enough grace to float them into Heaven, the keel of their vessel grating on the gravel all the way."[152] The shadowiness of the understanding of grace, lack of intimacy with and devotion to Christ (Revelation 3:16), deficiency of the fullness of "all grace" (1 Peter 5:10), and the insufficiency or inability to cope effectively with temptation, hardship, grief, persecution, illness and pain are all indicators of the need to grow in grace. And I would presume that would include every born-again person, to one degree or another.

Peter specifically enumerates seven graces in which the believer ought to grow, starting with faith and ending with love (2 Peter 1:5–7).

Faith. The root-grace of all graces is trusting reliance upon the promises of God and God Himself (2 Peter 1:4). Faith is the sure foundation on which to "add" the following graces enumerated to your life; it will sustain them. Therefore, it is essential the believer grows in the grace of faith. Spurgeon said, "Know more of Christ; think more of Him, and your faith will increase. Your little faith would soon get strong if you lived more on Jesus."[153] He that grows in the grace of faith discovers more and more God's ableness and dependability to supply every need. Matthew Henry states, "Those who know Him to be a God of inviolable truth and faithfulness will rejoice in His word of promise and rest upon that. Those who know Him to be the everlasting Father will trust Him with their souls as their main care and trust in Him at all times, even to the end."[154]

Virtue. It is courage and fortitude in spiritual warfare. "Christian manliness and active courage in the good fight of faith."[155] It's the grace to stand as the three Hebrew children before Nebuchadnezzar, saying, "If it be so, our God whom we serve is able to deliver us from the burning fiery furnace, and he will deliver us out of thine hand, O king. But if not, be it known unto thee, O king, that we will not serve thy gods, nor worship the golden image which thou hast set up" (Daniel 3:17–18).

Knowledge. "The power of knowing, intelligence, comprehension."[156] True knowledge proceeds from God (Colossians 2:3; Ephesians 3:19). Paul passionately desired to know the power of Christ's suffering and resurrection more fully (Philippians 3:10). Spurgeon says, "There can be no growth in grace except as we grow in our knowledge of Christ. We may always test whether we are growing in grace by this question: 'Do I know more of Christ today than I did yesterday? Do I live nearer to Christ today than I did a little while ago?' For increase in the knowledge of Christ is the evidence as well as the cause of true growth in grace."[157] Spurgeon continues, "Seek to know more of Him in his divine nature, in His human relationship, in His finished work, in His death, in His resurrection, in His present glorious intercession, and in His future royal advent. Abide hard by the Cross and search the mystery of His wounds. An increase of love to Jesus, and a more perfect apprehension of His love to us is one of the best tests of growth in grace."[158]

Self-control. Jeremy Taylor says self-control is "reason's girdle as well as passion's bridle."[159] It is the mastery over evil inclinations. Charles Bridges counsels, "Diligently improve all the means of grace for keeping your heart in a vigorous state. Be daily—yea continually—abiding in the vine and receiving life and health from its fulness. Be much conversant with the Word of God, loving it for itself—its holiness, its practical influences. Be chiefly afraid of inward decays—of a barren, sapless notion of experimental truth; remembering, that except your profession be constantly watered at the root, 'the things that remain in you will be ready to die.' Specially 'commune with your own heart.' Watch it jealously, because of its proneness to live upon itself— its own graces or fancied goodness (a sure symptom of unsoundness)—instead of 'living by the faith of the Son of God.' Examine your settled judgment, your deliberate choice, your outgoing affections, your habitual allowed practice; applying to every detection of unsoundness the blood of Christ as the sovereign remedy for the diseases of a 'deceitful and desperately wicked heart.'"[160]

Patience. Endurance. "It is that quality of character which does not allow one to surrender to circumstances or succumb under trial."[161] Wuest says "to remain under trials and testings in a way that honors God."[162] Paul exhibited this grace with regard to the thorn in the flesh that he experienced (2 Corinthians 12:7–9).

Godliness. It refers to godly living, devoutness, reverence and the believers close-knit fellowship with God. Spurgeon cautions, "You cannot grow in grace to any high degree while you are conformed to the world,"[163] and, "You cannot expect to grow in grace if you do not read the Scriptures."[164] W. S. Plumer remarked, "Without meditation, grace never thrives, prayer is languid, praise dull, and religious duties unprofitable."[165] Maclaren says, "Peter says, 'Seeing that we look for such things, let us be diligent, that we may be found of Him in peace without spot, and blameless.' If we are to be 'found in peace,' we must be 'found spotless,' and if we are to be 'found spotless,' we must be 'diligent.'"[166] "Grace is at a low ebb," writes Spurgeon, "in that soul which can even raise the question of how far it may go in worldly conformity."[167]

Brotherly love. A special affection for and kindness toward the household of faith that flows from spiritual commonality (1 Peter 3:8; John 13:34 and Romans 12:10). "We shall," Spurgeon says, "as we ripen in grace, have greater sweetness toward our fellow Christians. He who grows in grace remembers that he is but dust, and he therefore does not expect his fellow Christians to be anything more. He overlooks ten thousand of their faults, because he knows his God overlooks twenty thousand in his own case."[168]

Love. The esteem, goodwill, affection, benevolence for mankind at large, even persecutors (1 Corinthians 13). J. C. Ryle says, "His love will show itself actively—in a growing disposition to do kindnesses, to take trouble for others, to be good-natured to everybody, to be generous, sympathizing, thoughtful, tender-hearted and considerate."[169]

Peter adds *humility* to these cited in 1 Peter 5:5. It is the opposite of pride and arrogance. Augustine said, "Humility is the vessel of all graces."[170] Solomon says, "When pride comes, then comes disgrace, but with humility comes wisdom" (Proverbs 11:2 NIV). Bunyan said, "It is hard to sit in the valley of humiliation, but it is fruitful, fertile and beautiful once we get there." Saith Spurgeon, "It is owing only to His grace toward us [that we have been blessed richly above others], and we will not exalt ourselves above our fellows. We will not be high-minded, but condescend to men of low estate; we will not lift our necks with the proud, but we will bow down our brows with the humble. Every man shall be called our brother, not merely those who are arrayed in goodly raiment, but those who are clothed in the habiliments [clothing] of toil, for what have we that we have not received, and what maketh us to differ from another (1 Corinthians 4:7)?"[171] Nothing but grace. He that grows in grace will emerge humble realizing that "every good gift and every perfect gift is from above, and cometh down from the Father of lights" (James 1:17). Charles Hodge said, "The doctrines of grace humble a man without degrading him and exalt a man without inflating him."[172]

We are to give "all diligence" ("to speed, urge, hasten, press, zeal."[173] "To take pains to do a thing."[174]) to grow in these graces (2 Peter 1:5). Let us ask ourselves, "Am I in possession of all these graces? And if so, to what measure? Am I detrimentally lacking in regard to any one?" The possession of some do not compensate for the lack of others. We are admonished to add *all* of them to each other (2 Peter 1:5). "Each grace being assumed, becomes the steppingstone to the succeeding grace: and the latter in turn qualifies and completes the former."[175]

Clarke says, "Every grace and Divine influence which ye have received is a seed, a heavenly seed, which, if it be watered with the dew of Heaven from above, will endlessly increase and multiply itself."[176] Growth in grace to some measure occurs in suffering and pain (James 1:2–5 and 1 Peter 5:10). Paul testified that his sufferings produced the grace of perseverance (Romans 5:3) and strength in weakness (2 Corinthians 12:9). Spurgeon said, "I am certain that I never did grow in grace one-half so much anywhere as I have upon the bed of pain."[177] Elizabeth Elliot states, "In my own life, I think I can honestly say that out of the deepest pain has come the strongest conviction of the presence of God and the love of God."[178]

Saith J. C. Ryle: "We can never have
too much humility,
too much faith in Christ,
too much holiness,
too much spirituality of mind,
too much love,
too much zeal in doing good to others."[179]

Let me, then, be always growing,
   Never, never standing still,
Listening, learning, better knowing
   Thee and Thy most blessed will.
Till I win the glorious race,
Daily let me grow in grace.
          ~ Frances Ridley Havergal (1836–1879)

26   Song of Grace

Barnes says, "Rejoice that there 'is' a throne of grace. What a world would this be if God sat on a throne of 'justice' only, and if no mercy were ever to be shown to people! Who is there who would not be overwhelmed with despair? But it is not so. He is on a throne of grace. By day and by night, from year to year, from generation to generation, He is on such a throne. In every land He may be approached, and in as many different languages as people speak may they plead for mercy. In all times of our trial and temptation we may be assured that He is seated on that throne, and wherever we are, we may approach Him with acceptance."[180]

Let's be mindful not to slight the grace received from the hand of Him to whom it cost so much. Grace is free, but it's not cheap (it cost Jesus' agony, torment and death on a cross to make it possible). With this in mind, it is no wonder that Peter instructs all that have obtained grace to "ascribe glory, dominion, and power, to him [Christ Jesus] for ever and ever" (1 Peter 5:11).[181] Let him that possesses grace prize it and render praise to God. W. S. Plumer wrote, "The greater the trial, the greater is the deliverance, and the more joyous and louder should be the song which we sing to the praise and glory of God. To praise God for redemption only as we do for a cup of water is shocking."[182]

Believers are to live "to the praise of the glory of his grace, wherein he hath made us accepted in the beloved" (Ephesians 1:6). That is, grace's work in man prompts him to render gratitude to God with both life and lips which brings glory ("splendor, grandeur, power, praise, honor"[183]) to Him. Vincent says, "The grace is not merely favor, gift, but it reveals also the divine character. In praising God for what He does, we learn to praise Him for what He is. Glory is another of the ruling words of the epistle [Ephesians], falling into the same category with riches and fullness."[184] Spurgeon wrote, "Whatever others may think or say, the redeemed have overwhelming reasons for declaring the goodness of the Lord. Theirs is a special redemption, and for it they ought to render special praise. The Redeemer is so glorious, the ransom price so immense, and the redemption so complete that they are under sevenfold obligations to give thanks unto the Lord, and to exhort others to do so. Let them not only feel so but say so; let them both sing and bid their fellows sing."[185]

Praise Him for His grace and favor
    To His people in distress.
Praise Him, still the same as ever,
    Slow to chide and swift to bless.
Alleluia, alleluia!
    Glorious in his faithfulness!
                                    ~ Henry Francis Lyte (1834)

Consider grace's twofold praise. Praise God for saving grace that converts the soul, cleanses from sin, changes conduct and reconciles to God, granting abundant and eternal life. Paul says, "Let us praise God for his glorious grace, for the free gift he gave us in his dear Son! For by the blood of Christ we are set free, that is, our sins are forgiven. How great is the grace of God, which he gave to us in such large measure!" (Ephesians 1:6–8 GNT). See Titus 3:5–7.

Henry Moorhouse, English evangelist, was walking through a poverty-smitten section of a city when he noticed a little boy with a pitcher of milk in hand falling to the pavement. Rushing to the boy's side he found him unhurt but terrified. The lad said, "My mamma will whip me!" Moorhouse picked him up, went to a nearby store and purchased a new pitcher. He then returned to the dairy store and had it filled with milk. With that done, with boy and pitcher of milk in his arms, he took them home. Putting the boy down on his front porch, the evangelist handed him the pitcher of milk and asked, "Now will your mamma whip you?" A wide smile spread upon his tear-stained face, "Aw, no sir, 'cause it's lot better pitcher than we had before."

That's what saving grace has done for the believer. It has given him something "a lot better than we had before." It has brought about a complete transformation in life (2 Corinthians 5:17).

Wonderful Grace of Jesus, greater than all my sin;
How shall my tongue describe it; where shall its praise begin?
Taking away my burden, setting my spirit free;
Oh, the Wonderful Grace of Jesus reaches me!
~ Haldor Lillenas (1918)

But praise God also for the sustaining grace provided in the time of need. "Cast your burden on the LORD, and he will sustain you; he will never permit the righteous to be moved" (Psalm 55:22 ESV). Praise Him for the valleys and the storms that He has brought you through victoriously. See Psalm 103:1–5 and Lamentations 3:22–23.

Sustaining Grace till the end of it all,
Sustaining Grace till the last sunset falls,
Always there everlasting enough to see us through,
Sustaining grace is there for me and you.[186]
~ The Homeland Quartet (1994)

27 Salutation of Grace

"Grace and peace be multiplied unto you through the knowledge of God, and of Jesus our Lord" (2 Peter 1:2). Peter's salutation to the persecuted Christians living in five regions of Asia Minor encompasses a personal blessing and prayer. The text may be rendered, "My desire (good wish) for you and prayer unto God in your behalf is that He may multiply His grace (favor) and peace (fruit of grace) unto you through the knowledge of God and of Jesus our Lord." Encompassed in the general term *grace* (as used here) are blended all the mercies and favors of God for time and eternity.[187] It was a timely and edifying greeting to the discouraged, oppressed and hurting saints of Asia Minor.

Christian salutations ought to be extended in the routines of life to others to bestow a blessing, commend an action, share comfort, remind of a spiritual truth or as here in 2 Peter 1:2 to wish and pray for an increased measure of grace (benefits of God's favor and mercy). Such a custom was practiced widely by the apostle Paul (1 Corinthians 1:3; 2 Corinthians 1:2; Galatians 1:3; Ephesians 1:2; Philippians 1:2; Colossians 1:2; 1 Thessalonians 1:1; 2 Thessalonians 1:2; 1 Timothy 1:2; 2 Timothy 1:2; Titus 1:4). Without exception every believer stands in need of increased grace; therefore, its specific salutation (desire and prayer) is always proper and timely to extend. John Hendrix provides an excellent salutation in the composition of the hymn "Grace to You."

> Grace to you, God's grace to you,
>> As you walk through your life,
>> In joy or in strife,
> Grace, God's grace to you.

~ John Hendrix (1935)

28 Sign of Grace

"For who makes you differ from another" (1 Corinthians 4:7 NKJV). That is, who distinguishes you from the world? The child of God answers, the free grace and mercy of the Lord Jesus Christ (primarily saving grace but also sustaining grace). We humbly, and with greatest of gratitude for grace received, say with John Bradford, "There but for the grace of God go I," as we look out upon the lifestyle of the wicked and ungodly. Paul underscores this point in saying, "Do not be deceived: neither the sexually immoral, nor idolaters, nor adulterers, nor men who practice homosexuality, nor thieves, nor the greedy, nor drunkards, nor revilers, nor swindlers will inherit the kingdom of God. And *such were some of you*. But you were washed, you were sanctified, you were justified in the name of the Lord Jesus Christ and by the Spirit of our God" (1 Corinthians 6:9–11 ESV).

> What a wonderful change in my life has been wrought,
>   Since Jesus came into my heart!
> I have light in my soul for which long I have sought,
>   Since Jesus came into my heart!
>
> I'm possessed of a hope that is steadfast and sure,
>   Since Jesus came into my heart!
> And no dark clouds of doubt now my pathway obscure,
>   Since Jesus came into my heart!
>
> ~ Rufus H. McDaniel (1914)

The grace that made us "to differ" certainly is sufficient to make others "to differ." That's why the message of free and full grace must be proclaimed privately and publicly. "If grace does not make us differ from other men," says Spurgeon, "it is not the grace which God gives His elect."[188]

29 Strength of Grace

"Thou therefore, my son, be strong in the grace that is in Christ Jesus" (2 Timothy 2:1). Grace is the greatest untapped power source in the world. To withstand the foes of righteousness and suffer for the cause of Christ triumphantly, Timothy was exhorted by Paul to be strengthened ("keep on being strengthened"[189]) by the "means or power of"[190] the grace (God's gracious enabling power) afforded by Christ Jesus. See Philippians 4:13; 2 Timothy 4:17; Ephesians 6:10. This is not strength derived from others (though helpful) or one's own limited and insufficient strength and abilities. Grace saves us, secures us but also strengthens and motivates us, providing stamina in Christian duty and confrontation with trials. Simeon says, "Be strong in the grace that is in Christ Jesus, that is, know that there is grace treasured up for thee in Christ; and, in dependence upon that, thou shalt be able to sustain all the trials that shall come upon thee."[191] "What gives me the most hope every day is God's grace," saith Rick Warren, "knowing that His grace is going to give me the strength for whatever I face, knowing that nothing is a surprise to God."[192]

> What gives me the most hope every day is God's grace; knowing that his grace is going to give me the strength for whatever I face, knowing that nothing is a surprise to God.
> Rick Warren

Warren Wiersbe states of the power of grace, "God's grace enables us to overcome our three great enemies: the world (2 Timothy 2:4), the flesh (2 Timothy 2:22), and the devil (2 Timothy 2:26). God's grace enables us to endure hardship (2 Timothy 2:3, 10) as we fight the Lord's battles, so that we do not deny the Lord (2 Timothy 2:11–13). It helps us do work of which we are not ashamed (v. 15) and deal with problem people of whom we are not afraid (2 Timothy 2:23–26)."[193] W. S. Plumer remarked, "Divine grace and omnipotent power are necessary to bend the will, bow down the heart, and incline the affections to God. The reasons are: 1. the heart is naturally wrong; 2. many things present themselves to allure us from God."[194] By grace Paul's 'strength was made perfect [achieved its purpose[195]] in weakness' in bearing (victoriously coping, enduring) the thorn (2 Corinthians 12:9b). The outward man may be taxed beyond measure with pain, illness, fatigue, anxiety and despair and yet inwardly experience perfect peace all because of the gracious gift of amazing grace. "John Bunyan said that he could pray for a darker, damper dungeon, because, as his physical discomforts increased, his spiritual comforts and joys were multiplied."[196]

Grace gives success in ministry. "And with great power gave the apostles witness of the resurrection of the Lord Jesus: and great grace was upon them all" (Acts 4:33). Not only was favor ("great grace") among the people to whom they ministered manifested, but also success in their preaching and labor. Barnes explains that it was the 'great grace of God upon them' that enabled the disciples to preach the message of the resurrection with success, that great favor or success attended their preaching (Acts 4:33).[197] The ministry and labor of the devoted servant of the Lord will be met with success when enveloped with "great grace." Grace thwarts cowardice and instills courage to stand against ruthless opposers of the Gospel. Alan Redpath said, "The Christian who, by God's grace, learns to confess the Lord Jesus in circumstances which might normally be calculated to silence him is a Christian whose life is a tremendous challenge to other people."[198]

How is the believer to keep on being "strong in the grace that is in Christ Jesus"? Hughes and Chapell say, "By constantly calling to mind that *you have* this grace, Christ's grace—'grace upon grace.'—by humbly realizing that there is always more grace (James 4:6). We remain strong by prayerfully asking for the [empowering] grace that is in Christ Jesus."[199] Simeon adds, "We should have it as a settled principle in our minds that there is no strength in man, nor any other source of grace than Christ Jesus; and without hesitation we should go to Him from day to day, and from hour to hour, to receive it out of His fulness. We should not dream of meriting it at His hands or of earning it by anything that we can do; we should receive it as freely as the Israelites did the waters that issued from the rock and should go to it as the only source of all that we need. He has told us that, whatever be our necessities, 'his grace is sufficient for us'; and therefore, instead of dreading trials, lest we should be vanquished by them, we should 'take pleasure in them, that the power of Christ may rest upon us and his strength be magnified in our weakness.'[200]

> I need the influence of Thy grace
> To speed me in Thy way,
> Lest I should loiter in my race
> Or turn my feet astray.

When sore afflictions press me down,
    I need Thy quick'ning powers;
Thy Word that I have rested on
    Shall help my heaviest hours.

Are not Thy mercies sovereign still,
    And Thou a faithful God?
Wilt Thou not grant me warmer zeal
    To run the heav'nly road?

Does not my heart Thy precepts love
    And long to see Thy face?
And yet how slow my spirits move
    Without enliv'ning grace!

Then shall I love Thy Gospel more
    And ne'er forget Thy Word,
When I have felt its quick'ning power
    To draw me near the Lord.

~ Isaac Watts (1835)

30   Seeing of Grace

"And of His fullness have all we received, and grace for grace" (John 1:16). That is, one grace succeeds another, as if to take its place.[201] Christians are the recipient of bountiful, limitless and immeasurable grace(s) not only in salvation but provision, protection, and preservation. Ellicott said, "The fulness of the supply is constant; the power to receive increases with the use, or diminishes with the neglect, of that which we already have."[202]

Chambers says, "The moments of our lives drip with this grace, a pool collecting, a reflection of gifts. Do we see it?"[203] Sadly and shockingly many believers don't. With the proper spiritual lenses, we can see grace. Barnabas saw grace in the church at Antioch. "When he arrived and saw the grace of God [that was bestowed on them], he rejoiced and began to encourage them all with an unwavering heart to stay true and devoted to the Lord" (Acts 11:23 AMP). Gill explains that Barnabas witnessed "the many instances of the powerful and efficacious grace of God in regeneration and conversion [Acts 11:21]; the great goodness, love, and favor of God in enlightening, quickening, and converting so many souls; and the wonderful gifts of the Spirit bestowed upon many of them, fitting them for public use and service."[204] Henry says, "He took time to make his observations, and not only in their public worship, but in their common conversations and in their families, he saw the grace of God among them. Where the grace of God is, it will be seen, as the tree is known by its fruits; and, where it is seen, it ought to be owned. What we see which is good in any we must call God's grace in them and give that grace the glory of it; and we ought ourselves to take the comfort of it and make it the matter of our rejoicing. We must be glad to see the grace of God in others, and the more when we see it where we did not expect it."[205] Outside of seeing grace displayed in the church of Antioch, Barnabas also saw grace at work in the life of the apostle Paul (Acts 11:25–26; 9:27).

Barnabas witnessed grace in action and was "glad." When was the last time you actually saw grace at work? Don't be blind to the graces of God at work in and around you. Don't miss seeing grace in action through its healing, helping, comforting, equipping, and saving. Don't miss showing joy over the goodness of grace toward others and yourself. Don't be too busy to observe the grace of God at work, as did Barnabas (Acts 11:23). Learn with him to look for grace at work in salvation and in assisting believers as yourself. And when you see it give praise unto the Lord for it.

31   Stimulus of Grace

"The goodness [kindness, mercy[206]] of God leadeth thee to repentance [the act of turning from sin unto Christ for forgiveness and salvation]" (Romans 2:4). MacArthur comments, "This word ['longsuffering'] indicates the duration for which God demonstrates His goodness and forbearance—for long periods of time. Together these three words ['goodness and forbearance and longsuffering'] speak of God's common grace—the way He demonstrates His grace to all mankind (Job 12:10; Psalm. 119:68; Psalm 145:9)."[207] Grace (common grace) is designed to prompt repentance toward God and faith in the Lord Jesus Christ as Lord and Savior. It amounts to contempt of God's goodness if its recipient ignores that its purpose is to bring him to repentance and faith.[208]

"The goodness of God to a man of evil life," states Spurgeon, "is not intended to encourage him to continue in his sin, but it is meant to woo and win him away from it. God manifests His infinite gentleness and love (grace) that He may thereby kill man's sin, and that by His tender mercy, He may win man's hard heart unto Himself, and that by His abundant lovingkindness, He may awaken man's conscience to a sense of his true position in his Maker's sight, that he may turn away from the sin which he now loves, and may seek his God, whom he has despised and neglected."[209] "God's good qualities," Fitzmyer says, "have a salutary end: they are meant to bring sinners to a recognition of what their status really is."[210] Henry states, "Means are mercies, and the more light we sin against, the more love we sin against."[211]

Warren Wiersbe writes, "Have you not heard lost sinners today say, 'Oh, I'm sure God isn't going to send me to Hell. Why, He's done so many good things for me.' Little do they realize that God's goodness is the preparation for His grace; and instead of bowing in humble gratitude, they harden their hearts and commit more sin, thinking that God loves them too much to condemn them."[212] But they couldn't be more wrong. God will not suspend His condition for salvation for any man (Galatians 6:7).

Thy mercy is more than a match for my heart,
Which wonders to feel its own hardness depart;
Dissolved by Thy goodness, I fall to the ground
And weep to the praise of the mercy I've found.
~ John Stocker (1776)

God's goodness lavished out to the believer in salvation (and afterwards) incites deeper love, louder praise, greater devotion and heightened allegiance to Christ. Spurgeon speaks of the impact of grace in the believer's life: "I expect that as I learn more of His goodness, it will always continue to lead me to repentance, and I trust, beloved brethren and sisters in Christ, you can bear me witness that I do but speak what is in your mind also. The dearer Christ is to us, the blacker is sin in our sight. The sweeter the love of God is to us, the more bitter is the thought of having so long sinned against it. The more you see, in these shoreless, bottomless deeps, what divine grace has done for you, and to you, the more you smite upon your breast and cry, 'How could I ever have sinned against the Lord as I have done, and how can I sin against Him as I still continue to do?'"[213]

R. C. Sproul states, "The more we understand how kind God has been to us and the more we are overcome by His mercy, the more we are inclined to love Him and to serve Him."[214] God's grace in us teaches how we are to live rightly and motivates us to live accordingly (Titus 2:12).

32 Security of Grace

Grace (lovingkindness, mercy, favor of God through Christ) guarantees the believer's salvation (eternal security). The moment one repents and in faith receives Jesus Christ as Lord and Savior, his or her name is written in permanent ink in the Lamb's Book of Life in Heaven. Pink quotes Abraham Booth, who states, "The Reign of Grace thus, 'It is the eternal and absolute free favor of God, manifested in the vouchsafement of spiritual and eternal blessings to the guilty and the unworthy.'"[215]

Oh, tell me that my worthless name
 Is graven on Thy hands!
Show me some promise in Thy book
 Where my salvation stands!
~ Isaac Watts (1674–1748)

"We are in Christ, who is God," says A. T. Robertson, "and no burglar, not even Satan himself, can separate us from the love of God in Christ Jesus (Romans 8:31–39)."[216] At the moment of salvation, by grace, God covers a person with the canopy of

Christ's perfected righteousness (imputes); and from that moment forward, when He looks at that person, He sees Christ's righteousness (2 Corinthians 5:21), not that person's wretchedness, making salvation eternally secure. J. I. Packer wrote, "Guidance, like all God's acts of blessing under the covenant of grace, is a sovereign act. Not merely does God will to guide us in the sense of showing us His way, that we may tread it; He wills also to guide us in the more fundamental sense of ensuring that, whatever happens, whatever mistakes we may make, we shall come safely home. Slippings and strayings there will be, no doubt, but the everlasting arms are beneath us; we shall be caught, rescued, restored. This is God's promise; this is how good He is."[217]

> The love of Christ is rich and free,
> Fixed on His own eternally.
> Nor earth, nor Hell, can it remove;
> Long as He lives, His own He'll love.
>
> His loving heart engaged to be
> Their everlasting Surety.
> 'Twas love that took their cause in hand,
> And love maintains it to the end.
>
> Love cannot from its post withdraw;
> Nor death, nor Hell, nor sin, nor law
> Can turn the Surety's heart away.
> He'll love His own to endless day.
>
> At death, beyond the grave, He'll love;
> In endless bliss, His own shall prove
> The blazing glory of that love
> Which never could from them remove.
>
> ~ William Gadsby (1773–1844)

Grace also guarantees the love of God and provision for every crisis, calamity, and care in the believer's life. The Bible says, "But from everlasting to everlasting the LORD'S love ['loving-kindness; steadfast love; grace; mercy; faithfulness;

goodness; devotion.'[218]] is with those who fear him" (Psalm 103:17 NIV).

> Lord, I would own Thy tender care
>   And all Thy love to me;
> The food I eat, the clothes I wear
>   Are all bestowed by Thee.
>
> 'Tis Thou preservest me from death
>   And dangers every hour;
> I cannot draw another breath
>   Unless Thou give me power.
>
> Kind angels guard me every night,
>   As round my bed they stay;
> Nor am I absent from Thy sight
>   In darkness or by day.
>
> My health, and friends, and parents dear,
>   To me by God are giv'n;
> I have not any blessing here
>   But what is sent from Heav'n.
>
> Such goodness, Lord, and constant care,
>   I never can repay;
> But may it be my daily prayer
>   To love Thee and obey.
>
> ~ Jane Taylor (1809)

A traveler crossed what he thought was a safe bridge during a terrific storm at night. The bridgekeeper, in seeing him, said, "In the name of God, where did you come from?" The traveler replied, "I crossed the bridge." The man lodged with the bridgekeeper for the night. The next morning, he took him back to the bridge which he had crossed. All the planks of the bridge had been torn away by the storm, and nothing remained except several beams stretching from one side to the other of the chasm. Somehow the traveler walked in the center of one of those beams the distance of a hundred feet, below which was a rushing swollen river. The man, in seeing how near he came to death, fainted.

All of God's children can look back and see that grace time and again has carried them safely across unbeknown dilapidated "bridges" on a single beam, sparing them from grievous hurt and harm. The Bible says, "He keeps his eye upon you as you come and go and always guards you" (Psalm 121:8 TLB).

33   Service of Grace

Peter wrote his two epistles (1 and 2 Peter) to enable the saints' growth in grace. Further, he prayed that God's grace would increase in measure to them. This speaks of the Holy Spirit's use of human agency to evince (reveal) the grace of God to others in various ways. The Bible says, "God has shown you his grace in many different ways. So be good servants and use whatever gift he has given you in a way that will best serve each other" (1 Peter 4:10 ERV). Spurgeon said, "If we have received the grace of God in our hearts, its practical effect has been to make us God's servants."[219] Matthew Henry states, "The serviceableness of this grace. Grace for grace is grace for the promoting and advancing of grace. Grace to be exercised by ourselves; gracious habits for gracious acts. Grace to be ministered to others; gracious vouchsafements for gracious performances: grace is a talent to be traded with. The apostles received grace (Romans 1:5 and Ephesians 3:8), that they might communicate it (1 Peter 4:10)."[220]

"Grace infuseth a spirit of activity into a person," saith Watson. "Grace doth not lie dormant in the soul; it is not a sleepy habit, but it makes a Christian like a seraphim, swift-winged in his heavenly motions."[221] Grace purges of laziness and slothfulness. Grace is not based upon good works but will result in good works in its recipient's life. See 2 Corinthians 8:1–3. It was grace, Paul testifies, that not only made him the new man that he was but enabled him to "labor" harder than all the other apostles (1 Corinthians 15:10a). But he says, "It was not I really; it was God's grace that was with me" (1 Corinthians 15:10b ESV). That is, it wasn't natural ability or desire that prompted the radical change in his life or enabled the tremendous works (therefore, there was no reason to boast), but the grace of God alone. "Paul attributes all to the grace of God," states Gill, "and nothing to himself; it was the grace of God that made him an apostle of Christ, and preacher of the Gospel; it was that which being bestowed on him qualified him for it; it was that which enabled him to labor and toil, to do and suffer all he did, and which gave success to all his ministrations."[222] See Colossians 1:28. Paul's life is a testimony that grace doesn't turn a person into a "couch-potato" but energizes and equips him for profitable kingdom work which involves "hard work" in biblical study and the harvest field.

Spurgeon said, "We must ever keep in mind that we are only channels for grace. We are not even pools and reservoirs; we must have a continual supply of Divine gifts. We must have *an abiding union* with the Fountain of all good, or we should soon run dry; and only as fresh streams flow into us are we kept from becoming mere dry beds of sand and mire, but we know that He will never fail us."[223]

Let us determine to use the grace (loving-kindness, mercy, abilities, virtues) we possess to minister in behalf of Christ, like Paul, less it had been 'bestowed on us in vain' (1 Corinthians 15:10). Henry remarks that believers "should cherish, and exercise, and exert, this heavenly principle [grace]. So did Paul, and therefore labored with so much heart and so much success."[224] See 2 Corinthians 9:6. Any and all good that we might do to enhance the cause of Christ and alleviate the hurts and sorrows of man will flow from the grace of God within us. Spurgeon said, "The fact is, all of us need grace. You who preach the Gospel, you who are deacons, you who are elders, you who teach the infant class, you who can only give away a tract—you must do all these works with grace or else you will not really do them at all."[225]

Ways to share God's grace to others

To the grief-stricken, minister the grace of comfort that was received when experiencing death of a loved one.

To the devastated, minister the grace of hope that was received in a time of hopelessness.

To the guilt-ridden sinner, minister the grace of God's forgiveness that you have experienced numerous times.

To the crushed and brokenhearted over the breakup of their home (divorce, abandonment by parents), administer by the Holy Spirit that grace which was received that enabled you to withstand the horrendous ordeal. Use your pain for their gain in Jesus' name.

To the addicted (drugs, alcohol, pornography), be a channel of deliverance by sharing that grace of God that freed you from its power, tyranny and captivity.

To the terminally ill, minister the grace of God received that has enabled you to face its reality and eventual end calmy and courageously.

To the offender of your heart, minister the grace received from God in your transgression against Him.

To the pain-ridden sufferer, instill the grace of God received that prompted your endurance.

To the persecuted Christian, administer that same grace that sustained you in maltreatment and oppression for the faith.

To the downcast ("empty"), share that marvelous grace of God in Christ Jesus that filled you to overflowing with joy unspeakable, meaning, and significance. Saith Spurgeon, "Oh! tell it the wide world over. Tell it in time and in eternity, free grace hath done it. Free grace hath done it from the first to the last. I was a brand in the fire, but he plucked me from the burning, quenched me in his blood, and now He declares I shall be with Him forever in Heaven."[226]

To the heavy burdened, minister the grace of God that alleviated your cares and concerns.

The help that we received in the "time of need" is sharable through the leadership and empowerment of the Holy Spirit. Don't allow the grace received to terminate with you; use it at God's hand to help alleviate another's grief, pain, hardship and trial. MacArthur writes, "If I'm not showing grace…have I forgotten the grace I've been shown."[227]

Paul testified in Romans 1:14, "I am debtor both to the Greeks, and to the Barbarians; both to the wise, and to the unwise." Vincent quotes Godet as saying, "All men, without distinction of nation or culture, are Paul's creditors, He owes them his life, his person, in virtue of the grace bestowed upon him, and of the office which he has received."[228] Maclaren states, "Every servant of Jesus Christ who has received the truth for himself has received it as a steward, and is, as such, indebted to God, *from* whom he got the trust, and to the men *for* whom he got it. The only limit to the obligation is, as Paul says in the context, 'as much as in me is.' Capacity, determined by faculties, opportunities, and circumstances, prescribes the kind and the degree of the work to be done in discharge of the obligation; but the obligation is universal. We are not at liberty to choose whether we shall do our part in spreading the name of Jesus Christ. It is a debt that we owe to God and to men."[229]

Saith Spurgeon, "There are foes behind us as well as before us. Attacks may come from any quarter. We read that Amalek fell upon Israel and slew some of the hindmost of them. The experienced Christian will find much work for his weapons in aiding those poor doubting, desponding, wavering souls, who are hindmost in faith, knowledge, and joy. These must not be left unaided, and therefore be it the business of well-taught saints to bear their standards among the hindmost. My soul, do thou tenderly watch to help the hindmost this day."[230] See Numbers 2:31. The bottom line, Henry says, "If redeemed by the blood, and converted by the grace of the Lord Jesus, we are altogether His; and for His sake we are debtors to all men, to do all the good we can. Such services are our duty."[231]

34   Solution of Grace

"Therefore, brethren, we are debtors" (Romans 8:12). For debts incurred, a statement is received for "payment due." Man's sin against Holy God incurred spiritual indebtedness, the eternal separation from God in the domain of Hell. This debt is beyond man's means to pay, for it's not payable with good deeds, self-righteousness, philanthropy, church ordinances (baptism/Lord's Supper) or religious affiliation and rituals. Therefore, man has "no hope" (Ephesians 2:12) to personally remedy the problem.

But there is Good News: God has provided man a solution to remedy the sin problem. The Bible says, "When we were utterly helpless, with no way of escape, Christ came at just the right time and died for us sinners who had no use for him. Even if we were good, we really wouldn't expect anyone to die for us, though, of course, that might be barely possible. But God showed his great love for us by sending Christ to die for us while we were still sinners. And since by his blood he did all this for us as sinners, how much more will he do for us now that he has declared us not guilty? Now he will save us from all of God's wrath to come" (Romans 5:6–9 TLB). "He came to pay a debt He didn't owe because we owed a debt we couldn't pay." Jesus Christ at Calvary paid our sin debt in full with His precious, redeeming blood and stamped upon its statement (invoice), "Paid in Full." Nothing more is to be done. "It is finished" (John 19:30). It is a settled debt for time and eternity. Undeserved and unmerited and totally free, it was made possible by the grace of God. Hallelujah!

Handel's *Messiah* premiered on April 13, 1742, as a charitable benefit for those in debtors' prison. Enough funds (400 pounds) were received to set free 142 men. The Messiah (Jesus) paid the ultimate price on the Cross for man's release from sin's debtors' prison. As with the 142, all one must do to be saved, released from captivity, is to act upon the offer. (Revelation 22:17; Acts 16:31)

Spurgeon eloquently says, "Grace steps forth to be glorified *at Calvary*. Having given man blessings through long ages, Grace comes up to Calvary and there gives its last—no, its first, its all, its grandest gift! Grace gives up the Incarnate Son of God to die! He gives up His own life and bows His head upon the Cross. There may be much of shame and ignominy about the Cross— assuredly there is, for there we see sin punished—but how much there is of Glory and of majesty, for there we see Grace triumphant over itself—Grace in the heart of Christ leading Him to save others while Himself He cannot save!"[232]

All mankind fell in Adam's fall;
One common sin infects them all.
From sire to son the bane descends
And over all its curse impends.

Through all man's pow'rs corruption creeps
And him in dreadful bondage keeps;
In guilt he draws his infant breath
And reaps its fruits of woe and death.

From hearts depraved, to evil prone,
Flow thoughts and deeds of sin alone;
God's image lost, the darkened soul
Nor seeks nor finds its heav'nly goal.

But Christ, the second Adam, came
To bear our sin and woe and shame,
To be our Life, our Light, our Way,
Our only Hope, our only Stay.

As by one man all mankind fell
And, born in sin, was doomed to Hell,
So by one Man, who took our place,
We all received the gift of grace.

We thank thee, Christ; new life is ours,
New light, new hope, new strength, new pow'rs.
May grace our ev'ry way attend
Until we reach our journey's end!

~ Lazarus Spengler (1524)

But wherein grace is a "gift" of God for man's soul redemption (forgiveness of sin and reconciliation to God) without obligation, it nonetheless bears the believers indebtedness of gratitude. As Arnot says, "The forgiven sinner is clear in the book of God's judgment, but he owes much to his Redeemer. He is as deeply in debt as ever, but it is now a debt of gratitude. It is greater than he can ever pay; but the more he realizes its greatness, the happier he grows."[233] Spurgeon states, "Christ has paid the debt His people owed. I am a debtor to God's love, I am a debtor to God's grace, I am a debtor to God's power, I am a debtor to God's forgiving mercy; but I am no debtor to His justice—for He Himself will never accuse me of a debt once paid. But then because we are not debtors to God in that sense [justice], we become ten times more debtors to God than we should have been otherwise. Because He has remitted all our debt of sin, we are all the more indebted to Him in another sense. Consider how much you owe to His forgiving grace, that after ten thousand affronts He loves you as infinitely as ever; and after a myriad of sins, His Spirit still resides within you."[234] Amen and Amen.

When this passing world is done,
When has sunk yon glaring sun,
When we stand with Christ on high
Looking o'er life's history,
Then, Lord, shall I fully know,
Not till then, how much I owe.

When I stand before the throne,
Dressed in beauty not my own,
When I see Thee as Thou art,
Love thee with unsinning heart,
Then, Lord, shall I fully know,
Not till then, how much I owe.

~ Robert M. McCheyne (1837)

35　Setting Apart of Grace

Grace makes possible the call to ministry. It qualifies man for that for which he is disqualified (1 Corinthians 15:10). In Ephesians 3:7 Paul says, "Whereof I was made [at a specific moment of time and place[235]] a minister, according to ["in consequence of"[236]] the gift of the grace of God given unto me by the effectual working of his power." And again, in Galatians

1:15 he states, "But God chose me before I was born. By His loving-favor [grace] He called me to work for Him" (NLV). Bruce says, "There the general call of God to all His people is in view; here that is included, but it involves also the special call of God to Paul for his personal life-work."[237] See Romans 1:5. Saith Barnes, "It was a mere matter of grace that Paul was called into the ministry"[238]—and for me as well (1 Corinthians 1:28).

Paul is clarifying (in both texts) that his role (position) as an apostle (minister) was not man-appointed or self-chosen (Gill: "He did not thrust himself into this work."[239]) or based upon any human means or merits but solely upon the gift of God's grace founded and revealed through Jesus Christ. Note, grace (God's unmerited loving-kindness and favor in Christ Jesus) made possible the divine call to a religiously strict but spiritually blinded Pharisee, Jesus' hater, Christian persecutor and "chief of sinners" to declare the unsearchable riches of Christ Jesus. See Acts 22:4–5; Acts 26:10–11; Acts 7:58–8:1 and Acts 9:1–2. Now that's amazing grace! Saith Spurgeon, "In a moment Paul saw everything in a different light; and from a foe he was changed into a staunch and loyal friend of Jesus. He was not disobedient to the heavenly vision."[240]

Nothing but grace can change a wretched sinner like Paul into a workman for God, a persecutor into a preacher. Grace not only suddenly qualified the unqualified for gospel ministry but just as suddenly readied him for the task (1 Corinthians 15:10).

Barclay comments "It was to Paul an amazing thing, that he, the arch-persecutor, had been chosen as the missionary and the pioneer of Christ. It was not only that Jesus Christ had forgiven him; it was that Christ had trusted him. Sometimes in human affairs we forgive a man who has committed some mistake or who has been guilty of some sin, but we make it very clear that his past makes it impossible for us to trust him again with any responsibility. But Christ had not only forgiven Paul, but He had entrusted him with His work to do. The man who had been the persecutor of Christ had been made the ambassador of Christ."[241]

Let this encourage all that feel disqualified for Christian ministry due to past sin but who now "are washed,…are

71

sanctified,…are justified in the name of the Lord Jesus, and by the Spirit of our God" (1 Corinthians 6:11). Grace is the fountain out of which the call to ministry flows. Grace takes the unfit and unworthy, making them *eligible* candidates for vocational Christian work. Many may experience that extravagant grace without divine summons to vocational Christian work. But none receive that sacred summons apart from the work of grace in their heart. See 1 Corinthians 15:10 and 1 Timothy 1:16.

36 Standard of Grace

The Apostle Paul says that we should 'therefore walk [conduct] worthy [honorably] of the calling [grace] we have received' (Ephesians 4:1). "Therefore" points back to the previous three chapters (Ephesians 1–3) that recite the story of the Christian's transformation from sin to righteousness, captivity to freedom, darkness to light, and Hell to Heaven all through the loving-kindness (grace) and mercy of Jesus Christ. The believer's response to this bestowal of free grace should prompt a walk (conduct, lifestyle) worthy (standard, criterion of walk honorably) in expression and gratitude of the grace that made it possible.

To walk worthy of grace, Simeon says, "is a vocation [calling] from death to life, from sin to holiness, from Hell to Heaven."[242] See Romans 12:1. It is to walk a holy, blameless, loving, faith-based, witnessing, and devoted, and happy life. It is to exemplify Christ in all of life and educate and edify people to the riches of His grace. See Philippians 1:27; Colossians 1:10; and 1 Thessalonians 2:12. It is to trust in what Christ promises (2 Corinthians 1:20) and to perform what He commands (John 14:15).[243] Simeon continues, "Shew that the welfare of the Church and the honor of your Lord lie near your heart, and let no effort be wanting on your part to promote so glorious an object. Be willing to sacrifice any interest or wish of your own for the attainment of it, even as Paul 'became all things to all men' and 'sought not his own profit, but the profit of many, that they might be saved.'"[244]

Grace ought to permeate the whole of life. Every part of the camphor tree is impregnated with precious perfume that exudes from the highest twig to the lowest root.[245] Just so, the precious perfume of grace should permeate and be manifest in every relationship (parental, spousal, sibling, friendship, etc.), conversation, action and pursuit. Such is the high and honorable standard of grace that all ought to demonstrate. And if not, there is need for "growth in grace" (2 Peter 3:18).

> Love of God, so pure and changeless!
> Blood of Christ, so rich and free!
> Grace of God, so strong and boundless!
> Magnify them all in me.
>
> ~ Elizabeth Codner (1860)

Grace leads the believer to live differently and make a difference for the "sake of Christ." It may lead him to a remote mission field in India to bear testimony for Christ, or to the rescue mission to serve food, or to stand up for the unborn, or to visit the prison to set the captive free in Jesus' name from the chains of sin. It leads us to tell to one and all (the corrupt politician, pornographer, alcoholic, drug addict, sex addict, blasphemous, anti-Christian) the glorious riches of His grace that they may know the liberty, love and life that we embrace and enjoy.

And all this the believer willingly does not out of mere "duty" but the "delight" that flows from a grateful heart that has been set free. This is his new standard of conduct and behavior (state of grace). As a partaker of grace, honor it, be grateful for it, use it worthily by manifesting it in your life, demonstrating it unto the world and extending it to the broken in heart and needy. Make sure it has not been bestowed upon you in vain (2 Corinthians 6:1). Be ever as the prodigal's father, looking for and awaiting the opportunity to exhibit the grace of Christ to him that is in its great need (Luke 15:20–24).

37 Substitutes of Grace

"Make sure that no one falls short of the grace of God" (Hebrews 12:15 CSB). The text speaks not of one that has received grace and then falls back, but him that is near to obtaining it but doesn't. He appears to be a Christian (speech, conduct, profession), but he has never been born again (never experienced the grace of God in salvation). He stands on the edge of salvation and eternal life but fails to cross over to its saving and redeeming side by God's grace. Of these Jesus says, "Thou art not far from the Kingdom of God" (Mark 12:34). Make sure that you are not among the almost saved, but the altogether saved (2 Peter 1:10).

> So near to the Kingdom! yet what dost thou lack?
> So near to the Kingdom! what keepeth thee back?
> Renounce every idol, though dear it may be,
> And come to the Savior now pleading with thee!
>
> So near that thou hearest the songs that resound
> From those who, believing, a pardon have found;
> So near yet unwilling to give up thy sin,
> When Jesus is waiting to welcome thee in.
>
> To die with no hope! hast thou counted the cost?
> To die out of Christ, and thy soul to be lost?
> So near to the Kingdom! Oh, come, we implore;
> While Jesus is pleading, come enter the door!
> ~ Fanny Crosby (1875)

A second application of the text is cited in Jude 4. "For there are certain men crept in unawares, who were before of old ordained to this condemnation, ungodly men, turning the grace of our God into lasciviousness, and denying the only Lord God, and our Lord Jesus Christ." Satan allures men away from partaking of saving grace through various counterfeit substitutes such as good works, baptism, the Lord's Supper, church attendance, a clean life and religious disciplines (prayer, Bible study, witnessing, etc.). Spurgeon cautions, "If there be one stitch in the celestial garment of our righteousness which we are to insert ourselves, then we are lost; but this is our confidence: the Lord who began will perfect. He has done it all, must do it all, and will do it all. Our confidence must not be in what we have done, nor in what we have resolved to do, but entirely in what the Lord will do."[246]

"Salvation comes from the LORD alone" (Jonah 2:9 NLT). This text, to Spurgeon, was the sum and substance of salvation by grace alone.[247] Salvation is all of grace, not in degree or part, but in the whole. Any "substance or thing" added to God's grace adulterates its power to forgive sin and reconcile to God. Stott is correct in stating, "We cannot rely on church tradition for our message, for we cannot accept the 'two-source' theory of divine revelation, namely that Holy Scripture and holy tradition are independent, equal, and authoritative sources of doctrine. Rather, we see tradition standing alongside Scripture as a fallible interpretation of an infallible revelation."[248]

> No tears can wash my sins away;
>   I'm saved by grace alone.
> No deeds of love my debt can pay;
>   I'm saved by grace alone.
>
> Out from the depths of sin I cried
> Unto the Lord once crucified;
> He gently drew me to His side.
> I'm saved by grace alone.
>
> ~ Lizzie DeArmond (1903)

It is the pastor's duty to "make sure that no one falls short of the grace of God" (Hebrews 12:15 CSB) through exhorting members of the church to examine (investigate seriously) the basis for their hope of eternal life (Hebrews 13:7; 2 Corinthians 13:5). With the words of Paul, he is to urge them to "examine yourselves, to see whether you are in the faith. Test yourselves. Or do you not realize this about yourselves, that Jesus Christ is in you—unless indeed you fail to meet the test!" (2 Corinthians 13:5 ESV). He must warn of the deceptive trickery of the enemy to blind eyes to the truth of one's spiritual identity (Matthew 7:21–23) in an effort to prevent possession of a false hope. May his passion be that of John Welch who was seen in the coldest of winter nights on the ground wrestling and pleading with the Lord for his flock by his wife. Upon inquiry concerning his great despair, he said, "I have the souls of three thousand to answer for, while I know not how it is with many of them." Oh, that every pastor might manifest such concern and burden for the souls of his congregational membership. (The task ought to be supplemented by every teacher, officer, deacon, elder, and member in the church.) Spurgeon says, "The tares grow in the same furrows as the wheat. There is no floor which is as yet thoroughly purged from chaff. Sinners mix with saints, as dross mingles with gold. God's precious diamonds still lie in the same field with pebbles."[249]

Pink says, "Sin darkens the understanding, so that man is unable to perceive his real state before God. Satan 'hath blinded the minds of them which believe not' (2 Corinthians 4:4). The deep-rooted pride of our hearts makes us think the best of ourselves, so that if a question is raised in our hearts, we are ever prone to give ourselves the benefit of the doubt. A spirit of sloth possesses us by nature, so that we are unwilling to go to the trouble which real self-examination calls for. Hence the vast majority of religious professors remain with a head knowledge of the Truth, with outward attention to forms and ceremonies, or resting on a mere consent to the letter of some verse like John 3:16, refusing to 'make their calling and election sure.'"[250] The genuine Christian will bear fruit! See John 15:5 and Matthew 13:8. "It is expected," states Matthew Henry, "from those who enjoy the mercies of grace that, both in the temper of their minds and in the tenor of their lives, they comply with the intentions of that grace, and then they bring forth fruit."[251]

Therefore, to you, the reader, I implore, 'Look [examine; give attention to] diligently lest any man fail [to lack] of the grace of God.' Are you trusting totally in the free grace of God (not rituals, rites, adherence to the commandments, ordinances, good deeds or morality) provided through the death, burial and resurrection of Jesus Christ for the forgiveness of sins and rightness with God? Grace brings freedom in Christ Jesus (John 8:36); the law, bondage to rules and regulations (Romans 6:14).

Only through grace, oh, wonderful story!
    Only through grace, prolong the sweet sound!
Only through grace, it echoes in glory!
    Only through grace, the lost has been found!

Only through grace, our Father in Heaven
    Sent His dear Son to die in our place.
Life and salvation through Him are given—
    Wonderful love! Oh, wonderful grace!

Only through grace, we press on our journey,
    Kept by the power of God till the end.
Only through grace we'll enter the portals;
    Then to the Father grace will commend.

Wonderful story! wonderful Savior!
    Jesus has died and rose from the grave!
Join the glad chorus; praise Him forever—
    Jesus had died, lost sinners to save!

~ J. P. Lane (1909)

Maclaren and Gustart were both ministers in Edinburgh. When Maclaren was on his deathbed, Gustart asked, "What are you doing, brother?" Maclaren replied, "I'll tell you what I'm doing, brother. I am gathering together all my prayers, all my sermons, all my good deeds, all my evil deeds; and I am going to throw them all overboard and swim to Glory on the plank of free grace."[252] That's the only "plank" that will get us to the shores of Glory.

38   Speech of Grace

"Tongues are more terrible instruments than can be made with hammers and anvils, and the evil which they inflict cuts deeper and spreads wider."[253] Therefore Paul instructs, "Let your speech be alway with grace, seasoned with salt" (Colossians 4:6). That is, let your speech always be full of "graciousness, attractiveness," that which delights and charms"[254] to the ungodly.

77

As Piper says, "Make your mouth the means of grace."[255] Criswell says, "'Grace' denotes undeserved favor; 'salt' suggests that one should allow the Holy Spirit to convict others of sin, righteousness, and judgment to come (John 16:8). The salt that stings and pricks the conscience of the nonbeliever should be accompanied by undeserved favor and unconditional love."[256]

Jamieson, Fausset and Brown say, "Even the smallest leaf of the believer should be full of the sap of the Holy Spirit (Jeremiah 17:7–8). His conversation should be cheerful without levity, serious without gloom."[257] Expositors says: "*We* must strive to cultivate the gift of pleasant and wise conversation, so that *we* may be able to speak appropriately to each individual (with his peculiar needs) with whom *we* come in contact."[258] See Ephesians 4:29.

The believer's speech is to flow from the grace of God known and experienced in the heart. It is not condemnatory, belittling, rude or cruel, but gracious, sweet, gentle, hopeful and kind. It is to be appetizing, not tasteless. This precept is to be uniformly applied. Solomon says, "The tongue [words] of the just is as choice silver: the heart of the wicked is little worth" (Proverbs 10:20), and, "From a wise mind comes careful and persuasive speech" (Proverbs 16:23 TLB). Jesus said, "For every one shall be salted with fire, and every sacrifice shall be salted with salt" (Mark 9:49). Ignatius said in Magnesians 10:3: "Be salted in him [Christ]"[259] and then be seasoned salt unto others in deeds and words. Matthew Henry says, "Grace is the salt which seasons our discourse, makes it savory, and keeps it from corrupting."[260] It alone penetrates, pulverizes and purifies the heart from all iniquity through the empowerment of the Holy Spirit. See Proverbs 18:21.

The speech of grace knows how to answer man's inquiries and objections to the Gospel (Psalm 119:42) with meekness (gentleness) and fear (1 Peter 3:15). But it also knows how to respond to the brokenhearted to provide comfort and to the afflicted in times of their distress, granting hope and relief. Solomon says, "The words of the wise bring healing" (Proverbs 12:18 NET). See Proverbs 25:11. Grace speech flows from the lips by the free grace of God "without our merit, for we do not deserve to be trusted with a single good word."[261] And we all need plentiful grace to know what to say, when to say it, how much to say, and how to say it with effectualness. "The fountain of sound speech is knowledge drawn from the Word of God, laid up in the speaker's mind."[262] See Proverbs 19:7 and Psalm 19:8.

> Lord, speak to me, that I may speak
> In living echoes of Thy tone;
> As Thou hast sought, so let me seek
> Thy erring children lost and lone.
>
> Oh, teach me, Lord, that I may teach
> The precious things Thou dost impart;
> And wing my words, that they may reach
> The hidden depths of many a heart.
>
> Oh, give Thine own sweet rest to me,
> That I may speak with soothing power
> A word in season, as from Thee,
> To weary ones in needful hour.
>
> Oh, fill me with Thy fulness, Lord,
> Until my very heart o'erflow
> In kindling thought and glowing word,
> Thy love to tell, Thy praise to show.
>
> ~ Frances Ridley Havergal (1872)

By speech with grace Paul is not just referencing religious conversations but all interactions (child, spouse, friend, opponent). Care must be made not to be injurious or discourteous but kind and loving in all that is said. Such can only spring and surely will spring from a grace-filled heart. James cautions, "If anyone appears to be 'religious' but cannot control his tongue, he deceives himself and we may be sure that his religion is useless" (James 1:26 PHILLIPS). What's the cure to vain and painful talk? James says, "Understand this: Everyone should be quick to listen, slow to speak, and slow to anger" (James 1:19 BSB).

Keep me from saying words
   That later need recalling;
Guard me, lest idle speech
   May from my lips be falling.
But when, within my place,
   I must and ought to speak,
Then to my words give grace,
   Lest I offend the weak.

       ~ Johann Heermann (1630)

What's the cure for uncontrolled hostile and hateful speech? It is to fervently pray, "Set a watch, O LORD, before my mouth; keep the door of my lips" (Psalm 141:3). What is it that bridles the tongue? James says, "All kinds of animals, birds, reptiles and sea creatures are being tamed and have been tamed by mankind, but no human being can tame the tongue. It is a restless evil, full of deadly poison" (James 3:7–8 NIV). He that bridles the tongue does so by the grace of God, not mere determined intent. The more a person is "salted" with God's grace the more the tongue is controllable. Piper says, "The question for your mouth will not merely be the moral question: Am I avoiding dirty words? but the Christian question: Am I building the faith of others by what I say? Is my mouth a means of grace?"[263]

39 Spectacle of Grace

The Bible says, "That in the ages to come he might show the exceeding riches of his grace in his kindness toward us through Christ Jesus" (Ephesians 2:7). That is, at some point in the future God will point at all the redeemed as a trophy of His amazing grace. Barnes explains, "The sense is, that the riches of divine grace, and the divine benignity, would be shown in the conversion of Christians and their salvation, to all future times. Such was his love to those who were lost, that it would be an everlasting monument [trophy] of His mercy, a perpetual and unchanging proof that He was good. The sense is, we are raised up with Christ and are made to partake of His honor and glory in order that others may forever be impressed with a sense of the divine goodness and mercy to us."[264]

In Heaven there will be a parade of all the saved by grace. Amongst them will be some of the most notorious, worst, meanest, vilest, most profane and evil men. God will point to them all saying, "These are examples of the exceeding riches of grace; they are trophies of My grace." He will showplace Paul (the chief of sinners) as one that persecuted His people who by the riches of His grace was transformed into a minister of the Gospel. He will showplace Manasseh who was changed by grace from being a wicked and vile, contemptible king into being a child of God (2 Chronicles 33:11–13). He will showplace the thief that hung next to Jesus on the Cross whose strong faith led to the experience of the riches of God's grace in salvation. And He also will point at Billy Graham, Charles Finney, John Wesley, Billy Sunday, D. L. Moody, and the remainder of the host of Heaven as trophies of the riches of His grace (examples of what His grace did in a man and through a man for His glory). And one day, thankfully, because we have experienced the riches of His grace, He will point at us similarly.

In the midst of that great parade, I can envision the saints in union crying out, "saying in a loud voice, Deserving is the Lamb, Who was sacrificed, to receive all the power and riches and wisdom and might and honor and majesty (glory, splendor) and blessing!" (Revelation 5:12 AMPC). Amen and Amen.

James R. Fanning, Jr., a personal friend, wrote prior to his death a poem about the triumph of grace. Note especially the third stanza.

> Someday I'll receive my summons
>   To cross the great divide.
> I'll not journey by myself;
>   He'll be there by my side.
>
> As I cross the river,
>   My Savior's face I'll see.
> Sin will be gone forever;
>   Grace reigns triumphantly!

On that exhibition day,
    All things will have their place.
God's children will be on display
    As trophies of His grace.

Then through all eternity,
    We'll shout the glad refrain:
"Sin is driven from the throne;
    In victory grace reigns!"

Grace reigns in righteousness reckoned unto me;
Grace reigns by Jesus Christ who died on Calvary;
Grace reigns in spite of sin and strife;
Grace reigns in victory unto eternal life.

              ~ Used by permission of Julia Fanning

40   Slighting of Grace

Paul admonishes, "As God's fellow-workers we also urge you not to receive his grace and then do nothing with it" (2 Corinthians 6:1 CJB). Grace is the most magnificent gift that Christ has given man but also the most slighted, neglected and taken for granted. It is slighted when its redeeming power to rescue from sin is scorned or shunned (Hebrews 2:3; John 5:40). Lapide cites Anselm: "He receives grace into a vacuum...who does not work with it, who does not give it his heart, and who, through sloth, makes that grace ineffectual, by not doing all that he can to express it in good works."[265]

O souls who spurn salvation,
    See this eternity
Of darkness, desolation,
    And constant agony.

The torments none can banish,
    Nor aught can peace restore;
And hope itself shall vanish,
    When time shall be no more!

Awake! the voice still soundeth;
   'Tis now the accepted hour.
The grace of God aboundeth
   To save from sin's dread power.

Make haste, implore Christ's favor,
   Thy sins confess, and bow
Before Thy Lord and Savior;
   The accepted time is now.
          ~ Frans Mikael Franzen (1772–1847)

Grace is slighted when believers fail to take advantage of the access to God it affords in times of trouble and trial (Hebrews 4:16). It is slighted when we fail to allow it to enable change in our carnal attitudes, appetites, affiliations, and affections; when we hinder its transformation of our total being to the glory of God. It is slighted when we neglect to share it to benefit others. It is slighted when it is not cultivated continuously. It is slighted by absenteeism from church. It is slighted in unreal worship, unreal prayer, unreal humility, unreal purity, unreal service, and unreal repentance. It is slighted when it is merely a counterfeit of the genuine.

Concisely, grace is slighted when the believer fails to fashion his walk, belief, thought, and talk after that of Christ (Romans 12:1–2 and Ezekiel 33:31). Slighting the grace of God robs not only of Christian bliss and usefulness, but also of a heavenly reward for service to Christ (2 Corinthians 5:10, 15; 1 Corinthians 3:15).Spurgeon says, "Never neglect the means of grace; God may bless us when we are not in His house, but we have the greater reason to hope that He will when we are in communion with His saints."[266] J. Vernon McGee says, "The problem is that many of us do not avail ourselves of His grace. Tell Him you need grace. We all need grace, and it is available, but we've got to apply for it. We need to ask Him for it. Do not fail of the grace of God."[267] See Hebrews 12:15.

The Bible cautions, "For, brethren, ye have been called unto liberty [by and through grace]; only use not liberty for an occasion to the flesh, but by love serve one another" (Galatians 5:13). Since the time of conversion have you progressed in grace? Have you gradually become a better Christian and saintlier? Has the grace that made you free been used "for an occasion to the flesh" (to entertain carnal habits, and appetites)? Have you used it to love and serve others? Has grace been slighted to the end that little spiritual growth and advancement has been achieved? If so, resolve to allow grace to transform you until you are more like Jesus.

Simeon passionately appeals, "Many hate it [the Gospel of grace], and oppose it with all their might; either regarding it as foolishness, through their philosophic pride, or making it a stumbling-block, through their self-righteous habits. To all such it comes in vain, or rather, worse than in vain, seeing that it proves to them a savor of death to their more aggravated condemnation. In truth, all receive it in vain, who do not welcome it into their hearts and conform to it in their lives. Oh, that it might be embraced thus by all to whom it now comes! Receive it, brethren, as the most stupendous effort of Divine Wisdom for the salvation of your souls."[268] See 1 Corinthians 1:18.

41   Sermon Subject of Grace

Since the Gospel stands or falls upon the doctrine of grace, its preaching and teaching ought to be paramount. But, alas, it is a doctrine that seldom is expounded soundly and thoroughly, to the hurt of the man in the pew. G. Campbell Morgan stated preaching was "the declaration of the grace of God to human need."[269] Further he said, "The mass of men are waiting for preaching of the New Testament kind, with a great message of grace to meet human need."[270]

To preach with New Testament results, the preacher must preach the New Testament message of grace. Paul testified, 'I consider my life worth nothing to me, if only I may finish the race and complete the task the Lord Jesus has given me—the task of testifying to the Gospel of God's grace' (Acts 20:24). Paul's preaching was grace-centered preaching. Regrettably there is much preaching about the Gospel but little preaching of the Gospel (the great theological doctrines of the faith whose platform is grace).

42 Stories of Grace

"Come and hear, all ye that fear God, and I will declare what He hath done for my soul" (Psalm 66:16).

Story of delivering grace. Mel Trotter was an alcoholic. He promised his wife time and again that he would give up booze, but the longest he ever abstained was eleven and a half weeks. As is the case with most alcoholics, his wife and son suffered greatly due to his sin. One day Mel went home to find his two-year-old son dead in his wife's arms.

He recounts the story. "I went home after a ten-day drunk and found him dead in his mother's arms. I'll never forget that day. I was a slave, and I knew it. It pretty nearly broke my heart. I said, 'I'm a murderer. I'm anything but a man. I can't stand it, and I won't stand it! I'll end my life.'" But he didn't. Instead, he promised his wife once again, swearing on his son's coffin he would never taste liquor again. Two hours after the funeral he staggered home blind drunk.

On January 19, 1897, having giving up all hope of ever being delivered from the tyranny of alcohol, Trotter planned suicide by jumping into the frigid Lake Michigan. The path to the lake led by the Pacific Garden Mission where he heard Harry Monroe, recovered alcoholic, leading the singing. He was welcomed inside and heard Monroe's testimony of his deliverance from booze through Jesus Christ. That night Mel listened and believed and through God's grace was delivered from the addiction of alcohol. Asked later how he knew he was saved, Mel replied, "I was there when it happened, January 19, 1897, 10 minutes past 9, Central time, Pacific Garden Mission, Chicago, Illinois, USA." Never turning to alcohol again, he founded rescue missions throughout the United States to help enslaved men escape the addiction to alcohol.[271]

Story of transforming grace. Nicky Cruz was the leader of the renowned gang Mau Maus—the toughest in New York City. By his own admission he was an animal. He said, "New York was a jungle. The law of the jungle...you behave like an animal. Animals don't know the difference between right and wrong. An animal has to kill another animal for survival." He continued, "You can get high on sex. You can get high on alcohol. You can get high on all kinds of drugs. I was high on hate and violent."

Being raised by parents that practiced satanic worship and blood sacrifices and a mother that abused him violently led Nicky to harbor hate and ill-will for everybody. He says, "I wanted to do to others what my mother did to me. I used to feel good when I hurt some people."

David Wilkerson, a Christian minister, sought to rescue Nicky. "I heard his voice: 'God has the power to change your life.' I started cursing loud," says Nicky. "I spit in his face, and I hit him. I told him, 'I don't believe in what you say, and you get out of here.'" Wilkerson replied, "You could cut me up into 1,000 pieces and lay them in the street. Every piece will still love you." That triggered the subject of love in Nicky's heart that burned for two weeks. Nicky took his gang to a Wilkerson rally where they one by one gave their heart to Christ.

"I was choked up with pain, and my eyes were fighting, and tears became to come down and more tears, and I was fighting, and then I surrendered," says Nicky. "I let Jesus hug me, and I let my head rest on His chest. I said, 'I'm sorry. Forgive me,' and for the first time, I told somebody, 'I love you.' When I had opened my eyes, I got a new heart. I'd been born again. I'm a child of the Lord." He left the gang scene, attended Bible college and has since been pointing millions to the grace of Christ that set him free.[272]

Stories of coping grace. Coupled with the deaths of his children, financial disaster, and unrelenting physical pain, Job had to contend with the negative attitudes of his wife and friends, which exacerbated his suffering (Job 2:13). His life was marked with hardship, headache, and heartache. He felt hopeless and helpless; miserable and mournful; devasted and defeated; humiliated and broken. (Much like us in the pit of the unknown.) The pain, agony and loneliness drove Job to his knees where God gave added sustaining grace and, ultimately, recovery (Job 42:16–17). Note, the suffering believer, like Job, is never a moment outside the caring grace of God, though its vivid manifestation at times is not visible. Swindoll says, "Grace, grace, marvelous grace. The Book of Job teaches about grace. When He blesses Job, He doesn't bless a perfect man; He blesses an imperfect man. If he were perfect, he wouldn't be repenting. When are we going to get it? Because of His grace, God wonderfully blesses us. He does it better than *anyone!*[273]

John Donne, English poet and cleric in the Church of England, was smitten with typhus in the winter of 1623. While he was quarantined from others, the sickbed became an altar where he cried out to God for help. "My God, my God, thou hast made this sick bed thine altar, and I have no other sacrifice to offer but myself."[274]

"As long as I remain in this great hospital, this sick, this diseaseful world, as long as I remain in this leprous house, this flesh of mine, this heart, though thus prepared for Thee, prepared by Thee, will still be subject to the invasion of malign and pestilent vapors."[275]

"But I have my cordials in Thy promise: when I shall know the plague of my heart and pray unto Thee in Thy house, Thou wilt preserve that heart from all mortal force of that infection; and the peace of God which passeth all understandings shall keep my heart and mind through Christ Jesus."[276] In the midst of Donne's near-death experience he was sustained by the grace of God and wrote *Devotions upon Emergent Occasions*.

Martin Luther, German theologian, suffered numerous health maladies, including Meniere's disease (inner ear disorder that causes episodes of vertigo and tinnitus), fainting, severe constipation, kidney and bladder stones and arthritis which forced him into extended times of isolation in contemplation. Yet he found God's grace sufficient to sustain.

C. H. Spurgeon, English Baptist minister, battled severe bouts of depression and was afflicted by a combination of rheumatism, gout, neuritis, and Bright's disease. Yet he testified, "I am certain that I never did grow in grace one-half so much anywhere as I have upon the bed of pain."[277]

Unknown to many, Susannah Spurgeon (Spurgeon's wife), due to a botched surgery, suffered tremendously the rest of her life. The suffering prompted her to form The Book Fund to raise money to freely distribute her husband's book *Lectures to My Students* to impoverished ministers. At her death in 1902 she had distributed 199,315 theological resources throughout England without cost to the recipients.[278] Amidst her suffering, God gave her sustaining grace to accomplish a great work.

Grace, upon being requested and relied upon, enables coping, endurance, and perseverance through the darkest storm and deepest valley, as it did sufficiently for Job, Donne, Luther, Spurgeon and his wife.

Story of persecuting grace. A camp doctor that witnessed Bonhoeffer's hanging wrote: "The prisoners...were taken from their cells, and the verdicts of court martial read out to them. Through the half-open door in one room of the huts, I saw Pastor Bonhoeffer, before taking off his prison garb, kneeling on the floor praying fervently to his God. I was most deeply moved by the way this lovable man prayed, so devout and so certain that God heard his prayer. At the place of execution, he again said a prayer and then climbed the steps to the gallows, brave and composed. His death ensued in a few seconds. In the almost 50 years that I have worked as a doctor, I have hardly ever seen a man die so entirely submissive to the will of God." What a testimony to God's grace!

The Holy Spirit works powerfully and intimately in God's people, awakening them in times of needed counsel and support to hear from the pages of Scripture the Father's voice, to experience "new grace" and to see His loving hand enveloping them.

> Grace makes a way for us,
>   When all hope is gone;
> It flows freely from Calvary
>   To grant strength to press on.
>
> ~ Frank Shivers (2021)

43 Sweep of Grace

Is there an unforgiveable sin that is beyond the reach of God's mercy and grace to forgive and cleanse? Is grace available to someone that has committed a hideous, shameful and vile act?

The Bible is clear on the answer. "Where sin abounded, grace did much more abound" (Romans 5:20). Your sin may be great, but grace stands bigger. Regardless of the sin committed, grace is available through turning to Jesus Christ. Hear the Word of God. "Come, let's talk this over, says the Lord; no matter how deep the stain of your sins, I can take it out and make you as clean as freshly fallen snow" (Isaiah 1:18 TLB). Grace will "wash you" (blot out sin) and make you right with God through calling on the name of the Lord (1 Corinthians 6:11 NLT). Isaiah says, "Let the wicked forsake his way, and the unrighteous man his thoughts: and let him return unto the LORD, and he will have mercy [grace] upon him; and to our God, for he will *abundantly* pardon" (Isaiah 55:7).

"He canceled the record of the charges against us and took it away by nailing it to the cross" (Colossians 2:14 NLT). On the Cross of Christ every sin that man every committed or would commit was nailed, for which He bore the punishment of cruel torture and excruciating death to atone. The Bible says, "Who his own self bare our sins in his own body on the tree, that we, being dead to sins, should live unto righteousness: by whose stripes ye were healed" (1 Peter 2:24). Christ "offered himself unblemished to God, [to] cleanse our consciences from acts that lead to death" (Hebrews 9:14 NIV). Paul asserts, "There is therefore now no condemnation to them which are in Christ Jesus" (Romans 8:1).

> There is no pit so deep, that God's love is not deeper still.
> Corrie ten Boom

Look at the work of God's free grace in regard to man's sin when it is confession. By grace Christ forgets them (Hebrews 10:17); washes them away (Isaiah 1:17–18); blots them out (Isaiah 43:25); wipes them out like a cloud (Isaiah 44:22); pardons them (Isaiah 55:7); buries them in the depths of the sea (Micah 7:19) and separates them from the sinner as far as the east is from the west (Psalm 103:12). Corrie Ten Boom said, "There is no pit so deep, that God's love is not deeper still."[279]

Saith Spurgeon, "Have you grossly sinned? Have you defiled your body with unhallowed passions? Have you been dishonest to your fellowmen? Does some scarlet sin stain your conscience, even as you sit in the pew? Have you grown hardened in sin by long perseverance in it? Are you conscious that you have frequently, willfully, and resolutely sinned? Have you persecuted the saints of God? Then hear this text: 'Where sin abounded, grace did much more abound'; and as it was in the beginning, it is now and ever shall be till this world shall end. The grace of God, if thou believest in the Lord Jesus Christ, will triumph over the greatness of thy wickedness. 'All manner of sin and blasphemy shall be forgiven unto men' (Matthew 12:31). Throw down your weapons of rebellion; surrender at discretion; kiss the pierced hand of Jesus which is now held out to you, and this very moment you shall be forgiven, and you shall go your way a pardoned man, to begin a new life, and to bear witness that 'where sin abounded, grace did much more abound'" (Romans 5:20).[280]

> My sin, oh, the bliss of this glorious thought!
> My sin, not in part, but the whole
> Is nailed to the cross, and I bear it no more.
> Praise the Lord, praise the Lord, o my soul!
> ~ Horatio Gates Spafford (1873)

Granted, grace does exceed rational explanation. Why would God freely forgive of sin against Himself without payment? There is but one answer that foundationally may be given. It's His extravagant love for man. John says, "In this was manifested the love of God toward us, because that God sent his only begotten Son into the world, that we might live through him" (1 John 4:9). Personal shame and guilt over sin committed bolts at such amazing love and grace, but it is freely bestowed to all that believe.

God's grace covers any scenario that might impact our life, not just with regard to the need of salvation. It sweeps with immeasurable and indescribable broad strokes across every facet of our life, providing "help in the hour of need."

44 Spur of Grace

"No man can come to me, except the Father which hath sent me draw him: and I will raise him up at the last day" (John 6:44). It is necessary for the Holy Spirit to draw unregenerate man to grace (Christ), for he lacks the desire or ability to come on his own due to his depravity (Romans 5:10). Clarke states, "Unless God thus draw, no man will ever come to Christ; because none could, without this drawing, ever feel the need of a Savior."[281]

How? The Holy Spirit draws the unsaved primarily through the instrumentality of His Word (its proclamation and reading). See Romans 10:17; 2 Timothy 3:15; James 1:18 and 1 Peter 1:23. The lightning force of divine truth (the hammer of the Word) empowered by the Holy Spirit brings conviction of sin, acknowledgement of God and needed repentance (John 16:8). "For the word of God is quick, and powerful, and sharper than any twoedged sword, piercing even to the dividing asunder of soul and spirit, and of the joints and marrow, and is a discerner of the thoughts and intents of the heart" (Hebrews 4:12).

Clarke says, "So God draws man. He shows him his wants— He shows the Savior whom He has provided for him. The man feels himself a lost sinner; and, through the desire which he finds to escape Hell and get to Heaven, he comes unto Christ, that he may be justified by His blood."[282] Prayer prepares the heart for the receptivity of the Word and its conviction of sin, judgment and righteousness unto salvation (John 16:8 and Romans 10:1).

A minister was confronted by a blasphemous infidel in a hotel lobby. The infidel said to the preacher, "You and your prayers! Let us see you pray for me and convert me." The humble preacher knelt by the chair of the infidel and prayed that he might be saved. Afterwards the man laughed, saying, "Ha, I'm just the same. Nothing has been changed in me."

The minister replied, "But wait. God is not done yet." Later that preacher noted an article in the newspaper from another town about a man that was conducting a Heaven-sent revival meeting—and it was the infidel for whom he had prayed.[283] God used the witness and prayer of a humble preacher to plant the seed of grace that spurred a miracle.

Barnes comments, "In the conversion of the sinner, God enlightens the mind (John 6:45), he inclines the will (Psalm 110:3), and he influences the soul by motives; by just views of His law; by His love, His commands, and His threatenings; by a desire of happiness, and a consciousness of danger; by the Holy Spirit applying truth to the mind, and urging him to yield himself to the Savior. So that, while God inclines him, and will have all the glory, man yields without compulsion; the obstacles are removed, and he becomes a willing servant of God."[284] Ironside states, "The very first evidence of awakening grace is dissatisfaction with oneself and self-effort and a longing for deliverance from chains."[285]

He that avoids, shuns or neglects hearing the Word preached or read has little expectation of being drawn to God's free and rich grace. This is why it is expedient to get the unsaved under the sound of the Gospel in revivals, crusades, Sunday worship services, etc., and to keep ourselves under it as well, to be drawn to the new grace He has afforded to believers.

45   Selection of Grace

"Did God predestine some people," says Adrian Rogers, "for Heaven and predestine some people for Hell? Are humans just pawns on the chessboard of fate? Absolutely not! There are some who...say that God has chosen some before they are born to go to Hell and others He has chosen to go to Heaven—and there's absolutely nothing they can do about it. I don't accept this for a moment."[286] Spurgeon stated, "You will find all true theology summed up in these two short sentences: Salvation is all of the grace of God. Damnation is all the will of man."[287]

> Wonderful inclusiveness here, in the outstretched and encircling arms of the Christian Gospel—'to everyone.' Nobody excluded. Everybody included.
> R. G. Lee

The Bible says, "He died in our place to take away our sins, and not only our sins but the sins of all people" (1 John 2:2 NCV). R. G. Lee states, "Wonderful inclusiveness here, in the outstretched and encircling arms of the Christian Gospel—'to everyone.' Nobody excluded. Everybody included."[288] Lee continues, "Just as there is universal guilt among men, so there is the universal offer of salvation from God....Repeatedly God declares that sin is universal, that no one escapes. Repeatedly, too, God declares the atonement to be universal. That does not mean that salvation is universal, for many will not be saved....God has done His part for man's salvation, but man fails or refuses to do his part. That is the sum and substance of all excuses and objections. Man's free and wicked will is the only barrier in the way of his salvation."[289]

The free grace of God in salvation is extended to all men in Scripture. Christ Jesus died for all (2 Corinthians 5:15; 1 Timothy 2:6; Hebrews 2:9). Christ desires all men to be saved (1 Timothy 2:6; 2 Peter 3:9). Paul says, "Who desires all people to be saved and to come to the knowledge of the truth" (1 Timothy 2:4 ESV). Christ invites all men to be saved (Acts 17:30; Revelation 22:17). God's grace that bringeth (makes possible) salvation has appeared to *all* men: "For the grace of God has appeared, bringing salvation for all people" (Titus 2:11 ESV). The Bible teaches that whosoever shall call upon the name of the Lord shall be saved (Romans 10:9–13). Christ's atoning death on the cross was for the entire human race (world). See Colossians 1:20. John writes, "He is the propitiation for our sins: and not for ours only, but also for the sins of *the whole world*" (1 John 2:2). Christ promises grace for salvation to all that believe in Him (John 3:16).

John R. Rice says, "It is true the saved are God's elect, 'chosen...in him before the foundation of the world' (Ephesians 1:4). But it is wrong to make this election a whim of God whereby He saves some, compels them to be saved, and damns some whom He has decided He does not wish to save. No, election is not 'unconditional.' It is simply that God knows who will trust Him when they hear the Gospel and chooses them to be carried through till they be "conformed to the image of his Son."[290] See 1 Peter 1:2.

Spurgeon, in preaching on the text of Isaiah 1:18, opens the door wide for all to be saved. "I have a big net this morning—oh, that we might all be caught in its meshes! There is not one of us today who can be exempt from this invitation; not even that poor soul yonder who shivers in his shoes because he fears that he has committed the unpardonable sin. The Gospel is preached to every creature and shuts none out."[291] Spurgeon continued, "We may say of the invitations of Holy Scriptures:

None are excluded hence, but those
    Who do themselves exclude;
Welcome the learned and polite,
    The ignorant and rude." [292]

Saving grace awaits him that realizes its need and requests it from a heart of contrition over sin (Psalm 51:17 and 1 John 1:9).

46   Second Chance of Grace (Part 1)

As a child, I played with a magic slate which enabled a drawing to be totally erased with the lifting of a thin plastic screen. The lifting of the screen gave me a second chance to do a better job with my drawing. Similarly, grace grants a person a clean slate and fresh start upon confession and repentance of sin.

God relishes opportunities to offer second chances (Joel 2:13). His grace affords him who falters the opportunity for a second chance (multiple chances) for recovery and restoration to Christian walk and service. This is made crystal clear in Scripture. God says in Jeremiah 15:19, "If you return to me, I will restore you so you can continue to serve me" (NLT). Micah 7:18 (NIV) says, "Who is a God like you, who pardons sin and forgives the transgression of the remnant of his inheritance? You do not stay angry forever but delight to show mercy." John Bunyan well said, "A returning penitent, though formerly bad as the worst of men, may by grace become as good as the best."[293] Spurgeon well said, "It is blessed to know that the grace of God is free to us at all times, without preparation, without fitness, without money, and without price! 'I will love them freely.' These words invite backsliders to return; indeed, the text (Hosea 14:4) was specially written for such—"I will heal their backsliding, I will love them freely."[294]

> A returning penitent, though formerly bad as the worst of men, may by grace become as good as the best.
> John Bunyan

The service may differ from that prior to the stumble, but the opportunity for productive ministry is not closed. Failure doesn't disqualify for service after repentance. That's grace! Peter's denial of Christ thrice on the eve of His crucifixion wasn't final. Grace was extended (John 21:15–19), a second chance received, and in several days, he was back preaching (Acts 2). Jonah was given a second chance. The Bible says following his disobedience, "The word of the LORD came to Jonah a second time" (Jonah 3:1 NIV) and this time he obeyed. The prodigal son got a second chance and took advantage of it (Luke 15:21–22). Moses, who murdered an Egyptian soldier, got a second chance (Exodus 2:11–15) and became the leader of the Israelites out of Egyptian bondage. David, who committed murder and adultery (2 Samuel 11:14–17), got a second chance and penned the Psalter that has comforted and consoled millions throughout history. Abraham got a second chance upon lying about Sarah's being his wife (Genesis 12:10–20) and became the Father of many nations.

God is the God of second chances. Max Lucado says, "Second chances are the specialty of our Savior!"[295] He continues, "We are presumptuous, not when we marvel at His grace, but when we reject it. And we're sacrilegious, not when we claim His forgiveness, but when we allow the haunting sins of yesterday to convince us that God forgives but He doesn't forget. You see, God is either the God of perfect grace...or He is not God. Grace forgets—period. He who is perfect love cannot hold grudges. If He does, then He isn't perfect love."[296] Theodore Epps states, "When God forgives, He at once restores."[297] That in part is why grace is so amazing.

"It is the God of all grace," saith Maclaren, "to whom we look for our perfecting. No emptiness can be so vast and so empty that that *"all"* cannot fill it. No man can have gone so far from the right way or had his nature so lacerated by sin's cruel fangs, that that *"all"* cannot heal and repair the damage. Therefore, the more we sound the height and length and breadth and depth of our imperfections and sins, the more joyfully should we think of the completeness of that power which overlaps them on all sides and surpasses them in every dimension, and the more confidently should we exclaim, "The God of all grace shall restore us and complete us." Grace is love exercised to inferiors and undeserving persons; and, if he is the God of all grace, boundless love for the lowliest and foulest is in His heart."[298]

O prodigal, don't stay away!
The Father is waiting today.
　　There's room and to spare;
　　There is raiment to wear.
O prodigal, don't stay away.

O prodigal brother, come home!
Why longer in wretchedness roam?
　　You're lonely and lost;
　　You are driven and toss'd.
O prodigal brother, come home.

O prodigal, what will you do?
Love's table is waiting for you.
　　Forgiveness so sweet,
　　Sure, your coming will greet.
O prodigal, what will you do?

O prodigal brother, arise!
For pardon, look up to the skies.
　　No longer then stray
　　From Thy Father away.
O prodigal brother, arise.

~ Jeremiah Eames Rankin (1906)

David Jeremiah says, "In the state of Grace, there is no such thing as opportunity lost that cannot be found. Grace means forgiveness—period. Forgiveness doesn't come in shades of gray in the state of Grace: You're either forgiven by God or you're not. If you are lacking opportunities to serve, it's not because God hasn't forgiven you—so who does that leave? (Yes, it's important to seek His forgiveness, be reconciled to other people, and repent and turn away from sin.)"[299] Chambers agrees, "Never let the sense of failure corrupt your new action."[300]

A veterinarian was asked, "If the broken wing of a sparrow who has fallen to the ground is repaired, could it ever fly as high as it once did?" The veterinarian replied, "It depends on who repaired its wing." God mends broken wings as good as new, so the "broken and crushed" can mount up with wings as eagles; run, and not be weary; and walk, and not faint (Isaiah 40:31). The famous evangelist D. L. Moody said, "A man does not get grace till he comes down to the ground, till he sees he needs grace. When a man stoops to the dust and acknowledges that he needs mercy, then it is that the Lord will give him grace."[301]

Thus our bless'd Savior wont despise
The contrite heart for sacrifice.
The deep-fetch'd sigh, the secret groan
Rises accepted to his throne.

He meets, with tokens of his grace,
The trembling lip, the blushing face.
His bowels yearn when sinners pray,
And mercy bears their sins away.

~ Benjamin Beddome (1769)

47 Second Chance of Grace (Part 2)

He that has experienced the second chance (or third chance, fourth chance, etc.) of grace ought to manifest a disposition of grace (leniency, kindness, compassion, mercy, forgiveness) to others that stumble. It is he to whom Christ has shown great mercy and grace that is the most willing to demonstrate it to others (Matthew 5:7). Joseph Benson said, "The very first grace that grows, like a beautiful spring flower, on the ground of righteousness is the grace of mercy, or compassion."[302]

"In nothing does God delight more," writes Barnes, "than in the exercise of mercy. To us, guilty sinners; to us, wretched, dying, and exposed to eternal woe, He has shown His mercy by giving His Son to die for us, by expressing His willingness to pardon and save us, and by sending His Spirit to renew and sanctify our hearts. Each day of our life, each hour, and each moment, we partake of His undeserved mercy. All the blessings we enjoy are proofs of His mercy. If we, then, show mercy to the wretched, the guilty, it shows that we are like God. And we have abundant opportunity to do it. Our world is full of guilt and woe, which we may help to relieve; and every day of our lives we have opportunity, by helping the wretched, and by forgiving those who injure us, to show that we are like God."[303]

How might you as a believer exhibit the grace of mercy to a fallen brother?

1. Recall the grace of mercy God extended to you which was undeserved (Matthew 5:7).

2. Consider his case as your own.

3. Treat him as you would want to be treated if in his shoes.

4. Dispel slander and aspersions about his sin.

5. Conceal it; don't expose it if within your power and authority (Proverbs 25:2; 1 Peter 4:8). Matthew Henry remarks, "Love, instead of proclaiming and aggravating the offence, conceals and extenuates it as far as it is capable of being concealed and extenuated."[304] See Proverbs 10:12.

6. Forgive and takes steps to restore.

The Bible admonishes us to "be kind to one another, tenderhearted, forgiving one another, as God in Christ forgave you. Therefore be imitators of God, as beloved children. And walk in love, as Christ loved us and gave himself up for us, a fragrant offering and sacrifice to God" (Ephesians 4:32–5:2 ESV).

Clarke says, "He who shows mercy [and grace] to men, God will show mercy to him; but to him who shows no mercy to man, God will show no mercy."[305] What might your story read like had not someone manifested the rich grace of mercy of God toward you?

48   Shunning of Grace

"Woe unto him that striveth with his Maker!" (Isaiah 45:9). Rejection of free grace and the invitation of God unto salvation is a sin of the worst ingratitude, deepest guilt and stubbornest rebellion. It is the resisting of our Sovereign God's gracious invitation by the Holy Spirit for recovery from sin and reconciliation to Himself through Jesus Christ, our only Savior. See Acts 7:51.

Paul states frankly that multitudes 'receive the grace of God in vain' (2 Corinthians 6:1). The grace of God here refers to the offer of reconciliation and forgiveness. "Vain" means the "equivalent to the phrase to no purpose,"[306] or useless. The text may be translated, "We entreat you not to offer God's grace an ineffectual welcome."[307]

How is God's free and full grace received in vain? It is received in vain when there is no contemplation or examination of the fact of Christ's death, burial and resurrection. It is received in vain when there is no grief over what Christ did to secure man's salvation, heart concern over sin and rebellion against Him, and repentance or acceptance of Christ. It is received in vain when a deaf ear is turned to gospel sermons, exhortations from the Holy Bible from holy ministers, and conviction of the Holy Spirit. It is received in vain when it is mocked, scoffed and ridiculed. It is received in vain when thought an insignificant doctrine. It is received in vain when its truth is heard but unheeded. It is received in vain when neglected (Hebrews 2:3). It is received in vain when its rich benefits are squandered. It is received in vain when adulterated with heresies. It is received in vain when it is not taken as prescribed (as a gift). It is received in vain in unscriptural manners of receiving Jesus Christ. It is received in vain when accepted doubtfully or upon manipulation. It is received in vain when it is not allowed to do its effectual work. "He," says Pelagius, "receives the grace of God in vain who, in the new covenant, is not himself new."[308]

To shun or renounce God's grace is to empty it of its power and thwart its intended purpose of reconciliation in your life

(1 Corinthians 1:17). Grace has effectual power to save from the gutter-most to the uttermost, but, alas, it must first be received and applied by faith (Hebrews 7:25). Healing medicine on the shelf renders the body no cure until ingested.

Henry states, "The Gospel is a word of grace sounding in our ears, but it will be in vain for us to hear it unless we believe it and comply with the end and design of it."[309] Scott states, "We can neither expect the comforts of His love, nor the protection of His powerful arm, except we are partakers of His converting grace."[310]

> The Gospel is a word of grace sounding in our ears, but it will be in vain for us to hear it unless we believe it and comply with the end and design of it.
> Matthew Henry

To neglect the Gospel of Christ (grace) is the greatest of calamities of life and the soul, bearing both temporal and eternal consequences. See John 5:40; Matthew 25:30; Revelation 21:8.

This is the opportune day of salvation. "For he saith, I have heard thee in a time accepted, and in the day of salvation have I succored thee: behold, now is the accepted time; behold, now is the day of salvation" (2 Corinthians 6:2).

Hindson and Kroll say, "The force of his statement is that God conveys His grace and salvation to men in the day and time suited to Him, and it is incumbent upon men to appropriate that grace in the time appointed by God."[311]

Matthew Henry states, "The gospel day is a day of salvation, the means of grace the means of salvation, the offers of the Gospel the offers of salvation, and the present time the only proper time to accept of these offers—today, while it is called today. The morrow is none of ours. We know not what will be on the morrow, nor where we shall be; and we should remember that present seasons of grace are short and uncertain and cannot be recalled when they are past."[312] See Hebrews 2:3.

I have long withstood His grace,
Long provoked Him to His face,
Would not hearken to His calls,
Grieved Him by a thousand falls.

I my Master have denied;
I afresh have crucified,
Oft profaned His hallowed name,
Put Him to an open shame.

There for me the Savior stands,
Shows His wounds and spreads His hands.
God is love! I know, I feel.
Jesus weeps but loves me still!

Now incline me to repent!
Let me now my fall lament!
Now my foul revolt deplore,
Weep, believe, and sin no more.

~ Charles Wesley (1740)

H. A. Ironside remarks, "Ah, dear, unsaved reader, if into the hands of such a one these pages fall, remember there is not only a world in which you can say 'No' to God, the God of all grace; there is also a world in which He will say 'No' to you, if you meet Him as the God of judgment. What can be worse for a lost soul than to have to remember, in the abyss of woe, gospel messages once indifferently listened to, the Word of God once treated as a subject unfit for serious consideration; and then to have to cry in despair, 'Jesus died, yet I'm in hell! He gave Himself for sinners. He provided a way of salvation for me, but, like the fool that I was, I spurned His grace till grace was withdrawn, the door of mercy was closed, and now I am to be on the wrong side of that closed door forever!'"[313]

Spurgeon appeals to the unsaved, "Today Christ is to be had! Today all that your soul needs is to be had—and to be had for nothing! To be had for the asking! To be had for the accepting; for whoever believes in Him receives Him, and so is saved."[314]

101

49 **Sedation of Grace**

Sinclair Lewis writes, "We sing about 'amazing grace' and speak of 'amazing grace,' but far too often it has ceased to amaze us. Sadly, we might more truthfully sing of 'accustomed grace.'"[315]

What has happened to the "amazing" in the amazing grace John Newton passionately spoke and sung? It appears across evangelical lines in pulpit and pew that the divine grace that converted, changed and conformed us to the image of Christ Jesus is waning in interest, vitality, awe, prominence and sharing. This is a strange and perplexing paradox that is shocking and baffling. Whereas the redeemed ought to jubilantly and constantly make mention of grace in light of all it has wrought for them and as a fundamental doctrine of their faith, they act as if they know little of it, scarcely believe in it or are fearful to mention it.

Grace is still amazing in the love that it brought. The Bible says, "For God so loved the world, that he gave his only begotten Son, that whosoever believeth in him should not perish, but have everlasting life" (John 3:16). "Wonder of wonders, that Jesus loves me."

Grace is still amazing in the pardon that it bought. "He is so rich in kindness and grace that he purchased our freedom with the blood of his Son and forgave our sins" (Ephesians 1:7 NLT).

> Nothing can my sin erase,
>> Nothing but the blood of Jesus!
> Naught of works, 'tis all of grace—
>> Nothing but the blood of Jesus!
>
> ~ Robert Lowry (1826–1899)

Grace is still amazing in the souls that it sought. The Bible says, "For the Son of man is come to seek and to save that which was lost" (Luke 19:10). God is not willing that any man perish but that all might come to experience His grace of forgiveness through repentance (2 Peter 3:9).

Grace sought me when I was astray,
    Entangled deep in sin,
And found me when I was away
    From God and dead within.

~ Thomas A. Arne (1762)

Grace is still amazing in the change that it wrought. The Bible says, "Therefore if any man be in Christ, he is a new creature: old things are passed away; behold, all things are become new" (2 Corinthians 5:17). The Bible again says, "And such were some of you: but ye are washed, but ye are sanctified, but ye are justified in the name of the Lord Jesus, and by the Spirit of our God" (1 Corinthians 6:11).

Glory be to him who loved us,
    Washed us from all sin and stain!
Hallelujah! Hallelujah!
    Praise the Lamb that once was slain!

~ Horatius Bonar (1866)

Grace is still amazing in the instruction that it taught. The Bible says, "For the grace of God that bringeth salvation hath appeared to all men, Teaching us that, denying ungodliness and worldly lusts, we should live soberly, righteously, and godly, in this present world; Looking for that blessed hope, and the glorious appearing of the great God and our Savior Jesus Christ" (Titus 2:11–13).

Grace is still amazing in the help it imparts. The Bible says, "Let us therefore come boldly unto the throne of grace, that we may obtain mercy, and find grace to help in time of need" (Hebrews 4:16).

The soul that on Jesus hath leaned for repose
I will not, I will not desert to his foes;
That soul, though all Hell should endeavor to shake,
I'll never, no, never, no, never forsake!

~ John Rippon (1787)

The psalmist declares, "Blessed is the people that know the joyful sound: they shall walk, O Lord, in the light of thy countenance. In thy name shall they rejoice all the day: and in thy righteousness shall they be exalted" (Psalm 89:15–16). God's grace bestowed upon the saved is ground for unceasing joy and praise. Matthew Henry says, "The Gospel [the Gospel of grace] is indeed a joyful sound, a sound of victory, of liberty, of communion with God, and the sound of abundance of rain; blessed are the people that hear it, and know it, and bid it welcome."[316]

Your grace still amazes me....
God's grace still amazes me
In its abundant provision and delivery.
Each day I give praise upon my knees
For the change it brought to me.

God's grace remains unsurpassed in me
By anything that the world might do for me.
It loosed my chains and set me free;
It therefore, will never cease to bring amazement to me.

~ Frank Shivers (2021)

Guard thine heart from taking grace for granted and treating it mundanely. Sing of it with greater sincerity. Tell of it with greater exuberance. Utilize it with greater frequency. Praise God for it with greater gratitude. Preach it with greater passion. Ponder it with greater intensity. Keep its sweet taste and fragrant aroma lively. Refuse to allow lethargy and indifference about grace rob you of its awesomeness and marvelousness.

50   Spinoff of Grace

The believer's grateful response to the doctrines of grace, embraced rightly, generate faithfulness to Christ and good works (Romans 12:1–2). Genuine grace, though wrought by Christ's work at Calvary inclusively (Ephesians 2:8), generates in its recipient works of righteousness (Ephesians 2:10). It is because of this grace bestowed that Paul exhorts believer's to "walk worthy of the vocation wherewith ye are called" (Ephesians 4:1b). Wuest says, "In other words, they are to see to it that they practice what they preach, that their experience measures up to their standing in grace. The words 'the vocation wherewith ye are called' are literally 'the calling with which you were called.' 'Calling' refers to that divine summons into salvation which God gives a sinner in which he is constituted willing to accept the salvation offered. It speaks of that effectual call into salvation which God in sovereign grace extends to a sinner. They are to be obedient to that heavenly calling or summons to be saints and live saintly lives."[317]

The bottom line: Walk in expression of the grace received as a good soldier and follower of Christ. This righteous and dutiful walk is the believer's delight (not chore) due to the work Christ wrought for him at Calvary and since. Its specifics are addressed forthrightly in Ephesians 4:14–31. Henry states, "Christians ought to accommodate themselves to the Gospel by which they are called, and to the glory to which they are called; both are their vocation. We are called Christians; we must answer that name and live like Christians. We are called to God's kingdom and glory; that kingdom and glory therefore we must mind, and walk as becomes the heirs of them."[318] See 1 John 2:6 and Philippians 1:21. Let us pray with Spurgeon, "Save us, we pray Thee, from the common religion; give us the peculiar grace of a peculiar people. May we abide in Christ; may we live near to God."[319]

51   Suspension of Grace

God has chosen to place upon some "graces" conditions for their attainment or bestowal. For example, God wills for all men to be saved but that grace is suspended until man meets His divine condition for its reception: repentance and faith (Acts 20:21; John 5:40). It is God's will that the carnal saint (backslider) experience restoration grace, but such is suspended until he returns to God with a broken and contrite spirit over sin (Psalm 51:17). Similarly, God's grace may be suspended in granting comfort, healing, consolation, strength and help upon man's failure to meet the divine condition to simply request it (Matthew 11:28–29; Psalm 107:13–14).

Paul sought deliverance from the thorn in his flesh three times without avail. Instead of giving him what was requested, God gave him the grace of strength to bear it. "My grace is sufficient for you, for my power is made perfect in weakness" (2 Corinthians 12:8–9 NIV). Desired "favor" of the Lord may be blocked by the failure to exhibit faith in requesting it (Matthew 21:22), improper motives in its request (James 4:3), wrong timing in its request (Ecclesiastes 3:3), or its contrariness to God's will and our best good (James 1:17). When such grace is withholden or suspended, know that God has something better in store (Romans 8:28).

Sin may block various graces of God. The Bible says that God is opposed to the proud and will give His grace only to the humble (James 4:6), so arrogant pride could suspend God's blessings, as was the case with King Uzziah. Uzziah was blessed with the favor of God, richly enabling wealth, power and success. The Bible says, "God helped him against the Philistines and against the Arabians who lived in Gurbaal and against the Meunites" (2 Chronicles 26:7 ESV). But the King failed to remember that all the goodness experienced was through the grace of God. He became proud and arrogant. The Bible says, "But when he was strong, he grew proud, to his destruction. For he was unfaithful to the LORD his God and entered the temple of the LORD to burn incense on the altar of incense" (2 Chronicles 26:16). Uzziah's life of arrogance blocked the blessings of God. Note, Scripture states that "as long as he sought the LORD, God made him prosper" (2 Chronicles 26:5 ESV). Obviously, as with the sin of pride, other forms of sinful conduct—bitterness (Hebrews 12:15); reliance upon self-works (Galatians 5:1)—may block the blessings of God. See Jeremiah 3:3 and Deuteronomy 28:1–14.

An employee who worked for a city located in a valley was fired. In anger the man plugged the primary pipe that supplied water to the city from the reservoir in the mountain. People fully expecting water to flow upon turning the nozzle or knob were sorely disappointed when nothing happened. Efforts to ascertain the cause were unsuccessful. In time the distraught employee confessed to the act, indicating the place the channel or pipe was plugged. Upon removal of the plug, the water flowed freely again. We wonder why certain graces aren't bestowed, why God's favor is withholden. The reason may be a sin that is clogging the channel between God and our heart. "God's best gift," says Maclaren, "is of such a sort as cannot be laid upon a dirty palm. A little sin dams back the whole of God's grace, and there are too many men that pray, pray, pray, and never get any of the things that we pray for, because there is something stopping the pipe, and they do not know what it is, and perhaps would be very sorry to clear it out if they did."[320] The suspension (caused by sin) is easily remedied through confession and repentance. John says, "If we confess our sins, he is faithful and just to forgive us our sins, and to cleanse us from all unrighteousness" (1 John 1:9). The Bible says, "Turn you at my reproof: behold, I will pour out my spirit unto you, I will make known my words unto you" (Proverbs 1:23).

Eternal or saving grace is beyond suspension (John 10:28). Nothing man or Satan does can undo that permanent work. But provisional graces may be suspended as aforementioned (sometimes totally innocently) at God's discretion to enhance devotion, quicken faith and reliance, rebuke and reprove of wrong, and thwart selfish pride. Even when a grace is suspended, God's love, companionship, and care for His child remains unchanged (Jeremiah 31:3).

52 Sowers of Grace

"Behold, a sower went forth to sow" (Matthew 13:3). *The seed of the Sower* is the grace of our Lord Jesus Christ that transforms lives.

The sowing of the Sower. Charles Spurgeon says, "I have heard our Lord likened to a man carrying a waterpot, and as he carried it upon his shoulder, the water fell dropping, dropping, dropping, so that everyone could track the water bearer. So should all His people be, carrying such a fulness of grace that everyone should know where they have been by that which they have left behind."[321]

The sorrow of the Sower is the suffering endured from anti-Christian irritators and persecutors, the enemies of the Cross (Philippians 3:18). Paul and Barnabas were bitterly opposed (Acts 14:2); every Christian similarly will suffer for the sake of Christ. Jesus said, "Blessed are you when they revile and persecute you, and say all kinds of evil against you falsely for My sake" (Matthew 5:11 NKJV). (See the author's book *The Storm Is Coming: Persecuted for Christ's Sake*.) The Christian sorrows mostly over the disdain and disrespect of man toward Christ and rejection of the offer of grace. See Psalm 119:136.

The strength of the Sower rests totally in the Holy Spirit. Note it was not the apostles that wrought miracles, wonders and signs, but the Holy Spirit (Acts 14:3). Failure to rely upon His enablement and empowering in sowing grace will be futile.

The support of the Sower is the attestation, proof evinced of its truth by the Holy Spirit through signs and wonders. "Paul and Barnabas stayed there for a long time, preaching boldly and fearlessly about the Lord. Many trusted in the Lord, for He backed up His message of grace with miracles, signs, and wonders performed by the apostles" (Acts 14:3 Passion Translation). In sowing grace (in contrast to sowing legalistic demands and judgmental condemnation) God will back it up (give attestation to its truth) with His power that it might bear miraculous fruit. That is grace at work. "We ought to look for 'signs' that God is with us in the word we speak and the work we do for others.'"[322]

The success of the Sower is the reaping of the seed sown. "But God does give increase for our own eyes to see and our own hands to reap. And of all the joys with which He fills our human hearts there are few, if any, comparable to that of seeing the pleasure of the Lord prosper in our hand (Isaiah 53:10)."[323] "God gives His servants power to work and to effect good [sowing grace]."[324] The psalmist says, "He that goeth forth and weepeth, bearing precious seed, shall doubtless come again with rejoicing, bringing his sheaves with him" (Psalm 126:6).

Unheeding winter's cruel blast,
We venture Heaven's seed to cast,
Both late and early plant the truth
In aged hearts and tender youth.

Then sow the seed in every field,
And grace will bring the golden yield.
We soon shall sing the joyful song
And shout the blessed harvest home.

Shall we be found with only leaves
When Jesus comes to gather sheaves?
Nay, sowing daily o'er the land,
We'll come with joyful sheaves in hand.

Nor is the precious labor hard;
Its glory is its own reward.
We plant in hearts of grim despair
A life that blooms as Eden fair.

Oh, were this life the utmost span,
The closing destiny of man,
No toil could half so blessed prove
As sowing seeds of peace and love.

But Heaven's bright eternal years
Have bottled up our sowing tears;
There we shall greet in holy bliss
The souls we turned to righteousness.

~ D. S. Warner (1887)

53   Stamina of Grace

The stamina of grace (suffering grace) is standing or staying grace to withstand the bitterest storms and battles that inflict the heart with horrendous sorrow and suffering. The saints of Hebrews 11 epitomized persevering grace amidst the worst of hardship, torture and suffering. Grace turned their weakness into strength (Hebrews 11:34), enabling endurance. Paul likewise bears witness to the same. He testified, "And he said unto me, My grace is sufficient for thee: for my strength is made perfect in weakness. Most gladly therefore will I rather glory in my infirmities, that the power of Christ may rest upon me. Therefore I take pleasure in infirmities, in reproaches, in necessities, in persecutions, in distresses for Christ's sake: *for when I am weak, then am I strong*" (2 Corinthians 12:9–10).

God's faithfulness to give abundant grace (His strength, power) in times of infirmity, affliction and adversary enables us to withstand whatever hardship or trouble confronted. In fact, to so stand bears evidence of grace.[325] Grace also enables the perseverance of the believer's salvation. Jesus said, "And I give unto them eternal life; and they shall never perish, neither shall any man pluck them out of my hand" (John 10:28). The grip of grace (His hand) upon the believer's soul is eternal. Paul states, "For I am persuaded, that neither death, nor life, nor angels, nor principalities, nor powers, nor things present, nor things to come, Nor height, nor depth, nor any other creature, shall be able to separate us from the love of God, which is in Christ Jesus our Lord" (Romans 8:38–39). In one of his last letters (1938), G. Campbell Morgan wrote, "I have found through all the 60 years that grace is sufficient, and I am quite sure it's never-failing grace, whatever life may bring, until earthly service merges into that of the life of the life Beyond."[326]

Evidence that a person is not born again is seen in his abandonment (desertion) of the faith. The Bible says, "They went out from us, but they were not of us [they really were not saved]; for if they had been of us [genuine and true Christians], they would no doubt have continued with us [persevered unto the end]: but they went out, that they might be made manifest that they were not all of us" (1 John 2:19). Barnes comments, "This affirms, without any ambiguity or qualification, that if they had been true Christians, they 'would' have remained in the church; that is, they would not have apostatized. There could not be a more positive affirmation than that which is implied here, that those who are true Christians will continue to be such; or that the saints will not fall away from grace."[327]

54   Sayings of Grace

Chuck Swindoll: "Grace is ours. Let's live it! Deny it or debate it, and we kill it."[328]

Harry Ironside: "Grace is the very opposite of merit.... Grace is not only undeserved favor, but it is favor shown to the one who has deserved the very opposite."[329]

Arthur Pink: "Grace can neither be bought, earned, or won by the creature. If it could be, it would cease to be grace."[330]

Dwight L. Moody: "A man can no more take in a supply of grace for the future than he can eat enough today to last him for the next six months, nor can he inhale sufficient air into his lungs with one breath to sustain life for a week to come. We are permitted to draw upon God's store of grace from day to day as we need it."[331]

Andrew Murray. "The absolute contrast between law and grace. Law demands; grace bestows. Law commands, but gives no strength to obey; grace promises and performs, doing everything for us. Law burdens, casts down, and condemns; grace comforts, makes strong and glad."[332]

Max Lucado: "When grace moves in…guilt moves out."[333]

Francis Dixon: "The most urgent need in the life of every born-again person is that of growth in grace."[334]

John Piper: "Grace is not simply leniency when we have sinned. Grace is the enabling gift of God not to sin. Grace is power, not just pardon."[335]

Thomas Watson: "None so empty of grace as he that thinks he is full."[336]

C. H. Spurgeon: "We are accustomed not only to say 'grace,' but 'free grace.' It has been remarked that this is a tautology. So it is, but it is a blessed one, for it makes the meaning doubly clear and leaves no room for mistake. We feel no compunction in ringing such a silver bell twice over—grace, free grace. Lest any should imagine that grace can be otherwise than free, we shall continue to say not only grace, but free grace, so long as we preach."[337]

Augustine: "Give me the grace [O Lord] to do as You command, and command me to do what You will! O holy God...when Your commands are obeyed, it is from You that we receive the power to obey them."[338]

Horatius Bonar: "The road is rugged, and the sun is hot. How can we be but weary? Here is grace for the weariness— grace which lifts us up and invigorates us, grace which keeps us from fainting by the way, grace which supplies us with manna from Heaven and with water from the smitten rock. We receive of this grace and are revived. Our weariness of heart and limb departs. We need no other refreshment. This is enough. Whatever the way be—rough, gloomy, unpleasant—we press forward, knowing that the same grace that has already carried thousands through will do the same for us."[339]

John MacArthur: "We are saved by grace (Ephesians 2:8) and in grace we stand (Romans 5:2). Grace upholds our salvation, gives us victory in temptation, and helps us endure suffering and pain. It helps us understand the Word and wisely apply it to our lives. It draws us into communion and prayer and enables us to serve the Lord effectively. In short, we exist and are firmly fixed in an environment of all-sufficient grace."[340]

Phillip Hughes: "The greater the servant's weakness, the more conspicuous is the power of his Master's all-sufficient grace."[341]

John Calvin: "We should therefore learn that the only good we have is what the Lord has given us gratuitously; that the only good we do is what He does in us; that it is not that we do nothing ourselves, but that we act only when we have been acted upon, in other words, under the direction and influence of the Holy Spirit."[342]

J. C. Ryle: "If there is any point on which God's holiest saints agree, it is this: that they see more, and know more, and feel more, and do more, and repent more, and believe more, as they get on in spiritual life, and in proportion to the closeness of their walk with God. In short, they 'grow in grace,' as Peter exhorts believers to do; and "abound more and more," according to the words of Paul (2 Peter 3:18; 1 Thessalonians 4:1)."[343]

Martyn Lloyd Jones: "Grace is favor shown to people who do not deserve any favor at all....We deserve nothing but Hell. If you think you deserve Heaven, take it from me, you are not a Christian."[344]

Thomas Watson: "The sight Christians have of their defects in grace, and their thirst after greater measures of grace, make them think they do not grow when they do."[345]

55 Sanctification of Grace

Sanctification differs from justification. While justification deals with man's guilt and forgiveness of sin (Romans 3:4), sanctification deals with thwarting sin's corrupting power in man in the aftermath of salvation. Justification secures man's right standing with God through Christ by grace; sanctification impacts and changes the whole of man's life for Christ.

Justification happens once and instantly; this is the New Birth (John 3:3). Sanctification occurs progressively over the entirety of man's life (a lifelong process). There are three stages of sanctification (past, present, and future) which are cited in 1 Thessalonians 3–4.

Positional or past sanctification: "I was sanctified." The Bible says, "For God did not call us to uncleanness, but in holiness" (1 Thessalonians 4:7 NKJV). Positional sanctification refers to the believer's permanent state or status with God at the moment of salvation. He no longer is under the wrath of God (delivered from the ultimate penalty of sin) but embraced ("set apart") as a child of God, a saint, a member of His royal family, separated from the world unto holiness for His "exclusive use" (Colossians 1:13 and 1 Corinthians 12:27).

Progressive or present sanctification: "I am being sanctified." The Bible says, "For this is the will of God, your sanctification" (1 Thessalonians 4:3 ESV). Progressive sanctification is grace at work in the believer's life to make him holier and more Christlike throughout life (John 17:17; Hebrews 10:14; Romans 5:17; Romans 6:17; 2 Corinthians 3:18).

Perfect or future sanctification: "I will be sanctified." The Bible says, "So that He may establish your hearts blameless in holiness before our God and Father at the coming of our Lord Jesus with all His saints" (1 Thessalonians 3:13 NASB). Perfect sanctification is the completion of grace's work in the believer's life at the moment of his exodus to Heaven (1 John 3:2; Colossians 1:27). He is made completely holy, free from any defect of sin.

Solomon likens the three facets of the believer's sanctification to the movement of the sun. "But the path of the just is as the shining light, that shineth more and more unto the perfect day" (Proverbs 4:18). The Christian is saved by grace through faith and repentance in an instant (sunrise), but godliness or holiness is progressive (as the sun rises in the sky) until clothed with Christ's perfection in Heaven (sun reaches noonday). The same grace that saves also changes. To profess salvation apart from a changed and changing life (righteousness, separation, service) is preposterous (2 Corinthians 5:17). MacArthur states, "Every biblical command toward sanctification assumes the necessary obedience of the ones commanded. That makes it clear that believers have a duty to faithfully and obediently use the means of grace to grow to maturity."[346] See Philippians 3:13–14, Philippians 2:12 and 2 Peter 3:18a. Maclaren says, "The intention of every Christian life should be a life of increasing luster, uninterrupted, and the natural result of increasing communion with, and conformity [continuous growth] to, the very fountain itself of heavenly radiance."[347] And this spiritual progress is enabled by Divine grace.

> Finish, then, Thy new creation;
>   True and spotless let us be.
> Let us see Thy great salvation
>   Perfectly restored in Thee.
>
> Changed from glory into glory,
>   Till in Heav'n we take our place,
> Till we cast our crowns before Thee,
>   Lost in wonder, love, and praise.
>
> ~ Charles Wesley (1747)

56 Sieve of Grace

Peter says, "But the God of all grace, who hath called us unto his eternal glory by Christ Jesus, after that ye have suffered a while, make you perfect, stablish, strengthen, settle you" (1 Peter 5:10). Suffering is severe, but in contrast to eternal glory with Christ it is a light affliction which "worketh for us a far more exceeding and eternal weight of glory" (2 Corinthians 4:17).

Suffering serves as a sieve of grace to purify, edify, solidify, and sanctify the believer. Spurgeon says, "Depend upon it. God often sends us trials that our graces may be discovered, and that we may be certified of their existence. Besides, it is not merely discovery; it is real growth that is the result of these trials."[348]

Peter notes four benefits of suffering when accompanied by divine grace. Through suffering the believer will be 'perfected.' Wuest says, "The word refers to God mending [like fishermen mend their nets to make useable] the lives of Christians, thus equipping them for greater effectiveness and usefulness in His service."[349] See Romans 5:3–4. Suffering is a means (among others) God uses to fit His children for greater usefulness.

Through suffering the believer will be "established" ("to set fast; to fix firmly; to render immovable"[350]). Grace enables the believer to exhibit steadiness and steadfastness in his Christian walk and work. Through suffering, the believer will be "strengthened" ("that you may overcome all force brought against you"[351]). Grace enables the believer to withstand all his sufferings (psychologically, mentally[352]) without wavering from the faith. The same wind that may extinguish a weak flame, inflames a strong one into a greater blaze.[353]

Through suffering the believer will be "settled" ("establish you on a firm foundation.") "The allusion is to a house which is so firmly fixed on a foundation that it will not be moved by winds or floods,"[354] (Matthew 7:24; "to abide, firmly founded, in the truth of grace."[355]).

Grace reinforces the believer's foundation of confidence and trust in God (Ephesians 4:14). Barclay says, "When we have to meet sorrow and suffering, we are driven down to the very bedrock of faith. It is then that we discover what are the things which cannot be shaken."[356] Warren Wiersbe says, "When an unbeliever goes through suffering, he loses his hope; but for a believer, suffering only increases his hope."[357]

MacArthur says, "These four words [perfected, established, strengthened and settled] all speak of strength and resoluteness. God is working through the Christian's struggles to produce strength of character. Christians are to live with the understanding that God's purposes realized in the future require some pain in the present."[358] Bengel summarizes the entire verse saying that God's grace in suffering "shall perfect, that no defect remain in you; shall stablish, that nothing may shake you; shall strengthen, that you may overcome every adverse force."[359]

> Oh, how wonderful Thy goodness,
>   Far beyond my highest thought!
> I can only take, rejoicing,
>   What Thy tender care has brought.
>
> Purged and tried as gold or silver,
>   This is what I long to be;
> Perfected, and wanting nothing—
>   Work Thine own sweet will in me.
>
> Grand assurance! Thou art watching
>   Most intently all the while.
> Welcome is the fining process
>   Carried on beneath Thy smile;
>
> Or, if Thou in love withholdest
>   Thy felt presence, it is well.
> Faith shall triumph over feeling;
>   Peace shall still within me dwell.
>
> Welcome, welcome every dealing,
>   Pain or pleasure, joy or woe;
> All is sent, O Great Refiner,
>   By a loving hand, I know.

116

Daily cares which fret and grieve me,
    Small and trifling, yet so keen,
Are on purpose to refine me,
    Though by human eyes unseen.

Do not let me miss one trial
    Which would make me purer still;
When Thine image shineth through me
    Cease the fining—not until!

When the silver gleams and glitters,
    From all earthly dross set free,
With no stain to mar its beauty,
    Satisfied Thou then shalt be!

                   ~ Ellen L. Goreh (1883)

"Perhaps, O tried soul," saith Spurgeon, "the Lord is doing this to develop thy graces. There are some of thy graces which would never be discovered if it were not for thy trials....God often takes away our comforts and our privileges in order to make us better Christians."[360]

57   Selflessness of Grace

The grace of liberality was provided to and manifested by the extremely poor saints of Macedonia. They gave selflessly and sacrificially to help the church in Jerusalem. Paul testifies of their gracious giving: "We want you to know, brothers, about the grace of God that has been given among the churches of Macedonia, for in a severe test of affliction, their abundance of joy and their extreme poverty have overflowed in a wealth of generosity on their part. For they gave according to their means, as I can testify, and beyond their means, of their own accord, begging us earnestly for the favor of taking part in the relief of the saints—and this, not as we expected, but they gave themselves first to the Lord and then by the will of God to us. Accordingly, we urged Titus that as he had started, so he should complete among you this act of grace. But as you excel in everything—in faith, in

117

speech, in knowledge, in all earnestness, and in our love for you—see that you excel in this act of grace also" (2 Corinthians 8:1–7 ESV).

The grace of liberality was a grace (God's enablement and unconditional kindness and love generously bestowed) given to the Macedonian saints (2 Corinthians 8:1–5), as to all believers.

Jamieson, Fausset and Brown say, "Their liberality was not of themselves naturally, but of God's grace bestowed on them, and enabling them to be the instrument of God's 'grace' to others (2 Corinthians 8:6, 19)."[361] Failure to recognize liberality as a grace makes it a burden,[362] a mere Christian obligation and loathsome duty. It is only when giving is exhibited out of gratitude for Christ's grace being liberally poured out upon us and viewed as operating through us that it becomes a delight.

This grace is manifested richly in him who has 'first given himself to the Lord' (2 Corinthians 8:5). The heart that is surrendered to Christ is willing to give graciously and generously as the Lord prompts and enables. A man received the gift of a house that was rented to tenants. At the point of the transaction the giver no longer could collect the rent payable by the tenants.[363] It now was the rightful possession, along with the house, of the new owner. In giving ourselves to Christ freely and completely, He becomes sole owner and possessor of all that we "own" (money, property, giftedness, time—all now are His) to utilize as He deems wise and best. We are to be just stewards of God's possessions motivated not only by His ownership of our very being and devoted love to Him but by Christ's example of sacrificial grace, the giving of His life at Calvary to purchase our salvation (2 Corinthians 8:9).

Paul makes plain that the grace of liberality ought to be engaged and cultivated. "But as you excel in everything—in faith, in speech, in knowledge, in all earnestness, and in our love for you—see that you excel in this act of grace also" (2 Corinthians 8:7 ESV). Exercise the grace of giving as you do those of prayer, Bible study, church attendance and demonstrations of love, and it will flourish and become spontaneous. Apart from exercise, it withers and even dies.

"Grace prepares the way for grace. Denial of self in one direction leads to cross bearing in other forms."[364] Warren Wiersbe says, "Grace giving means giving in spite of circumstances."[365] See 2 Corinthians 8:2–3.

"The reason 'God loves a cheerful giver' [2 Corinthians 9:7]," writes J. M. Bolland, "is because such giving can only flow from grace, and such giving is always a means of grace. Instead of a collection dissipating all religious feeling, our 'joy' ought 'to abound unto liberality.' If liberality is a Christian grace, and giving is a means of grace, why should not a man feel as religious while giving as he does while singing and praying?"[366]

> To Thee, Thou bleeding Lamb, I all things owe,
> All that I have and am and all I know.
> All that I have is now no longer mine,
> And I am not mine own, Lord; I am Thine.
>
> How can I, Lord, withhold life's brightest hour
> From Thee, or gathered gold, or any pow'r?
> Why should I keep one precious thing from Thee,
> When Thou hast giv'n Thine own dear self for me?
> ~ Charles E. Mudie (1872)

58   Stamp of Approval of Grace

To live life under the umbrella of another's man's praise and approval is to live life constantly in bondage, dread, and fear. The craving for man's approval is a cistern that cannot hold water or satisfy. "Saul's armor" wouldn't fit David; it proved to be more of an impediment than a help (1 Samuel 17:38–39). 'So he took it off.' And in doing so David avoided a huge mistake that might have cost him his life. The armor of others may work for them (Saul's armor proved worthy for him personally), but not for you. It's always best to dress in the "armor" God gave you (your personal identity, personality, abilities, giftedness). To seek to be someone that you are not (dress in another's armor) is not only frustrating but defeating. Refuse to be the cut-out caricature of another man. Be true to yourself. "Take your directions at first hand from God, and don't spoil your own little gift by trying to bend it into the shape of somebody else's. Flutes cannot be made to sound like drums. Be content to give out your own note, and leave the care of the harmony to God."[367]

And grace frees you to be "you." The Bible says, "It was for this freedom that Christ set us free [completely liberating us]; therefore keep standing firm and do not be subject again to a yoke of slavery [which you once removed]" (Galatians 5:1 AMP). Grace frees you to take off the armor of another's making to be yourself. It frees you to walk the path of God's choosing, not that which leads to another man's castle. Grace frees you to be the unique person God created (Psalm 139:14) and to follow the plan He designed (Jeremiah 29:11). Grace frees you from the pressure of impressing and pleasing others. Grace frees you from accepting the lies of the world about your self-worth and potential. Grace says whatever lies in the past doesn't have to jeopardize the present (God won't hold it over your head, as others may). Grace takes that which happened to you in the past and transforms it into use for His glory (Genesis 45:7). Grace gives you freedom from being controlled by the approval, criticism, and opinion of others.

Neither David's brothers' criticism nor Saul's unbelief kept him from trusting his divinely designed armor. Grace frees you from the stress of ever seeking to prove yourself to someone else. 'If the son sets you free, you are free indeed' (John 8:36). Grace frees you not only from the bondage of sin, but the bondage of the governing control of others. Grace frees you from the fear of disappointing man. Chappell says, "Fear of man is the enemy of the fear of the Lord. The fear of man pushes us to perform for man's approval rather than according to God's directives."[368] Grace frees you to understand that the approval of God is enough, and through grace you have that approval. Live to please Him, and it matters not what others say or think.

A young violinist, in ending his first concert, was applauded by a standing audience. Amid the approval of the crowd, his eyes stayed fixed the entire time upon an elderly man in the balcony.

The young violinist showed no emotion of joy until that man stood and applauded. You see, that elderly man was the young violinist's instructor, and he was concerned only with pleasing him.

Such was the attitude of the Apostle Paul with regard to Christ, for he testifies, "Obviously, I'm not trying to win the approval of people, but of God. If pleasing people were my goal, I would not be Christ's servant" (Galatians 1:10 NLT).

Grace frees you to live life before an audience of the ONE who has stamped upon your heart with indelible ink "Accepted in the Beloved" (Ephesians 1:6) and that fitted you with uniquely designed armor. It matters not if the armor is polished brass, as Saul's, or a sling and pouch of stones, like that of David. Accept it, rejoice in it, walk in it, and be content with it. And God will use it mightily.

59 Shining of Grace

Isaiah says that at times the believer may find himself walking in the dark without any light (Isaiah 50:10). And how dark that darkness is at times, none but he who walks in it understands. Its misery, gloom and discomfort defy tongue or pen to accurately tell. Its despair and distress are horrendous and bewildering. Its "blinding" darkness is like seeking passage through a deep fog, not knowing where to place the next foot. To walk in the vale of darkness and tears "sets all his songs to a minor key. It gives to all his prayers a wailing pathos. It takes away much of his buoyancy and elasticity for work."[369] And it would make "light" (peace and meaning to life) irrecoverable, were it not for God's amazing grace.

> Grace shines the brightest in our deepest darkness.

God's grace (the unmerited loving action of God for our good) is outpoured upon us daily, yet we often fail to see it until the hour of deep darkness when it sorely is needed and requested. The testimony of suffering saints is that grace shines the brightest in the soul's deepest darkness.

Grace is the anchor that will secure footing when our world tumbles into shambles. It is the light that illuminates the darkness to show us the way out. It is the balm of Gilead that will grant comfort, peace and hope to heal the brokenness. It is the gentle voice of Jesus who "speaks the drooping heart to cheer." It is the staying and coping power of the Holy Spirit to enable endurance through the storm. "The security of the saint is rooted in the fact that God has hold of him, and not at all in his consciousness that he has hold of God. His comfort may be affected by the latter, but his safety is due entirely to the former."[370] It is the supernatural hand of God at work using the "bad" for our "good" (Romans 8:28).

When grace shines into our darkness, the impossible becomes possible, the pain becomes consolable, the suffering becomes bearable, the struggle becomes manageable, the battle becomes winnable, and the future becomes sunny and bright.

> Engulfed in deep darkness,
>   My soul cried out for grace.
> It gave that which was needed
>   To withstand all that was faced.
>
> ~ Frank Shivers (2021)

60   Salvation of Grace

Salvation is the achievement of God's unmerited free gift of grace in man's repentant heart. Saith Paul, "We have redemption through his blood, the forgiveness of sins, according to the riches of his grace" (Ephesians 1:7). Salvation is totally based upon grace, and not on works in anywise (Ephesians 2:8–9). Simeon says, "Salvation must either be of grace or of works; the two cannot be mixed together or reconciled with each other. If it be of works in any degree, it is no more of grace."[371] Paul said, "The gospel of Christ…is the power of God unto salvation to every one that believeth" (Romans 1:16). The message of the Cross (the death, burial and resurrection of Jesus Christ) is the power of God that enables pardon through grace to everyone that believeth.

A chief of a tribal village, following many years in sin, was won to Christ by a missionary. Friends asked why the change in his life. Picking up a little worm, he placed it on a pile of leaves and ignited the leaves. As the flames drew near to the spot where the worm lay, the old chief thrust his hand into the burning pile snatching out the worm. Holding the worm gently, he bore witness to the grace of God: "Me...that worm." What a simple and wondrous picture of grace. It brings to mind Isaac Watts' hymn that says, "Alas! and did my savior bleed...for such a worm as I."

> Grace, grace, God's grace,
>   Grace that will pardon and cleanse within;
> Grace, grace, God's grace,
>   Grace that is greater than all our sin!
> ~ Julia H. Johnston (1910)

By free grace (provided by Christ's atoning death at Calvary and subsequent resurrection three days later) sin is blotted out (Isaiah 43:25), pardoned (Isaiah 55:7), buried in the depth of the sea (Micah 7:19), and removed from the sinner as far as the east is from the west (Psalm 103:12). See 1 Peter 1:18–19.

> They are covered by the blood;
> They are covered by the blood;
> My sins are all covered by the blood.
>   Mine iniquities so vast
>   Have been blotted out at last;
> My sins are all covered by the blood.
> ~ Nellie Edwards (1904)

Paul states in Acts 20:21 that this redeeming grace is attainable ("accessible") by faith placed in Jesus Christ as Lord and Savior, and godly repentance; and that, once approbated, it secures (surefootedness) the soul for all eternity (Romans 5:2: "grace wherein we stand"). "A present salvation," writes Spurgeon, "must be through grace, and salvation by grace must be through faith. You cannot get a hold of salvation by grace by any other means than by faith."[372] He continues, "Grace is the

123

first and last moving cause of salvation; and faith, essential as it is, is only an important part of the machinery which grace employs. We are saved 'through faith,' but salvation is 'by grace.'"[373]

Grace is what God provides; faith is the hand that receives it as a free and welcome gift (Ephesians 2:8–9). The link between the two cannot be broken—they ever stand together (Galatians 3:22; John 3:16). "Salvation is by grace. It does not come to us by an involuntary act, as light falls on our eyes, sounds on our ears, or air enters our lungs. When we are so far enlightened as to understand about it, there must be a personal reception of salvation by us, and that is by faith."[374]

"It [salvation] is not a casual or evanescent [momentary or fleeting] feeling, but a settled condition wrought for us and in us by the abounding mercy of the Lord."[375] The Bible says, "But when the kindness and love of God our Savior appeared, he saved us, not because of righteous things we had done, but because of his mercy. He saved us through the washing of rebirth and renewal by the Holy Spirit" (Titus 3:4–5 NIV).

A monument of grace,
    A sinner saved by blood,
The streams of love I trace
    Up to their fountain—God—
And in His heart of mercy see
Eternal thoughts of love to me![376]

~ John Kent (1766–1843)

61 Stumbling Block of Grace

"Behold, I thought" (2 Kings 5:11). Naaman's preconception of the means of his healing of leprosy became a barrier or stumbling block to it. He brought to Elisha "gifts of $20,000 in silver, $60,000 in gold, and ten suits of clothing" (2 Kings 5:5 TLB). But they were of no interest to Elisha, had no bearing on Naaman's healing, and were refused. See Isaiah 55:1. The simple instruction to Naaman for healing was to dunk himself seven times in the muddy river Jordan (2 Kings 5:10a), an action that required only faith. But misconceptions about the means of healing, and pride in Naaman's heart caused him to balk, get angry and almost miss the miracle that he sought (2 Kings 5:10b, 14).

A salvation by grace without works is too easy for some to accept. Like Naaman, they feel what is told them to do to be saved is too simple; surely, they say, it requires me doing my part in good deeds, sincere efforts to please God, morality and/or the sacraments. But the Bible says that such thinking is flawed (Ephesians 2:8–9). Human righteousness, religious rituals and works do not count one iota toward salvation. It is a free gift (grace), prohibitive of any additive.

A cake mix company promoted its product as requiring nothing but water to be added by the housewife to make a creamy and delicious cake. It did not sell. Marketing research discovered the reason for its failure was that the public felt uneasy about a mix that required only water to be added. It seemed too simple. The public felt they had to do more personally in making the cake batter. The company changed the cake formula, requiring an egg to be added. Immediately sales soared.[377] Sadly, far too many feel this same way about the means of salvation—saving grace.

Maclaren says, "Men would be a great deal more willing to accept God's way of salvation if it gave them some share in their own salvation. But its characteristic is that it will have none of our work—not even so much as this man [Naaman] had to do in his healing. The Gospel rejects our cooperation just because it demands our faith."[378] Joseph Parker said, "As in the case of Naaman, so now. The surprise of Christian revelation is always in the direction of simplicity. Naaman had a program; Elisha, a command. Naaman had a ceremony; Elisha, a revelation. Naaman required a whole sheet of paper on which to write out his elaborate scheme; Elisha rolled up his address into a military sentence and delivered his order as a mightier soldier than Naaman. Let us burn our theories, inventions, preconceptions, prejudices, and our forecasts about God, Providence, Inspiration, Redemption, and human destiny, and throw ourselves into the great arms, asking only to be and to do what God would have us be and do [to be saved]."[379]

Don't allow the simplicity of the means of salvation, grace through faith in the Lord Jesus Christ without personal contribution (works), and pride block the path to abundant and eternal life (Titus 3:5–7; John 14:6). Peter wrote, "Ye were not redeemed with corruptible things [like] silver and gold…but with the precious blood of Christ" (1 Peter 1:18–19). It's a no-brainer that if man's salvation could have been obtained by any other means than Jesus' sacrificial death, Calvary would have been avoided.

J. C. Ryle explains, "People seem to me to forget that all Christ's sufferings at Calvary were necessary for man's salvation. He had to bear our sins, if ever they were to be borne at all: with His stripes alone could we be healed. This was the one payment of our debts that God would accept; this was the great sacrifice on which our eternal life depended. If Christ had not gone to the cross and suffered in our stead, the just for the unjust, there would not have been a spark of hope for us; there would have been a mighty gulf between ourselves and God, which no man ever could have passed. The cross was necessary, in order that there might be an atonement for sin."[380]

Spurgeon remarks, "You are a sinner and want pardon; your nature is depraved and needs renewing. Should the plan of forgiving and regenerating you be shaped to please your tastes and whims? Should the great Lord of mercy wait upon you and consult you as to how He shall work out your salvation?"[381] Blasphemous arrogance answers yes, but the heart of humility and truth know better.

> It's not by works of righteousness
>> Which our own hands have done,
> But we are saved by sovereign grace
>> Abounding through His Son.
>
> It's from the mercy of our God
>> That all our hopes begin;
> It's by the water and the blood
>> Our souls are washed from sin.
>
> ~ Isaac Watts (1674–1748)

A woman complained about the life preservers to the captain of a vessel. "Just look at them," she said.

"What's the matter with them?" inquired the captain.

"Matter with them?" the woman replied. "Don't you see that they are dirty? If a woman with a nice summer dress on had to put one of those things over it, it would never be fit to wear again!" Man has a choice about being saved, not about its means.

62 Sustaining of Grace

It's God grace that bears us up in the storms of life. See Romans 5:2; Philippians 4:13 and 1 Timothy 1:12. Storms are opportunities to deepen spiritual roots, enlarge faith, and witness the power of God at work. Hudson Taylor said, "All our difficulties are only platforms for the manifestations of His grace, power and love."[382] John Piper says grace "is an influence or a force or a power or an acting of God that works in us to change our capacities for work and suffering and obedience."[383] Saith Watchman Nee, "Natural strength is what we receive from the hand of God as Creator. Spiritual strength is what we receive from God in grace."[384] "Grace," says Westcott, "is to be 'sought' by man according to his necessity."[385]

> All our difficulties are only platforms for the manifestations of His grace, power and love.
> Hudson Taylor

It's God's grace that enables standing in the midst of the "unfair" troubles of life, things you didn't deserve, initiate, orchestrate, or want. They just happen and turn your world upside down.

It's God's grace that sustains when you are confronted with unfixable situations, things not within your power to change. It's God's grace (infused through the Holy Spirit) that provides stamina (strength, energy and will-power) to press on when you feel like quitting, are taxed to the limit, or are worn and exhausted (Galatians 6:9).

Sustaining grace isn't prevention of trials. It is perseverance in the midst of them. Spurgeon said, "God grants to Satan permission to try His people in this way because He knows how He will overrule it to His own Glory and their good. There are certain graces which are never produced in Christians, to a high degree, except by severe temptation."[386]

Looking unto Jesus for sustaining grace,
That I may with "patience" run the heavenly race.
Looking unto Jesus when I'm weak or strong,
Looking unto Jesus I am helped along.
          ~ James L. Nicholson (1889)

The hymn "How Firm a Foundation" portrays God speaking to the believer with regard to His sustaining grace.

"Fear not; I am with you. Oh, be not dismayed,
For I am your God and will still give you aid!
I'll strengthen you, help you, and cause you to stand,
Upheld by my righteous, omnipotent hand.

"When through the deep waters I call you to go,
The rivers of sorrow shall not overflow,
 For I will be with you, your troubles to bless,
And sanctify to you the deepest distress.

"When through fiery trials your pathway shall lie,
My grace, all sufficient, shall be your supply.
The flames shall not hurt you. I only design
Your dross to consume and your gold to refine.

"The soul that on Jesus still leans for repose,
I will not, I will not desert to its foes.
That soul, though all Hell should endeavor to shake,
I'll never, no, never, no, never forsake!"
          ~ attributed to George Keith (1787)

63 Subjectiveness of Grace

In essence 1 Corinthians 10:27–33 states, "When at the table with meats which have been sacrificed to idols, from which a fellow-guest conscientiously abstains and reminds you of the fact, then out of deference to his weak conscience do not touch it—however delicious it may appear, and however hungry you may be. The most sacred thing is conscience, and the weakest should be respected."[387] The principle embraces all of life. Grace is mindful of and subject to the conscience of others. He that possesses grace willingly abstains from that which offends another (although he is at liberty to engage in it) in order to prevent the weaker brother from stumbling and to glorify God.

Warren Wiersbe states, "Humanly speaking, it may seem wrong for a strong Christian to bow to a weaker brother, but this is what glorifies God. Making that weaker brother stumble into sin would disgrace the church and the name of Christ."[388] Note, it is *needless offense* that causes another to stumble to which Paul refers, not offense for speaking the truth in love. The governing rule of grace is 'let everyone seek his neighbor's good' (1 Corinthians 10:24).

Jon Courson comments, "The underlying reason for giving up liberty is an awareness of how it affects the salvation or walk of another. As he brings to a close this important question of Christian liberty, Paul gives three questions to ask ourselves regarding any activity. Can I thank the Lord in it? (v. 30). Will God be glorified through it? (v. 31) Will someone be tripped up by it? (v. 32). Like a weathervane that changes direction depending upon which way the wind is blowing, the wise man will adjust his activities to the way the wind of the Spirit is moving."[389]

Grace grants liberty to engage in that which is lawful and acceptable to God, as well as forfeiting that right at certain times to prevent a weaker brother from stumbling or a lost man from being saved, and to glorify God.

64   Straying from Grace

Paul told the Galatian believers, "Christ is become of no effect unto you, whosoever of you are justified by the law; ye are fallen from grace" (Galatians 5:4). Judaizers had crept into the churches of Galatia, teaching circumcision as a part of justification and swaying believers to revert from the system of grace for salvation back to the law. George says, "What they advocated was a Christianity by amalgamation, a mingling of the grace of Christ with the merit of works. Yet, as Calvin put it so well, 'Whoever wants to have a half-Christ loses the whole.'"[390]

"Fallen from grace" (to loosen one's grip) does not mean losing of salvation. Criswell explains, "If the Galatians seek to be justified by the keeping of the Law, they will have abandoned grace as the means of salvation and will demonstrate that they were never saved in the first place."[391] MacArthur similarly says, "Paul's clear meaning is that any attempt to be justified by the law is to reject salvation by grace alone through faith alone. Their desertion of Christ and the Gospel only proves that their faith was never genuine."[392] "Grace and legal righteousness cannot co-exist" (Romans 4:4; 5:11–16).[393]

The same mistake is repeated today when a believer leaves a church that teaches salvation by grace through faith alone and unites with one which teaches that salvation depends on baptism, works, church membership and adherence to certain teachings.

65   Sanguinity of Grace

"Therefore, with minds that are alert and fully sober, set your hope [certainty] on the grace to be brought to you when Jesus Christ is revealed at his coming" (1 Peter 1:13 NIV). Believers are instructed not to abandon their hope in the Gospel (grace), despite opposition and trials, but to embrace those hopes until the coming of Christ. (Gird your hope with readiness to stand true to the end.) See 2 Thessalonians 2:16. At Christ's coming, He is to reveal perfected grace (salvation). The second grace that is to be revealed is perfect vindication of our faith.[394] Saith Scripture,

"That the trial of your faith, being much more precious than of gold that perisheth, though it be tried with fire, might be found unto praise and honor and glory at the appearing of Jesus Christ" (1 Peter 1:7). Spurgeon says, "Today they sneer at our faith, but they will not do so when Jesus comes; today we ourselves tremble for the ark of the Lord, but we shall not do so when He comes. Then shall all men say that believers were wise, prudent, philosophical. Those who believe in Jesus may be called fools today, but men will think otherwise when they see them shine forth as the sun in the Father's kingdom."[395] See 2 Thessalonians 1:7. "Christ's future ministry," states MacArthur, "of glorifying Christians and giving them eternal life in His presence will be the final culmination of the grace initiated at salvation."[396]

Ye servants of the Lord,
    Each in his office wait,
Observant of His heavenly Word
    And watchful at His gate.

Let all your lamps be bright,
    And trim the golden flame;
Gird up your loins as in his sight,
    For awful is His name.

Watch! 'tis your Lord's command,
    And while we speak, He's near;
Mark the first signal of His hand,
    And ready all appear.

Oh, happy servant he
    In such a posture found!
He shall his Lord with rapture see
    And be with honor crowned.

Christ shall the banquet spread
    With His own royal hand,
And raise that faithful servant's head
    Amid the angelic band.

~ Philip Doddridge (1755)

66 Spiritual Gifts of Grace

Peter says, "As each has received a gift, use it to serve one another, as good stewards of God's varied grace" (1 Peter 4:10 ESV). Through God's grace He gives grace gifts of various kinds (diversified, manifold, multicolored) for Christian service. The same Greek word for 'various' is used in the description of Joseph's "coat of many colors." It had many and varied colors. Joseph's coat serves as a picture of the grace of God. Though grace is one "coat" (one substance), it consists of multiple dimensions or colors or varied gifts.

Matthew Henry says, "True Christians are anointed ones; their names express this: they are anointed with grace, with gifts and spiritual privileges, by the Holy Spirit of grace."[397] With regard to the gifts of grace, Paul writes, "In his grace, God has given us different gifts for doing certain things well. So if God has given you the ability to prophesy, speak out with as much faith as God has given you. If your gift is serving others, serve them well. If you are a teacher, teach well. If your gift is to encourage others, be encouraging. If it is giving, give generously. If God has given you leadership ability, take the responsibility seriously. And if you have a gift for showing kindness to others, do it gladly" (Romans 12:6–8 NLT). Grace gifts, bestowed upon us by the Holy Spirit, have been given to enhance the body of Christ. Of these diverse gifts Paul says, "But unto every one of us is given grace according to the measure of the gift of Christ" (Ephesians 4:7). Barnes comments, "It comes through Him [measure of grace]. It is what He has purchased; what He has obtained by His merits. All have enough for the purposes for which God has called them into His kingdom, but there are not the same endowments conferred on all. Some have grace given them to qualify them for the ministry; some to be apostles; some to be martyrs; some to make them eminent as public benefactors. All this has been obtained by Christ; and one should not complain that another has more distinguished endowments than he possesses."[398] See Romans 12:3; 1 Corinthians 12; John 1:16.

Arrogance and boastful pride must be avoided by him that possesses gifts of grace that seem superior to others, as he who exhibits lesser grace gifts should avoid jealousy and envy. They equally are Christ's gifts of grace measured out as deemed needed for the edification and harmony of the Body. Identify the gift of grace measured out to you and operate within its element for the greater usefulness to the kingdom and personal pleasure and happiness (Ephesians 4:7). It is when the believer oversteps the boundary of the "gift" bestowed that frustration develops and productivity is impacted. Be content to use your own gift, not that of another (avoid King Saul's armor). Spurgeon comments, "We must minister as the Spirit has given us ability, and not intrude upon our fellow servant's domain. Our Lord taught us not to covet the high places, but to be willing to be the least among the brethren."[399] Whatever the gift(s) of grace possessed, it is vitally important and invaluable to the body of Christ's ability to function effectively, uniformly and harmoniously (1 Corinthians 12:15–31).

67   Showing of Grace

"We can say with confidence and a clear conscience that we have lived with a God-given holiness and sincerity in all our dealings. We have depended on God's grace, not on our own human wisdom. That is how we have conducted ourselves before the world, and especially toward you" (2 Corinthians 1:12 NLT). Saith Barnes, "It means that Paul had been influenced by such sentiments and principles as would be suggested or prompted by the influence of His grace. Locke renders it 'by the favor of God directing me.' God had shown him favor; God had directed him; and He had kept him from the crooked and devious ways of mere worldly policy. The idea seems to be not merely that he had pursued a correct and upright course of life, but that he was indebted for this to the mere grace and favor of God."[400]

The text speaks of *living grace* that impacts all of life and its relationships, enabling life to be lived with a clear conscience and "sincerity in all our dealings" (honesty, holiness, and purity of affection without intentional deviation, but not "faultlessness"). The believers' outward conduct is an extension of his inward state (Proverbs 4:23; John 15:4). Simeon says, "Whatever be our end, we must do nothing to accomplish it which will not bear the light and stand the test of the severest scrutiny. We must act simply under the influence of "the grace of God," and never in a way of carnal policy. Our ends, and our means, must be alike regulated by the Word of God and alike conducive to the glory of his name."[401] "Not with fleshly wisdom, 'but by the grace of God'—by its cleansings, its kindlings, its renewing," states Raleigh, "its growth; by its whole drift and discipline we have *'our manner of life'* in the world. And because it is 'the grace of God,' those who take it, and trust in it, and put it to use, cannot fail in some measure to realize and embody, and cannot fail, ultimately, to perfect the fair ideal of Scriptural holiness."[402]

Matthew Henry said, "Believers, in this world, need the grace of God to arm them against temptations, so as to bear the good report of men without pride; and so as to bear their reproaches with patience. They have nothing in themselves but possess all things in Christ."[403]

The greatest proof of the presence of grace in the heart is its manifestation in the affairs and relations of life. "If the majesty, grace, and power of God," Chambers says, "are not being exhibited in us, God holds us responsible. 'God is able to make all grace abound toward you, that you...may have an abundance....' (2 Corinthians 9:8 NKJV)."[404]

68 Salient Teaching of Grace

"The grace of God has appeared that offers salvation to all people. It teaches us to say 'No' to ungodliness and worldly passions, and to live self-controlled, upright and godly lives in this present age, while we wait for the blessed hope—the appearing of the glory of our great God and Savior, Jesus Christ" (Titus 2:11–13 NIV). Paul says that grace teaches five primary things.

It teaches us the universality of the opportunity for salvation. "That offers salvation to all people." Grace has made possible that which all men need, forgiveness of sin and reconciliation to God through the "riches of His grace." It is perfectly fitted to meet man's dire need because of estrangement from God.

It teaches us what to deny. "Ungodliness and worldly lusts." Raffles says, "Wherever this Gospel hath come 'in demonstration of the Spirit and with power,' it hath purified the polluted; it hath made the dishonest honest, the intemperate sober, the licentious chaste."[405] Barnes says, "The phrase 'worldly lusts' refers to all improper desires pertaining to this life."[406] Grace empowers the believer to deny sin and live the Spirit-controlled life.

It teaches us what to do. 'To live self-disciplined [exercise restraint in appetite and desire], righteous [justly], and godly [pious] lives in the present world.'

It teaches us what to anticipate. "Looking for that blessed hope and the glorious appearing of the great God and our Savior Jesus Christ." Clarke says, "This is what the Gospel teaches us to expect, and what the grace of God prepares the human heart for."[407]

It teaches us who to acknowledge. 'The God of grace.' Matthew Henry says, "Personal and relative duties must be done in obedience to His commands, with due aim at pleasing and honoring Him, from principles of holy love and fear of Him. But there is an express and direct duty also that we owe to God, namely, belief and acknowledgment of His being and perfections, paying Him internal and external worship and homage; loving, fearing, and trusting in Him; depending on Him, and devoting ourselves to Him; observing all those religious duties and ordinances that He has appointed; praying to Him, praising Him, and meditating on His Word and works."[408]

69 Solace of Grace

The believer possesses "everlasting consolation and good hope through grace" to comfort and sustain (2 Thessalonians 2:16). What is this "good hope through grace" that God supplies the believer? It is a hope based upon events that are to take place at the end of the age.

Scripture describes it as "the obtaining of the glory of our Lord Jesus Christ" (2 Thessalonians 2:14 ASV), "The hope of salvation" (1 Thessalonians 5:8 ASV), "The hope laid up for you in heaven" (Colossians 1:5 ESV), "Hope of eternal life" (Titus 1:2), "The hope of 'an inheritance incorruptible, and undefiled, and that fadeth not away, reserved in heaven for you'" (1 Peter 1:4), "Hope to the end for the grace that is to be brought unto you at the revelation of Jesus Christ" (1 Peter 1:13); and in Titus 2:13, Paul says, "Looking for that blessed hope, and the glorious appearing of the great God and our Savior Jesus Christ."

To possess hope in the imminent return of Jesus Christ to take us to a place free from sorrow gives "everlasting consolation" in battling life's present woes and pains (John 14:1–3; Revelation 21:4). Christian hope tranquillizes the mind (Romans 15:13), purifies the soul (1 John 1:1–3), grants endurance in trial (1 Thessalonians 1:3b) and peace in the moment of death (John 14:1–3). Thomas Watson says, "Hope is an active grace. It is like the spring in the watch: it sets all the wheels of the soul in motion. Hope of a crop makes the husbandman sow his seed; hope of victory makes the soldier fight; and a true hope of glory makes a Christian vigorously pursue glory."[409] See Romans 5:2. "The grace of hope is the fruit of the Lord's mercy" (1 Peter 1:3).[410]

This hope of consolation is as reliable as it is certain, for it is founded upon the unchanging grace of God and His eternal promises (Romans 15:4). Saith Miller, "In the 'good hope' of the Christian, uncertainty is no element. It is a deferred hope, a waiting hope, a tried hope; but not an uncertain hope, not a speculative hope. It rests not upon probability. Its security is the word, the character, the nature of the unchanging and unchangeable Jehovah."[411]

The everlasting consolation of this "good hope" is divinely imparted into the soul by grace (ascertained by faith in Jesus Christ). The hope of the Christian is securely founded on grace (1 Peter 1:13), but that of the ungodly will "evaporate" (Job 8:13 NLT; Job 27:10). Barclay says, "When a man's hope is in God, it cannot turn to dust and ashes. When a man's hope is in God, it cannot be disappointed. When a man's hope is in the love of God, it can never be an illusion, for God loves us with an everlasting love backed by an everlasting power."[412]

70 Standing of Grace

"The great day of his wrath is come; and who shall be able to stand?" (Revelation 6:17). Who is able to stand in the day (last day) of God's mighty wrath (a wrath never experienced by man before)? Not the unbeliever, hypocrite (masks will be removed), drunkard, coward, liar, immoral, religionist, or murderer. See Revelation 21:8. All these shall have their part in "the lake burning with fire and brimstone" (Revelation 21:8 BLB). Matthew Henry comments, "Sinners must bear all the blame of their own destruction. Therefore, the ungodly perish, because the very way in which they have chosen and resolved to walk leads directly to destruction; it naturally tends towards ruin and therefore must necessarily end in it."[413]

They that shall stand are those who are resting entirely upon the blood and righteousness of Christ for the salvation of their souls, which is accessible by faith through grace alone. Of "this grace wherein we *stand*" (Romans 5:2), Ironside says, "The believer in the Lord Jesus Christ stands before God in all the infinite value of the finished work of our blessed Savior, and no charge can be brought against him."[414] He has been justified by faith in Christ's atoning work at Calvary and stands in a state of reconciliation with God. Simeon says, "His sins are all washed away in the Redeemer's blood; and he is clothed from head to foot in the robe of the Redeemer's righteousness, so that in the sight of God he stands without spot or blemish."[415]

And this glorious state of grace is 'accessed by faith' in Christ" (Romans 5:1–2). All that possess this standing of grace attest with Ironside, "It is a great thing to be able to stand. It is a great thing to be able to say, 'Thank God, my standing is in the risen Christ! I claim nothing on the ground of my own merit but stand before God in His perfection.'"[416]

71 Skepticism of Grace

"The sin underneath all our sins," states Martin Luther, "is to trust the lie of the serpent that we cannot trust the love and grace of Christ and must take matters into our own hands."[417] Hasty conclusions and decisions fueled by panic are the mark of a fool. Solomon says, "To make rash, hasty decisions shows that you are not trusting the Lord. But when you rely totally on God, you will still act carefully and prudently. Self-confident know-it-alls will prove to be fools. But when you lean on the wisdom from above, you will have a way to escape the troubles" (Proverbs 28:25–26 TPT).

Instinctively some believers, instead of first looking to the Lord for help in the time of need, look to secondary sources and means, such as "chariots, and...horses" (Psalm 20:7). Like the unbeliever, they believe the more "chariots, and...horses" (human instrumentation instead of divine dependence) that are utilized the greater the chance for deliverance, healing or victory. But they are wrong and partake of the bitter consequences. "They (all that trust in 'chariots and horses') are brought down and fallen (defeat and collapse): but we (all that rely upon the Lord) are risen, and stand upright (successful, victorious)" (Psalm 20:8).

He that depends upon human ingenuity or ability or skill will be sorely disappointed and defeated, while the person that trusts in the Lord will be delighted and delivered. Such is affirmed time and again in Scripture: 2 Chronicles 14:11–12 (Asa); 2 Chronicles 20:12 (Jehoshaphat); 2 Chronicles 32:7–8 (Hezekiah); Psalm 33:17; 34:22; 118:8 (David). Spurgeon states, "Doubt discovers difficulties which it never solves; it creates hesitancy, despondency, despair. Its progress is the decay of comfort, the death of peace. 'Believe!' is the word which speaks life into a man, but doubt nails down his coffin."[418]

Placing trust in God first and foremost opens the door to Him to supply our needs through miraculous intervention or human agency. Every need is an opportunity for God to intervene and meet. Say with David, "The LORD is my strength and my shield; my heart trusted in him, and I am helped: therefore my heart greatly rejoiceth; and with my song will I praise him" (Psalm 28:7). See 1 John 5:15. God has proved through history His worthiness of man's trust. E. M. Bounds says, "Trust always operates in the present tense. Hope looks toward the future. Trust looks to the present. Hope expects. Trust possesses. Trust receives what prayer acquires. So, what prayer needs, at all times, is abiding and abundant trust."[419] "Our confidence must not be in what we have done, nor in what we have resolved to do, but entirely in what the Lord will do. We can never be too confident when we confide in Him alone, and never too much concerned to have such a trust."[420] See Proverbs 3:26.

> Whatever instrumentality we may employ, we will remember always that our hope is in God, and that he only can give success.
> Albert Barnes

Albert Barnes remarks, "We will not forget that our reliance is not on armies, but on God, the living God. Whatever instrumentality we may employ, we will remember always that our hope is in God, and that He only can give success."[421] "Great certainly is the Faith," says Luther, "which hath such courage by remembering the name of the Lord."[422] W. S. Plumer writes, "The righteous put nothing with God to form the basis of their joy and trust. He alone is enough. They need neither help, nor guidance, nor wisdom, nor strength, nor righteousness but in Him alone."[423] Thomas Brooks says, "We trust as we love, and where we love. If we love Christ much, surely, we will trust Him much."[424] Arthur Pink said, "Resist with the utmost abhorrence anything that causes you to doubt God's love and his loving-kindness [grace] toward you. Allow nothing to make you question the Father's love for His child."[425]

With Christ's grace, uncertainty is no element. It is a waiting grace at times, but not an uncertain grace, not an unsubstantiated grace. It rests not upon probability but actuality. Its certainty is intertwined with three unbreakable cords: Christ's unchangeableness, everlasting consolation and compassion, and divine Word. See Psalm 37:23 and Jeremiah 29:11. Thomas Aquinas said "Faith is to believe what you do not see; the reward of this faith is to see what you believe."[426] "The fanatic's hopes," saith Spurgeon, "will pass away with the vapors which produced them, but the believer's hope is founded in grace. Why is it, then, that some believers' hopes flicker? Because they get away from a hope in grace and look towards themselves."[427] "It is true that God reserves the right to fulfill His promises in His own time. But that does not impugn His trustworthiness. The Word of God over and over again declares that God does what He says He will do."[428] Therefore, "my soul, wait thou only upon God; for my expectation is from him" (Psalm 62:5).

72   Sophisms of Grace

There are seven fallacies (sophisms) about grace.

What you do impacts the degree of love God has for you. That's wrong. God can love you no more and no less than He loves you presently and eternally. And this is because His love for us is unconditional and unmerited, solely based on grace (Ephesians 3:19).

Man's efforts or works enhance grace. That's wrong. The two cannot be combined. Paul explains, "But if it is by grace, it is no longer on the basis of works; otherwise grace would no longer be grace" (Romans 11:6 ESV). Work and grace don't mix.

Grace gives free license to sin all that is desired. That's wrong. Jesus didn't die for our sin that we might continue in it. See Romans 6:15 and Romans 3:23.

Grace enables sinning without consequence. That's wrong. Although grace is promised upon repentance to grant forgiveness for the wrong done, it does not mean we can sin with impunity. The Bible says, "Be not deceived; God is not mocked: for whatsoever a man soweth, that shall he also reap" (Galatians 6:7). Consequences may result from a sinful act, although it is freely forgivable by grace.

Grace removes the trouble, hardship or sickness. That's wrong. Though grace may on occasion give rescue from the affliction, it always will give relief for the duration of the testing. The lesson of Paul's thorn in the flesh teaches this truth (2 Corinthians 12:6–8).

Grace will be always available. That's wrong. The opportunity for grace is in the present; tomorrow may be too late to experience it. The door to God's marvelous grace can shut without warning. "For he saith, I have heard thee in a time accepted, and in the day of salvation have I succored thee: behold, now is the accepted time; behold, now is the day of salvation" (2 Corinthians 6:2).

Grace is irresistible. That is wrong. The freeness of God's love, forgiveness, salvation and help is not forced upon any man. It is a matter of free choice. Paul said of the unsaved, "They perish because they did not accept the love of the truth in order to be saved" (2 Thessalonians 2:10 HCSB). That is, they resisted the gospel message of grace. In 1 Timothy 2:1–4 the Bible states it is "good and acceptable in the sight of God" that all men might be saved; therefore, we are to pray for their conversion. If grace were irresistible, then our prayers for their salvation would be senseless.

Billy Graham wrote, "There is also volitional resolution. The will is necessarily involved in conversion. People can pass through mental conflicts and emotional crises without being converted. Not until they exercise the prerogative of a free moral agent and will to be converted are they actually converted. This act of will is an act of acceptance and commitment. They willingly accept God's mercy and receive God's Son and then commit themselves to do God's will. In every true conversion the will of man comes into line with the will of God. Almost the last word of the Bible is this invitation: 'And whosoever will, let him take the water of life freely' (Rev. 22:17). It is up to you. You must will to be saved. It is God's will, but it must become your will, too."[429]

73 Steering Principle of Grace

Grace permeated Paul's life and theology. Hiebert writes, "Paul could not think of Christian truth and conduct apart from God's grace."[430] God's grace likewise was the driving factor of the brief life of Jim Elliot, missionary slain by the Auca Indians in Ecuador. At age 22, he wrote, "I see clearly now that anything, whatever it is, if it be not on the principle of grace, it is not of God. Here shall be my plea in weakness; here shall be my boldness in prayer; here shall be my deliverance in temptation; at last, here shall be my translation. Not of grace? Then not of God."[431]

The principle of grace is the foundation for salvation, the undeserved forgiveness and love of Christ changing the sinners' status from slaves to sons and transferring them out of the dark into the light (Ephesians 2:3–5). That miraculous transformation freely accomplished by the power of the Holy Spirit upon their repentance and exhibition of faith in Christ as Lord and Savior birthed them into a new realm of life governed by a new principle, the principle of grace as citizens of a new world order (1 Peter 2:9; Philippians 3:20). Apart from the intervention of grace (liberation), man is ruled by the principle of sin (1 John 5:19b), which orders rebellion, disdain and hostility toward God and the sacred (Holy Scripture, the Church, etc.), and prompts conduct divinely unacceptable and spiritually deplorable (Isaiah 64:6) to God and man. See Romans 6:14.

> Not under law, that could not save,
> But doomed me to a hopeless grave;
> But under grace, where I am free
> Through Jesus Christ who died for me.
> ~ Thomas O. Chisholm (1935)

Believers relate to God (access to, acceptance by, fellowship with, forgiveness through) not on the governing principle of the Law (bondage and its regulations) but that of grace (liberty and freedom), and order their lives accordingly (forgiveness to offenders, gracious behavior, service to others, abundant life and the glory of God).

By the living grace of God
    I will labor, watch, and pray,
Till this mortal life shall end
    In supernal day.

Work on, toil on,
    Till my work on earth is done;
By the living grace of God
    I will labor on.

By the living grace of God
    I'll defy the tempting throng;
High above the battle's din,
    Shout the victor's song.

By the living grace of God
    I will never doubt my Lord;
Till my eyes are closed in death,
    I'll believe His word.

By the living grace of God
    I will conquer, though I die;
The reward will come at last,
    In my home on high.

~ Daniel Otis Teasley (1911)

74   Streams of Grace

"And of his fulness [brimful] have all we received, and grace for grace" (John 1:16). "Grace for grace" is better rendered "grace on top of grace" or "one grace heaped upon another." Ponder the waves of the ocean—no more does one wave strike the shore than a fresh one arrives. F. F. Bruce says believers ever draw from the ocean of divine fullness grace upon grace—"one wave of grace being constantly replaced by a fresh one."[432] He continues, "The plentitude of divine glory and goodness which resides in Christ is an ocean from which all his people may draw without ever diminishing its content."[433]

143

The *Amplified Bible* renders the text, "For out of His fullness [the superabundance of His grace and truth] we have all received grace upon grace [spiritual blessing upon spiritual blessing, favor upon favor, and gift heaped upon gift]" (John 1:16). Paul states in Ephesians 1:3 something similar: "Blessed be the God and Father of our Lord Jesus Christ, who hath blessed us with all spiritual blessings in heavenly places in Christ."

Streams of grace are never ceasing from the throne of God to your soul to supply every deficiency, console every sorrow, enable every undertaking, conquer every temptation, and thwart every enemy. In Christ, the believer has access to the highest degree of grace, making all things possible.

Grace is given on top of grace to enable coping, conquest and comfort. The grace that forgives sin is topped with new grace to move past the sin victoriously; grace given to relieve the broken heart is topped with new grace to start life anew amidst the pain; grace for hatred of sin gives way to grace to live a holy and blameless life; grace that copes with the storms of life is topped at life's end with new grace to die; grace bestowed to be a minister of the Gospel is topped with empowering grace to fulfill the task effectively; grace given to suffer the "thorns" of life without complaint is topped with grace to patiently bear the discomfort; the grace for close communion with Christ is topped with grace to conform more perfectly to His image; the grace to live in isolation or loneliness is topped with the sweetest of graces of having Christ as one's "all in all."

And these perpetual "waves" of fresh grace gently keep washing upon the beach of the believer's life, bringing calm and assurances of His constant care, the one building upon the other ceaselessly. Matthew Henry states, "Grace for grace is one grace to improve, confirm, and perfect another grace. We are changed into the divine image, from glory to glory, from one degree of glorious grace to another (2 Corinthians 3:18). Those that have true grace have that for more grace (James 4:6). The grace we receive from Christ changes us into the same image (2 Corinthians 3:18), the image of the Son (Romans 8:29), the image of the heavenly (1 Corinthians 15:49)."[434] Spurgeon said, "The more the Lord gives, the more we may expect. Every blessing is not only in itself a mercy, but it is a note for more mercies. When we get the most of God's mercy that we can hold, we are, by its greatness, enlarged to receive still more. Realization begets expectation and expectation increases realization. Each mercy, as it comes, makes room for another larger than itself, even as the narrow end of the wedge opens the way for its wider portion. Every mercy bears a thousand mercies in its heart."[435]

How is that grace received? Alexander Maclaren said, "Here on the one hand is the boundless ocean of the Divine strength, unfathomable in its depth, full after all draughts, tideless and calm, in all its movements never troubled, in all its repose never stagnating; and on the other side is the empty avidity of our poor, weak natures. Faith opens these to the impulse of that great sea, and 'according to our faith,' in the exact measure of our receptivity, does it enter our hearts."[436]

A peddler entered at a cottage in Scotland, threw down his pack, and asked for a glass of water. Upon receiving the water, he was asked, "Do you know anything of the water of life?" "By the grace of God, I do." After drinking the water, he said, "Let us pray." And this was his prayer: "O Lord, give us grace to feel our need of grace. O Lord, give us grace to receive grace. O Lord, give us grace to ask for grace. O Lord, give us grace to use grace when grace is given." He then picked up his pack and walked away.[437] What a powerful sermon he preached in those few words!

"How highly privileged are all true believers! The believer may survey all the fulness that there is in Christ and claim it all as his own. All which Christ possesses in Himself, all which He can do on earth, and all which He can bestow in Heaven is the portion of the weakest saint, according to the measure of the grace that is in him, and according to the capacity which he has for receiving more grace. Every vessel of the sanctuary, from 'the smallest cups to the largest flagons' shall be filled."[438]

75 Slaying by Grace

Grace grants deliverance from sin's captivating power. "But where sin abounded, grace did much more abound [superabounds]" (Romans 5:20). Whatever may be the vice or sinful indulgence that plagues, pains and paralyzes life, the grace of God is more than capable to grant rescue, remedy and recovery. To see where grace abounded (its proof), one has only to look at people in whom sin first abounded. David committed an adulterous act and murderous scheme; Peter bluntly denied he knew Jesus three times; Manasseh engaged in every imaginable evil and perversion and was a murderer; Saul of Tarsus was a relentless pursuer and persecutor of Christians; Rahab was a harlot; John Newton was a slave trader; Mel Trotter was a drunkard and gambler; and Freddie Gage was a drug addict. But with them all, where sin abounded, grace did much more abound (superabounded), granting forgiveness and deliverance. Whatever the addiction or indulgence, even if counted among the worst, God's grace is supernaturally able to grant freedom and victory over its clutches if upon Him you believe and to Him you cleave. Grace has power to break the prison chains and set the captive free. It has power to relieve the misery of and remove the guilt of the sin. "It not merely justifies the person, but renovates the nature, implants new principles, induces new feelings, inspires love to prayer, and communicates that strength and consolation which we require while residents in this world."[439]

"But," you ask, "Does Christ have any superabounding grace for me to emancipate me from the tyrant of my sin?" Overwhelmingly, the Bible answers a thousand times over, yes (1 John 1:7, 9; Revelation 22:17 and Psalm 103:8). Partake of this amazing, free grace. Grace to blot out your sins, wash you white as snow and purify your heart and set you free from sin's domination awaits. See John 8:36. Trust Christ, rely upon Him, surrender all to Him, and in an instant all sin will be forgiven, and hitherto you will bear witness that 'where sin abounded, grace did much more superabound.'

76 Strait for Grace

Not all that speak or sing of grace know grace, for they understood it theoretically but not theologically and experientially. The basis for grace is man's utter sinfulness against a Holy God, its damnable consequences and its only source of hope. Not until a person experiences deep contrition of sin, repents of it and looks to Christ Jesus for help is saving grace appropriated. This is why the preaching of the Law is necessary. It is a mirror that reveals man's sin. Paul said, "Through the law we become conscious of our sin" (Romans 3:20 NIV). Spurgeon said, "Lower the law [the Ten Commandments], and you dim the light by which man perceives his guilt. This is a very serious loss to the sinner rather than gain, for it lessens the likelihood of his conviction and conversion....They will never accept grace till they tremble before a just and holy law. Therefore, the Law serves a most necessary purpose and must not be removed from its place."[440] The Mosaic Law is the start-off to grace, for it produces the guilt of sin that prompts the cry for grace.

Junior Hill, speaking at a revival at New Orleans Baptist Theological Seminary, said, "A pivotal trait of 'itching-ear churches' is that they are dominated by grace without guilt." He explained, "A grace without guilt will eventually cause you to have a salvation without any joy. If you don't know what you have been forgiven of and you don't know from whence you have come, you don't have much to shout about in this generation." Hill continued, "The reason the shout has left many of our Baptist churches is that we have a congregation of men and women who have done nothing more than cultural reforms and have sociological blemishes removed and they have never seen the guilt of unbelief and the devastation of wicked sin."[441] Shouting Christians are those that testify with the hymn writer:

In loving-kindness Jesus came
My soul in mercy to reclaim,
And from the depths of sin and shame
Through grace He lifted me.

From sinking sand He lifted me;
   With tender hand He lifted me.
From shades of night to plains of light,
   Oh, praise His name, He lifted me!

~ Chas. H. Gabriel (1905)

Arthur W. Pink said, "Fellow-preachers, the knowledge of God's law is absolutely necessary in order to have a true knowledge of sin. The greatest and most deplorable defect in modern 'evangelism' is the near absence of preaching of the Law."[442] Spurgeon says, "The law comes before the Gospel [grace], the sense of need before the supply of it."[443] Preach the Law, for it opens up man's awareness of the need of God's grace. Guilt precedes grace.

77   Secret of Grace

The open secret to grace revealed in Scripture is that the approval and acceptance of God is not performance based. How's that for good news! The Bible says, "Not by works of righteousness which we have done, but according to his mercy he saved us, by the washing of regeneration, and renewing of the Holy Ghost; Which he shed on us abundantly through Jesus Christ our Savior; That being justified by his grace, we should be made heirs according to the hope of eternal life" (Titus 3:5–7). Our standing with God is not determined by a list of *do*s and *don't*s, nor is the measure of His love. Albert Barnes says it perhaps the clearest, "Whatever we have done or can do, when we come to receive salvation from the hand of God, there is no other element which enters into it but mercy. It is not because our deeds deserve it; it is not because we have by repentance and faith wrought ourselves into such a state of mind that we can claim it; but, after all our tears, and sighs, and prayers, and good deeds, it is a mere favor."[444] Spurgeon says, "God as much accepts a sinner who only believed in Christ five minutes ago as He will a saint who has known and loved Him 80 years, for He does not accept men because of anything they do or feel but simply and only for what Christ did, and that is finished!"[445]

Therefore, stop working at being saved. The work is already done to make it possible. Nothing more need be done or can be done than has been done. Rest in the finished work of Christ at Calvary for the atonement of your sins and rightness with Him (John 19:30). Curtis Hutson said, "Notice that forgiveness of sins is through His blood (1 John 1:7). It is not the death of Christ, plus sorrow; the death of Christ, plus tears; the death of Christ, plus mourning; or even the death of Christ, plus pleading. No, no, no! It is the death of Christ—period. The Word of God makes it clear that salvation is based entirely upon the death of Christ and the believer's faith or trust in Him."[446] Rely upon His free gift of grace through faith and repentance for the eternal transaction (Ephesians 2:8–9). "True conversion," states Spurgeon, "is in all men attended by a sense of sin, by a sorrow for sin or holy grief at having committed it, by a hatred of sin which proves that its dominion is ended, and by a practical turning from sin which shows that the life within the soul is operating upon the life without. True belief and true repentance are twins. It would be idle to attempt to say which is born first."[447] See Romans 10:9–13.

Let the message of grace free you from bondage to the Law and/or works to attain or help acquire salvation. Only grace affords genuine liberty, joy and peace in the Christian life. The Bible says, "It was for this freedom that Christ set us free [completely liberating us]; therefore keep standing firm and do not be subject again to a yoke of slavery [which you once removed]" (Galatians 5:1 AMP).

Though salvation is by grace through faith in Christ, the Christian is to dig out of his salvation its fullest blessings, beliefs and benefits (Philippians 2:12).

78 Staggering Question of Grace

What might your heart look like outside of the impact of grace? At times the Holy Spirit draws back that curtain to remind you that in you (that is, in your flesh) dwelleth no good thing (Romans 7:18), that human nature separated from God is mere spiritually decadent, corrupt, depraved and enslaved by sin. And yet even in its renewed (regenerate) state by grace there remains the still-abiding impulses and propensities to evil. And that is humiliating to acknowledge to ourselves, much less to others in the church. But that's exactly what Paul did.

But whereas Paul says there dwelleth no good thing in us in the flesh, much good that God hath done abides in the believer. Gill comments, "There were many good things dwelt in him [Paul]. There was the good work of grace and the good word of God in him; and even Father, Son, and Spirit dwelt in him. But his meaning is that there was no good thing naturally in him; no good thing of his own putting there; nothing but what God had put there; no good thing but what was owing to Christ, to the grace of God, and influence of the Spirit. Or as he himself explains it, there was no good thing in his 'flesh'; in the old man that was in him, which has nothing in his nature good. No good thing comes out of him, nor is any good thing done by him."[448] What a picture of man's total depravity apart from grace!

Why the occasional reminders of the work of grace in us?

To remind us of the grace of God that sought us—unworthy, unfit by sin to enter His presence, yet His love saw in us something redeemable and lovable; totally amazing!

To remind us of the utter depravity from which grace brought us.

To remind us where we might be today had not grace found us.

To remind us that without due discipline and diligence relying upon the Spirit of grace, the deeds and desires of the old man can resurrect; by grace the coffin lid of the "flesh" must be continuously nailed thoroughly shut. (See Romans 7:24–25.)

To remind us that what grace did for us, as wretched as we were, it can do for any man.

Christians don't shout praises to God long or loud enough about the work of grace that changed them.

150

79   Serenity of grace

"Grace be to you and peace from God the Father, and from our Lord Jesus Christ" (Galatians 1:3). Note, Henry says, "First grace, and then peace; there can be no true peace without grace."[449]

Rest is the fruit of grace which grants peace and calm in raging storms. Spurgeon said, "My soul's rest must be a grace-given rest and can only be found in Thee."[450] He continues, "'I will give you rest' (Matthew 11:28). If His hand gives it, this ensures you're getting it. Jesus does not say, 'I will send you rest.' It might be lost in the post. He does not say, 'I will commission an angel to bring you rest.' He might miss his way. It is, 'I will give you rest.' Come you to Jesus, and you shall have rest, out of His own hand put into your hand; nay, put into your heart. You shall certainly get it; there will be no missing it; between the cup and the lip there shall be no slip."[451]

Far away in the depths of my spirit tonight
   Rolls a melody sweeter than psalm;
In celestial strains it unceasingly falls
   O'er my soul like an infinite calm.

What a treasure I have in this wonderful peace
   Buried deep in the heart of my soul,
So secure that no power can mine it away
   While the years of eternity roll.

I am resting tonight in this wonderful peace,
   Resting sweetly in Jesus' control,
For I'm kept from all danger by night and by day,
   And His glory is flooding my soul.

And me thinks when I rise to that city of peace
   Where the Author of peace I shall see,
That one strain of the song which the ransomed will sing
   In that heavenly kingdom shall be:

Peace, peace! wonderful peace
    Coming down from the Father above,
Sweep over my spirit forever, I pray,
    In fathomless billows of love.

Ah! soul, are you here without comfort and rest,
    Marching down the rough pathway of time?
Make Jesus your friend ere the shadows grow dark;
    Oh, accept this sweet peace so sublime!

~ W. D. Cornell (1889)

80   Success of Grace

The benefits of grace are incalculable. It frees from the penalty and power of sin (and one day its very presence), reconciling man to God. It grants strength to face the adversities and afflictions of life successfully and unwaveringly. It grants boldness to enter into the throne room of Holy God to seek help in the time of need. It empowers for kingdom work. It assures peace and comfort in death. The same marvelous grace that was manifested at Calvary, that was bestowed to us upon our faith and repentance, that raised us from spiritual death and destitution and delivered us out of the darkness into His marvelous light is able to sustain us triumphantly to the day of the coming of the Lord.

Jonathan Edwards said, "Grace is but Glory begun, and Glory is but Grace perfected."[452] Grace never faints, fails, lessens, gives up or quits its work in the believer. Warren Wiersbe says, "He has 'called us unto His eternal glory by Christ Jesus' (1 Peter 5:10). This is the wonderful inheritance into which we were born (1 Peter 1:4). Whatever begins with God's grace always leads to God's glory (Psalm 84:11)."[453]

Through many dangers, toils and snares
    I have already come;
'Tis grace has brought me safe thus far,
    And grace will lead me home.

~ John Newton (1779)

81 Survey of Grace

Grace is progressive in the believer's life (steps of grace).

1. Saved by grace. The only means of introduction into the family of God is through the grace of the Lord Jesus Christ, that is the New Birth (Ephesians 2:8–9).

2. State of grace. Paul says, "So that, [just] as sin has reigned in death, [so] grace (His unearned and undeserved favor) might reign also through righteousness (right standing with God) which issues in eternal life through Jesus Christ (the Messiah, the Anointed One) our Lord" (Romans 5:21 AMPC). Grace declares us righteous and in good standing with God. At the moment of salvation, the believer's spiritual footing becomes secure eternally in Christ Jesus through the riches of His grace.

3. Sanctified by grace. See 2 Timothy 2:19. The believer, although positionally sanctified at salvation (set apart for God's holy purposes and service), progresses in sanctification throughout life. Titus says, "It teaches us to reject ungodliness and worldly (immoral) desires, and to live sensible, upright, and godly lives [lives with a purpose that reflect spiritual maturity] in this present age" (Titus 2:12 AMP). The Christian grows more Christlike. See Proverbs 4:18.

4. Schooled through grace. Development in grace is taught in the school of the Holy Scriptures by the Holy Spirit. Peter instructs, "But grow in grace, and in the knowledge of our Lord and Savior Jesus Christ. To Him be glory both now and forever. Amen" (2 Peter 3:18). Grace's growth foundation is faith and the knowledge of Christ.

5. Speaking in grace. Paul said, "Let your speech be always with grace, seasoned with salt, that ye may know how ye ought to answer every man" (Colossians 4:6). "The 'salt' is the power of Christ's grace, banishing all impurity of motive and all uncleanness of allusion, and at the same time giving the pleasant 'savor' of sound and nourishing 'food for thought.'"[454]

6. Serving in grace. Peter says, "God has given each of you a gift from his great variety of spiritual gifts. Use them well to

serve one another" (1 Peter 4:10 NLT). Grace equips the believer with spiritual gifts by the Holy Spirit for the general welfare of all. And all believers have a gift(s). Adam Clarke says, "Whatever gifts or endowments any man may possess, they are, properly speaking, not his own; they are the Lord's property and to be employed in His work and to promote his glory."[455]

7. Sustaining of grace. Grace sustains the believer in trials, troubles, afflictions, and infirmities. Christ says, "My grace is sufficient for thee: for my strength is made perfect in weakness" (2 Corinthians 12:9). Plenteous is the grace (manifold forms) at the throne of God to supply every need.

8. Success by grace. The final step of grace will be to usher us into the presence of God in Glory successfully. Newton is right: "Grace has brought us safe this far, and grace will lead us home." See Titus 2:11–14.

82   Supreme Cost of Grace

Grace is free but was not without supreme cost to provide. It cost God His only Son. Imagine His heart of love mingled with pain the moment He sent Jesus on the mission to save the world, and the sorrow He bore in abandoning Him on the Cross (Matthew 27:46).

It cost Jesus untold suffering, torment, and excruciating death by crucifixion. Spurgeon says, "If you would know love, you must repair to Christ, and you shall see a Man so full of pain, that His head, His hair, His garments bloody be. 'Twas love that made him sweat as it were great drops of blood. If you would know love, you must see the Omnipotent mocked by His creatures, you must hear the Immaculate slandered by sinners, you must hear the Eternal One groaning out His life and crying in the agonies of death, 'My God, my God, why have you forsaken me?'"[456]

Jesus experienced Roman flogging, a cruel and barbarous punishment (Mark 15:15; Matthew 27:26–30). Stripped of clothing to the waist and with hands tied to a pole, Jesus was beaten mercilessly with forty lashes from a Roman cat-o'-nine-tails (a handle with several leather thongs as much as three feet in length attached to jagged pieces of bone, metal and rock). "Victims lost eyes and teeth," states W. A. Criswell, "were occasionally disemboweled, and were always horribly disfigured."[457] Church historian Eusebius of Caesarea records the testimony given of a scourging. "For they say that the bystanders were struck with amazement when they saw them lacerated with scourges even to the innermost veins and arteries, so that the hidden inward parts of the body, both their bowels and their members, were exposed to view."[458]

With Jesus exhausted and injured from the beating, Simon of Cyrene (Matthew 27:32) had to be compelled to help Him carry His cross the distance to Golgotha, where the torment continued with the hammering of seven-inch iron spikes through Jesus' feet and hands (Mark 15:24; Luke 23:33; John 19:18, 24), the crown of jagged thorns (two–three inches long) that were pressed deeply into His scalp, the spear that was thrust into His side. Additionally consider the pain of the open wounds on His back (caused by the flogging) as they scraped against the post, the railing accusations, and conscious mental agony. This anguish and torment Jesus endured for over three hours.

Then looking up to Heaven, Jesus said, "It is finished" (John 19:30). "When Jesus gasped those final words, 'It is finished!,' what did He mean? What was 'it'? The malice of His persecutors was now finished. The command of God concerning His sufferings was now fulfilled. The types and prophecies of the Old Testament were now accomplished. Sin was finished. Christ made an end to transgression by bringing in an everlasting righteousness (Daniel 9:24; Hebrews 9:26). His sufferings were now finished. His life was now finished (John 17:11). The work of our redemption and salvation was completed (John 17:4)."[459] The mission of grace is now accomplished, making possible the reconciliation of unrighteous man with Holy God (Ephesians 2:8–9; 2 Corinthians 5:17–21 and Romans 5:8–11).

Yes, grace is free, but it does not come cheap. "For God so loved the world, that he gave his only begotten Son, that

whosoever believeth in him should not perish, but have
everlasting life" (John 3:16).

> Oh, the love that drew salvation's plan!
> Oh, the grace that brought it down to man!
> Oh, the mighty gulf that God did span
> At Calvary!
>
> ~ William Reed Newell (1868-1956)

83   Start of Grace

"God chose him as your ransom long before the world
began, but now in these last days he has been revealed for your
sake" (1 Peter 1:20 NLT). Prior to the day of modern communica-
tion, it was learned that two trains were about to have a head-on
collision. Without any way to make contact with the engineers of
the two trains, it was decided to put on the track behind one of
them a hospital train complete with doctors, nurses, medicine,
etc. In so doing, it assured that though the collision could not be
stopped, medical help would be on the scene to help the injured.
So it is with God's provision of grace for man's salvation.
Knowing that man was going to sin, God put a "hospital train"
on the tracks in the person of His Son, Jesus Christ ("from the
foundation of the world"). As early as Genesis 3:15, it is stated
that the "hospital train" was in motion (the seed of the woman
refers to Jesus' virgin birth). John says, "And all the inhabitants
of the earth will fall down in adoration and pay him homage,
everyone whose name has not been recorded in the Book of Life
of the Lamb that was slain [in sacrifice] from the foundation of
the world" (Revelation 13:8 AMPC).

Grace had its beginning at the foundation of the world. Long
before sin was in the heart of man, the Cross was on the mind of
God. Spurgeon remarks, "Pause here, my hearer, awhile, and
think before this world was made, before God had settled the
deep foundations of the mountains or poured the seas from the
laver of the bottom of His hand, He had chosen His people and
set His heart on them. To them He had given Himself, His Son,

His Heaven, His all. For them did Christ determine to resign His bliss, His home, His life; for them did the Spirit promise all His attributes, that they might be blessed. O grace divine, how glorious you are, without beginning, without end. How shall I praise you? Take up the strain you angels; sing these noble themes, the love of the Father, the love of the Son, the love of the Spirit."[460]

84 State of Grace

Sins, regardless of their innumerability or heinousness, upon confession are thoroughly expunged (blotted out) and forgiven by grace. Jesus said, "For I will be merciful to their unrighteousness, and their sins and their iniquities will I remember no more" (Hebrews 8:12). Note the scope of the forgiveness that Jesus promises.

The Freeness of God's Forgiveness ("I will be merciful")

The Fullness of His Forgiveness (all "their sins and... iniquities")

The Forever of His Forgiveness ("remember no more")

Grace preserves the believer from the penalty of sin (Hell) forever. Jude attests to this fact when he addresses the believer as those "preserved in Jesus Christ" (Jude 1). Albert Barnes comments, "What the apostle here says of those to whom he wrote is true of all Christians. They would all fall away and perish if it were not for the grace of God keeping them."[461] Believers are safekept by the guardianship of Christ Jesus from having their salvation stolen by Satan or any other power. Saith Spurgeon, "Some people tell us that God forgives men and yet they are lost. A fine God yours! They believe that the penitent sinner finds mercy, but that if he slips or stumbles, in a little while he will be taken out of the covenant of grace and will perish. Such a covenant I could not and would not believe in; I tread it beneath my feet as utterly despicable. The God whom I love, when He forgives, never punishes afterwards. By one sacrifice there is a full remission of all sin that ever was against a believer, or that ever will be against

157

him. Though you should live until your hair is bleached thrice over, until Methuselah's thousand years should pass over your furrowed brow, not a single sin shall ever stand against you, nor shall you ever be punished for a single sin; for every sin is forgiven, fully forgiven, so that not even part of the punishment shall be executed against you."[462] See Hebrews 8:12 and Micah 7:19.

> There's pardon for transgressions past;
> It matters not how black their cast.
> And, oh! My soul, with wonder view,
> For sins to come there's pardon too.
> Now freed from sin I walk at large,
> My Savior's blood my full discharge;
> At His dear feet my soul I lay,
> A sinner saved, and homage pay.
> ~ John Kent (1766–1843)

Grace is not confined to salvation, because it continues its work in making possible forgiveness and change in the believer's life by the power of God. Forgiveness of sin that sealed the believer's eternal destiny to Heaven is a once and forever transaction by grace through faith upon confession of Jesus as Lord. However, forgiveness of sin committed post-conversion is yet needed in the believers' day-to-day fellowship with Christ. Christians can and do sin because of man's dualistic nature—the flesh (carnal) and the spirit (spiritual). These two wrestle each other, competing for dominion throughout the believer's life (Galatians 5:17).

It is when the believer yields to the carnal nature that he or she sins, and although divine discipline may come for the rebellious act, the Christian's salvation is never in jeopardy (Romans 8:1). But there is forgiveness available when sin occurs. It is supplied freely by grace upon request (1 John 1:9–10). It is for this reason John wrote to Christians saying, "My little children, I am writing these things to you so that you may not sin. But if anyone does sin, we have an advocate with the Father, Jesus Christ the righteous" (1 John 2:1 ESV). Aim not to sin, but when you do sin, know that grace is available through Christ to forgive it (1 John 2:2).

85 Self-Appropriation of Grace

We don't have grace to forgive ourselves upon wrongdoing, but God does. His grace is sufficient to both forgive the sin and heal its wound. Undeserved, yes, but nonetheless, out of God's abundance of love, grace and mercy stand always ready to do this for us. It just has to be accepted and appropriated. When we deny that grace, then guilt, anxiety, and gloom rule instead of the calm, peace and joy that the acceptance of it brings.

Before the throne of God above
I have a strong, a perfect plea,
A great High Priest, whose Name is Love,
Who ever lives and pleads for me.

My name is graven on His hands;
My name is written on His heart.
I know that while with God He stands
No tongue can bid me thence depart.

When Satan tempts me to despair
And tells me of the guilt within,
Upward I look and see Him there,
Who made an end of all my sin.

Because the sinless Savior died,
My sinful soul is counted free;
For God, the Just, is satisfied
To look on Him and pardon me.

Behold Him there, the risen Lamb;
My perfect, spotless Righteousness;
The great unchangeable I AM;
The King of glory and of grace!

One with Himself, I cannot die;
My soul is purchased by His blood.
My life is hid with Christ on high,
With Christ, my Savior and my God.

~ C. L. Bancroft (1863)

86 Stance for Grace

Standing for biblical grace may come with a hefty cost. Adrian Rogers said, "It is better to be divided by truth than to be united in error. It is better to speak the truth that hurts and then heals, than falsehood that comforts and then kills. It is better to be hated for telling the truth than to be loved for telling a lie. It is better to stand alone with the truth than to be wrong with a multitude. It is better to ultimately succeed with the truth than to temporarily succeed with a lie. There is only one Gospel."[463]

Martin Luther's stance for the Gospel (grace by faith alone in Christ Jesus for salvation) is an example to all believers under fire for the faith. He opposed the church's practice of selling "indulgences" to atone for man's sin. To the tribunal at the Imperial Diet of Worms, boldly and unapologetically, he said, "Since your majesty and your lordships desire a simple reply, I will answer without horns and without teeth. Unless I am convicted by Scripture and plain reason—I do not accept the authority of popes and councils, for they have contradicted each other—my conscience is captive to the Word of God. I cannot and I will not recant anything, for to go against conscience is neither right nor safe. Here I stand; I cannot do otherwise, God help me. Amen."

For his stance for grace over indulgences (and more) he was excommunicated from the church by the pope and later declared by the emperor to be an outlaw and heretic.

We will not falter in the battle,
    For by the grace of God we'll stand;
And while we use our Captain's armor,
    No one can pluck us from His hand.

He is our confidence and courage;
    While we obey we'll never fall.
Let us be true and fight in Jesus' might,
    Follow our mighty Captain's call.

Lord, I need grace to be Your soldier—
　　Grace that will bear the battle's din;
Strengthen me at my post of duty,
　　That I may conquer every sin.

You are my confidence and courage;
　　Not a defeat You've ever known.
I will not quit nor yield, but trust Your shield,
　　Strong in the strength You give Your own.

We will not fear the foe's appearance,
　　For we are led by Christ our King.
He is the Captain of Salvation,
　　And of His conquests we will sing.

He is our confidence and courage;
　　He is the One Who set us free.
And with our hearts aglow we'll rout the foe,
　　For He has promised victory!

　　　　　　　　　　　~ Joel A. Erickson (2007)

87　Statutory Limitation of Grace

Grace for salvation will not always be available. The Bible states that four things will forever close its door.

1. Blaspheming the Holy Ghost or committing the unpardonable sin (Matthew 12:31–32; Luke 12:10; Numbers 16:29–34). The sin is attributing to Satan the miracles of Christ, despite irrefutable proof to the contrary. The unpardonable sin is not rejecting Christ (despite years of stubborn rebellion the sinner yet may be saved).

2. The hardening of the heart against the claims of Christ. The Bible says, "He, that being often reproved hardeneth his neck, shall suddenly be destroyed, and that without remedy" (Proverbs 29:1). "Hardening the neck" is a picture of an obstinate, stubborn bull that resists the yoke. H. A. Ironside remarks, "In this way, men, in their obstinacy, persistently refuse

161

to heed reproof, and set their wills stubbornly against what would be for their own best interests, thus insuring their destruction. [Though God is longsuffering] Yet even *His* patience with the unrepentant comes to an end at last. He will plead and strive and warn till it is manifest the heart is fully set upon having its own way. Then He leaves the hardened soul to its doom, giving it up to sudden destruction."[464] See Hebrews 3:8.

Examples in Scripture of hardening of the neck are numerous. The list includes Pharaoh (Exodus 9:34); Eli's sons (1 Samuel 2:25); Ahab (1 Kings 18:18); Korah, Dathan, and Abiram (Numbers 16); Jezebel (2 Kings 9:32–37); Belshazzar (Daniel 5:22–23).

George Lawson comments, "But woe to that man who is stubborn and obstinate after many reproofs. He despises a merciful appointment of God for his recovery and tramples upon precious pearls. He refuses to bow before the Lord—and he shall be dashed in pieces like a potter's vessel! He perhaps designs to reform at some other time—but he is hardened in sin, and puts off his intended repentance until judgment comes upon him unexpectedly, and he is ruined forever! The reproofs which he received will then be like hot thunderbolts to him, and the remembrance of them will feed the worm that never dies."[465]

The Proverb states that upon man's 'sudden' and 'unexpected' end, he will be "without remedy." Charles Bridges elucidates, "No remedy—not even the Gospel—can remedy the case. As they lived, so they die; they stand before God *without remedy*. No blood—no advocate—pleads for them. As they sink into the burning lake, every billow of fire, as it rolls over them, seems to sound—*without remedy*."[466] They are without remedy, for they are without Christ.

3. Death. The Bible says, "And as it is appointed unto men once to die, but after this the judgment" (Hebrews 9:27). John Webster said, "Death hath ten thousand several doors for men to take their exits."[467] And for the unbeliever that takes one of those exit doors, unbeknown as to when, where or how, the door to salvation forever shuts behind him. There are no second chances after death to be saved.

4. The second coming of Christ for His people. Hear and heed the Word of God: "Someone asked him, 'Lord, are only a few people going to be saved?' He said to them, 'Make every effort to enter through the narrow door, because many, I tell you, will try to enter and will not be able to. Once the owner of the house gets up and closes the door, you will stand outside knocking and pleading, "Sir, open the door for us." But he will answer, "I don't know you or where you come from." Then you will say, "We ate and drank with you, and you taught in our streets." But he will reply, "I don't know you or where you come from. Away from me, all you evildoers!" There will be weeping there, and gnashing of teeth, when you see Abraham, Isaac and Jacob and all the prophets in the kingdom of God, but you yourselves thrown out'" (Luke 13:23–28 NIV).

Jesus plainly is teaching that at His coming, the "drawbridge" to Heaven is lifted and those left behind have no chance of gaining entrance but will experience the wrath of God in Hell for all eternity.

The door of opportunity remains open for you to experience the grace of God unto salvation. Enter that door now. Tomorrow may be one day too late. C. H. Spurgeon says, "What I am when death is held before me, that I must be forever. When my spirit goes, if God finds me hymning his praise, I shall hymn it in Heaven; doth He find me breathing out oaths, I shall follow up those oaths in Hell. Where death leaves me, judgment finds me. As I die, so shall I live eternally."[468]

88 Scriptures of Grace

Exodus 34:6–7: "Yahweh! The LORD! The God of compassion and mercy! I am slow to anger and filled with unfailing love and faithfulness. I lavish unfailing love to a thousand generations" (NLT).

Psalm 5:7: "Because of your great love, I can come into your Temple" (NCV).

Psalm 86:15: "But thou, O Lord, art a God full of compassion, and gracious, long suffering, and plenteous in mercy and truth."

Psalm 89:33: "But I will never stop loving him nor fail to keep my promise to him" (NLT).

Luke 2:52: "And Jesus increased in wisdom and stature, and in favor with God and man."

John 1:14: "And Christ became a human being and lived here on earth among us and was full of loving forgiveness and truth. And some of us have seen his glory—the glory of the only Son of the heavenly Father!" (TLB).

John 1:16–17: "And of his fulness have all we received, and grace for grace. For the law was given by Moses, but grace and truth came by Jesus Christ."

Acts 4:33: "And with great power gave the apostles witness of the resurrection of the Lord Jesus: and great grace was upon them all."

Romans 5:2: "By whom also we have access by faith into this grace wherein we stand, and rejoice in hope of the glory of God."

Ephesians 1:2: "Grace be to you, and peace, from God our Father, and from the Lord Jesus Christ."

Ephesians 2:8–9: "For by grace are ye saved through faith; and that not of yourselves: it is the gift of God: Not of works, lest any man should boast."

1 Peter 4:10: "As every man hath received the gift, even so minister the same one to another, as good stewards of the manifold grace of God."

1 Peter 5:10: "But the God of all grace, who hath called us unto his eternal glory by Christ Jesus, after that ye have suffered a while, make you perfect, stablish, strengthen, settle you."

2 Peter 3:18: "But grow in grace, and in the knowledge of our Lord and Savior Jesus Christ. To him be glory both now and forever. Amen."

2 Timothy 1:9: "Who hath saved us, and called us with an holy calling, not according to our works, but according to his own purpose and grace, which was given us in Christ Jesus before the world began."

Titus 2:11: "For the grace of God that bringeth salvation hath appeared to all men."

Hebrews 2:9: "But we do see Jesus, who was made lower than the angels for a little while [by taking on the limitations of humanity], crowned with glory and honor because of His suffering of death, so that by the grace of God [extended to sinners] He might experience death for [the sins of] everyone" (AMP).

Hebrews 12:15: "Look after each other so that none of you fails to receive the grace of God" (NLT).

Hebrews 4:16: "Let us therefore come boldly unto the throne of grace, that we may obtain mercy, and find grace to help in time of need."

Some of the parables of Jesus teach grace. The parable of the laborers in the vineyard (Matthew 20:1–16) teaches that Christ has the sole right to determine the grace gifts He distributes. The parable of the great supper (Luke 14:16–24) reveals that salvation is open to all. The prodigal son teaches that the most undeserving are always welcomed back home by the Father (Luke 15:20–24).

89 Seeking of Grace

The love, kindness, mercy and goodness of God (grace) took the initiative to pursue the ungodly. It's not that man first sought grace. John said, "We love him, because he first loved us" (1 John 4:19). Jesus stated, "For the Son of man is come to seek and to save that which was lost" (Luke 19:10). "Sovereign grace," saith Spurgeon, "waiteth not for man, neither tarrieth for the sons of men. The love of God goes forth to men when they have no thought after Him; when they are hastening after all manner of sin."[469] In a sense grace is like the barking hound that possesses the blood scent of a vile criminal. It is determined to chase and apprehend the fugitive with the greatest of intensity.

> Jesus comes with all His grace,
> Comes to save a fallen race;
> Object of our glorious hope,
> Jesus comes to lift us up.
>
> ~ Charles Wesley (1749)

Christ seeks out the fugitive from God to grant forgiveness of crimes committed against Him.

Matthew Henry explains, "The gracious design of the Son of God: He came to seek and save, to seek in order to saving. He came from Heaven to earth (a long journey), to seek that which was lost (which had wandered and gone astray), and to bring it back (Matthew 18:11–12); and to save that which was lost, which was perishing, and in a manner destroyed and cut off. Christ undertook the cause when it was given up for lost, undertook to bring those to themselves that were lost to God and all goodness. Observe, Christ came into this lost world to seek and save it. His design was to save when there was not salvation in any other. In prosecution of that design, He sought, took all probable means to effect that salvation. He seeks those that were not worth seeking to; He seeks those that sought Him not and asked not for Him, as Zacchaeus here."[470]

"Such is the grace of God. It does not visit us," writes Spurgeon, "because we ask it, much less because we deserve it, but as God wills it; and the bottles of Heaven are unstopped, so God wills it, and grace descends. No matter how vile and black and foul and godless men may be, He will have mercy on whom He will have mercy; and that free, rich, overflowing goodness of His can make the very worst and least deserving the objects of His best and choicest love."[471]

> Come, Thou Fount of every blessing;
>   Tune my heart to sing Thy grace.
> Streams of mercy, never ceasing,
>   Call for songs of loudest praise.

Here I raise my Ebenezer;
   Hither by Thy help I'm come,
And I hope, by Thy good pleasure,
   Safely to arrive at home.

Jesus sought me when a stranger,
   Wandering from the fold of God;
He, to rescue me from danger,
   Interposed His precious blood.
      ~ Robert Robinson (1735–1790)

Grace continuously is seeking out sinners unawares to them at most times, through the convicting power of the Holy Spirit to the conscience, witness of believers and sermons of ministers, Christian books and movies, and His gracious goodness which is designed to bring man to repentance and faith. Though we often do not realize it at this very moment, grace is seeking out the hardest of sinners and the Gospel's greatest antagonists. Pray for grace to be multiplied throughout the earth and for it to be graciously received by all in need of it.

90   Slur of Grace

Don't live a life disgraceful to grace after being delivered from a life of disgrace. Believers that say they are saved by grace, therefore it matters not how they live, are a disgrace to grace. Grace itself infused in man becomes a teacher to guide in the governing of behavior.

Paul says, "For the grace of God (His unmerited favor and blessing) has come forward (appeared) for the deliverance from sin and the eternal salvation for all mankind. It has trained us to reject and renounce all ungodliness (irreligion) and worldly (passionate) desires, to live discreet (temperate, self-controlled), upright, devout (spiritually whole) lives in this present world, Awaiting and looking for the [fulfillment, the realization of our] blessed hope, even the glorious appearing of our great God and Savior Christ Jesus (the Messiah, the

Anointed One)" (Titus 2:11–13 AMPC). Listen and heed its invaluable instructions as a good student of Christ. Not to do so is to walk in disgrace to the undeserved gift of grace received.

A day is forthcoming when the believer will give an account for what he did with the grace (new life) he possessed. This will be at the Judgment Seat of Christ (2 Corinthians 5:6–10). This judgment, which takes place in Heaven, is not to deem the believer worthy or unworthy to enter Heaven—he will already be there. That already will have been established on earth through the New Birth (John 3:15–16). *Tickets* to Heaven were purchased at a great cost by Jesus but are provided without charge to all that receive Him as Lord and Savior (grace). See Romans 8:1; Titus 3:5; Ephesians 2:8–9.

For what, then, is the saint to be judged? All believers, without exception, will give an accounting for their works (Romans 14:12; 2 Corinthians 5:10). No believer will be permitted to give *answer* for another or plead *excuses* for another. Masks will fall off, and the fakery and deception displayed in life will be known. We all shall be seen for *what* we are in heart. This is the meaning of "appear" in 2 Corinthians 5:10.

That which shall be examined includes not only our actions, but our words, thoughts, inclinations, motives and dispositions.[472] "Every act of man leaves its mark, and hereafter our life will be judged by these marks."[473] The judgment will take into consideration the believer's abilities, gifts, talents, capabilities, and opportunities. Its overarching purpose is to reward faithfulness and devotion through the presentation of five crowns and assign positions or heavenly assignments to the saints.

At our court date in Heaven, it will be far too late to wish that we had taken the Christian life and commitment to Christ more seriously. The time to do that is now. So, walk, work and witness that you may receive a "full reward" on that day (2 John 8). Walk worthy of the grace you received at the hand of a gracious God.

91 Stewards of Grace

"As every man hath received the gift, even so minister the same one to another, as good stewards of the manifold grace of God" (1 Peter 4:10). We are prone to forget grace's manifoldness of spiritual gifts—variety of forms, shapes and sizes and their intended purpose. John MacArthur says, "A spiritual gift is a graciously given supernaturally designed ability granted to every believer by which the Holy Spirit ministers to the body of Christ. Each believer has one specific gift, often a combination of the various categories of gifts blended together uniquely for each Christian."[474] Wuest states, "The word 'gift' here is not the usual Greek word, but one that refers to the special spiritual enablements given graciously to certain Christians as an aid in the discharge of the special duties to which God has called them, as in 1 Corinthians 12 and 13."[475]

The Christian is not the owner of the gift; God is. Therefore it is to be used according to His designed purpose—to benefit the body of Christ. William MacDonald says, "We are not meant to be the terminals of God's gifts to us; His grace reaches us but should not end with us. We are intended to be channels through whom the blessing can flow to others."[476] See 1 Peter 4:8. Believers are to be "good stewards" of the gifts (good managers of the gifts God has entrusted in their care by using them as intended). "There should be not only exactness, but also grace and beauty in their stewardship—the beauty which belongs to holy love and flows from the imitation of Him who is 'the good Shepherd.'"[477] Believers ought to utilize their *own* gifts, not those of another, with unblemished honor, fervency and diligence. "The point is," writes Schreine, "that spiritual gifts are given to serve and to help others, to strengthen others in the faith. They are bestowed for ministry, not to enhance self-esteem."[478]

Peter states in 1 Peter 4:11 that the believers' gifts fall under two categories: speaking gifts (Romans 12:6–7; 1 Corinthians 12:10, 28–30; Ephesians 4:11) and serving gifts (Romans 12:8; 1 Corinthians 12:9–10, 28–30). Every good gift we possess we owe to the unmerited favor of Christ. "What hast thou that thou didst not receive?" Therefore, as you have freely received, freely give or use your gift to His cause and purposes. What gifts has God endowed you with by grace? Are you using it as a "good steward" of the Lord? Every believer possesses at least one gift. Discover it and use it wisely.

92 Spots of Grace

The white pearly spots of the pearl fish distinguish it from all others. But it's not the white spots that make the pearls, although pearls do have many spots. A person may be spotted with various traits of the Christian, yet not be a Christian. Christians ought to have spots that distinguish them from the ungodly, but it's not the spots that make them His children (Galatians 3:26).[479] See 2 Corinthians 13:5 and Matthew 7:21–23.

The Bible says, "Therefore if anyone is in Christ [that is, grafted in, joined to Him by faith in Him as Savior], he is a new creature [reborn and renewed by the Holy Spirit]; the old things [the previous moral and spiritual condition] have passed away. Behold, new things have come [because spiritual awakening brings a new life]" (2 Corinthians 5:17 AMP). What are some distinguishing *spots* of him who genuinely has experienced the grace of God?

A new heart. He that is saved by grace bears a new allegiance and love toward Christ. "I will give you a new heart and put a new spirit in you; I will remove from you your heart of stone and give you a heart of flesh" (Ezekiel 36:26 NIV). He has a new heart of love for God and hatred for sin. Someone wrote, "When God touches a life, He breaks the heart. Where He pours out the spirit of grace, there are not a few transient sighs that agitate the breast; there are heart-rending pangs of sorrow."[480]

A new purpose. It is to live to bring honor and glory to the Lord. The self-gratification life is dead. He says with Paul, "I am crucified with Christ: nevertheless I live; yet not I, but Christ liveth in me: and the life which I now live in the flesh I live by the faith of the Son of God, who loved me, and gave Himself for me" (Galatians 2:20). He lives in denial to self, to live pleasing to the Savior. "And he said to them all, if any man will come after me, let him deny himself, and take up his cross daily, and follow me" (Luke 9:23). John MacArthur says, "I believe that true saving faith is marked by the desire to glorify God above everything else. And there's a certain sense in which you have as a life focus the setting aside of your own glory and your own attainment and your own designs and your own will and your own comfort and your own enterprise for the seeking of that which brings honor to God. The person who is truly experiencing salvation is one who is consummately committed to God's glory."[481]

A new work. "For we are his workmanship, created in Christ Jesus unto good works, which God hath before ordained that we should walk in them" (Ephesians 2:10). "Now then we are ambassadors for Christ, as though God did beseech you by us: we pray you in Christ's stead, be ye reconciled to God" (2 Corinthians 5:20). The believer is enlisted in the King's service (to witness, teach, preach, sing, testify, help others, etc.).

A new hope. He possesses a God-given confidence and assurance of salvation based upon the Word of God. "He that hath the Son hath life; and he that hath not the Son of God hath not life. These things have I written unto you that believe on the name of the Son of God; that ye may know that ye have eternal life, and that ye may believe on the name of the Son of God. And this is the confidence that we have in him, that, if we ask any thing according to his will, he heareth us" (1 John 5:12–14).

A new identity. The saved by grace bear a new identity; they are new creatures belonging to a new family. "So then you are no longer strangers and aliens, but you are fellow citizens with the saints and members of the household of God, built on the foundation of the apostles and prophets, Christ Jesus himself being the cornerstone, in whom the whole structure, being joined together, grows into a holy temple in the Lord. In him you also are being built together into a dwelling place for God by the Spirit" (Ephesians 2:19–22 ESV). The genuine believer no longer shares the same commonalities with the ungodly; his affinities now are with like-minded believers. See 2 Corinthians 6:14–17.

Here we are gathered, one family in the Lord;
    His life is the bond that we share.
Although we are many, we are in one accord,
    And as the members, know the family care.

And blending with the saints we know,
    Our joy has just begun;
    We blend together and we blend as one.
And blending with the saints we know,
    The building has begun;
    We build together and we build as one.

When we're together our joy is made so full;
    The love of the Lord fills our hearts,
And we all partake of the Spirit bountiful.
    We've found, here in the family life, a part.

Here we will stay, Lord, according to Your plan,
    For here in the church life we're one;
And we will be built up to be the corp'rate man
    To consummate the New Jerusalem.

                                ~ M. S.

A new future. A change in eternal destiny takes place at true conversion. The saved by grace look forward to an eternity in Heaven with Christ and the saints (Revelation 21:4), whereas their former address was the Lake of Fire (Revelation 21:8)

93   Stillness of Grace

"Be still, and know that I am God: I will be exalted among the heathen, I will be exalted in the earth" (Psalm 46:10). A biblical narrative that illustrates the truth and instruction of this text is the story of the two sisters of Bethany, Mary and Martha, recorded in the Luke's Gospel. "While Jesus and his followers were traveling, Jesus went into a town. A woman named Martha let Jesus stay at her house. Martha had a sister named Mary, who was sitting at Jesus' feet and listening to him teach. But Martha was busy with all the work to be done" (Luke 10:38–40a NCV). At times the believer needs to be more of a Mary ("Be still, and know that I am God") than a Martha. Certainly, that which both sisters did for Christ was needed and pleasing to the Lord. It is as E. M. Bounds said, "A holy life does not live in the closet, but it cannot live without the closet."[482]

The Christian life involves stillness and service. It's just that to "live in the closet" supersedes in value "life outside the closet." (But this can be taken to the extreme where one lives a totally monastic life without interaction in the world in service to Christ).

> A holy life does not live in the closet, but it cannot live without the closet.
> E. M. Bounds

The point of the biblical narrative is that there must be a time in our busy lives for stillness, quietude and private communion with the Lord regularly. And this takes a special measure of grace, for it contradicts our human inclination that wants to be teaching, preaching, witnessing, helping and visiting the hurting instead of doing "nothing" but praying.

Communion or fellowship time with Christ must be prioritized. Plan the day around it, not it around the day. Don't do it on the run. "God's acquaintance is not made hurriedly," says E. M. Bounds. "He does not bestow His gifts on the casual or hasty comer and goer."[483] He continues, "Prayer is no petty duty, put into a corner; no piecemeal performance made out of the fragments of time which have been snatched from business and other engagements of life; but it means that the best of our time, the heart of our time and strength must be given."[484] Adjust the attitude toward it from being a daily duty to that of a disciplined delight. Restrain impulsive reaction while waiting for divine interaction. Don't panic. Remain calm. Let God speak, instruct and console.

"The one concern of the Devil," states Samuel Chadwick, "is to keep Christians from praying. He fears nothing from prayerless studies, prayerless work, and prayerless religion. He laughs at our toil, mocks at our wisdom, but trembles when we pray."[485] Ask God for special grace to practice the discipline of stillness in His presence.

> Be still, my soul; your God will undertake
>   To guide the future as He has the past.
> Your hope, your confidence let nothing shake;
>   All now mysterious shall be bright at last.
> Be still, my soul; the waves and winds still know
> His voice who ruled them while He dwelt below.
>
> ~Katharina von Schlegel (1855)

94   Salute to Grace

"I thank my God always on your behalf, for the grace of God which is given you by Jesus Christ" (1 Corinthians 1:4). Paul gives recognition of and a salute to the grace given to the saints at the Corinthian church which stimulated their great encouragement in the faith in a distraught time of despair. "He extracts from a disquieting situation all the comfort possible."[486] The salute to grace serves to do the same for all that are disquieted, despairing and depressed.

A salute to its Provider. Observe that no less than ten times in the first ten verses of 1 Corinthians 1, the name of Jesus Christ is mentioned (the only time in Scripture where this happened). Chrysostom hits the nail on the head: "Nowhere in any other epistle does the name of Christ occur so continuously in a few verses; by means of it he [Paul] weaves together the whole...not by chance or unwittingly."[487] Paul makes it absolutely clear, leaving no room for misunderstanding at all, that it was Jesus Christ by whom the grace was bestowed, not by religion or man.

We don't rightly give Christ the praise and glory for the riches of the grace He provided that has forever changed every aspect of our life for time and eternity. Today let's salute Him for that great grace. See John 1:17 and Titus 2:11.

A salute to its pardon. Paul salutes the grace that enabled the Corinthians' salvation (1 Corinthians 1:4). John Gill said this free grace in its entirety is not to be attributed "to man's free will and power, or to any merits of his; and all come through the hands of Christ, and are given forth by Him, as the Mediator of the covenant, and in consequence of His blood, righteousness, sacrifice, and merit."[488]

A salute to its possession. His grace "is given you by Christ Jesus" (1 Corinthians 1:4). Paul affirmed the sure evidence upon which they had received the Gospel. They had sure grounds for assurance that their faith was sincere and genuine.

A salute to its provision (profit). Paul says that the saints have been "enriched" in every way (1 Corinthians 1:5). Redeeming grace looks chiefly at transformation and sanctification, while the gifts of grace look primarily at edification and service (1 Peter 4:10). John Gill says, "For the grace which is given you by Jesus Christ includes all sorts of grace: adopting, justifying, pardoning, regenerating, and sanctifying grace; every particular grace of the Spirit, as faith, repentance, hope, love, fear, humility, self-denial; and all are gifts of God."[489] Give praise to God for the provision of His manifold grace (various forms and degrees) to supply the saint's every need. All good gifts are attributable to the Lord (preaching, teaching, singing, perseverance, helping, etc.).

A salute to its plentifulness. Of grace's supply there is no shortage. "For out of His fullness [the superabundance of His grace and truth] we have all received grace upon grace [spiritual blessing upon spiritual blessing, favor upon favor, and gift heaped upon gift]" (John 1:16 AMP).

A salute to its promise. "He will also keep you firm to the end, so that you will be blameless on the day of our Lord Jesus Christ" (1 Corinthians 1:8 NIV). Paul affirms that at the coming of Christ their grace will be fully perfected. Grace's work will only conclude when the saint is safe before the throne of God in Heaven. That which grace begins in man, it will end with man.

175

By the grace of God I am saved today;
I will walk by faith in the narrow way.
I will trust His grace to preserve my soul;
I will rest secure while the billows roll.

By the grace of God I will live for Him;
I will trust His power to keep from sin.
I will never doubt, but resist the foe;
I will grow in grace as I onward go.

By the grace of God I will never yield
To the tempter's pow'r, but with sword and shield
I'll defeat the foe with an ardor strong,
In the name of Christ sing the victor's song.

By the grace of God I will testify;
I will watch and pray as the moments fly.
I will live for Him in despite of all;
I will hear and heed the Redeemer's call.

By the grace of God I will never fear;
What can harm my soul when the Lord is near?
If I keep low down in humility,
If I walk by faith, He'll abide with me.

By the grace of God I will keep my eyes
On the Lord alone and the promised prize.
I will bear all things in His precious name;
I will trust His grace and His promise claim.

~ Barney Elliott Warren (1897)

95   Sparing of Grace

"He that spared not His own Son, but delivered Him up for us all, how shall He not with Him also freely [this word means 'to bestow out of grace.'[490]] give us all things?" (Romans 8:32). God did not spare the Cross for His Son that man might be spared the condemnation for sin. Had God spared Christ from the anguish and death of the Cross, man would be hopelessly and eternally lost due to sin's corruption and penalty. Had Jesus been spared the Cross, there would be no atonement or forgiveness for sin (Romans 5:1; Hebrews 9:22), no liberation from the bondage to sin (Luke 4:18), no chance of escape from eternal damnation (John 3:16), no hope of reunion with family and friends beyond the grave, no anticipation of ever dwelling eternally with God in Heaven (Revelation 7:9–10), and no means to have access to God (1 Timothy 2:5). Had Jesus been spared the Cross, life would be empty, meaningless and miserable. Had Jesus been spared the Cross, to really know and love God would be impossible (1 John 4:9–10). Despite what anti-Christians advocate, had Christ been spared the Cross, this world be far poorer.

Spurgeon wrote, "He says, 'Except a corn of wheat fall into the ground and die, it abideth alone' (John 12:24). Our Lord seems to say that it was absolutely necessary that He should die— that even His perfect life would have been of no use to us if He had not died. So you see, brethren, that if Christ, after having come to this earth as He did, had not died, He would, as far as mankind is concerned, have had to abide in Heaven alone. As God, the word 'alone' would have had no reference to Him, for the holy angels, as well as His Father and the ever-blessed Spirit would always have been near Him. But if our Lord could have come here and then have gone back to Heaven without dying, it would not have been possible for any other man to ever have gone to Heaven, and Christ would have been the only man in the whole of that land of joy. It is dreadful even to think of such a thing as that. If that could have happened, where must all the saints of God and all mankind have gone? There is but one other region— the land of darkness and of death, the land of pain, of horror, and of woe unutterable. And there must we all have gone if Christ had not died upon the cross—not only the thief on the left hand of Christ, but the thief on His right hand too; not only Judas, but Peter, John, and all the apostles; not only Demas, but Paul, and Silas, and all the early Christians; not only Ahithophel, but David also; not only the unrighteous, but the righteous too—all! All! ALL, having sinned, would have been condemned to eternal wrath if Jesus had not died."[491]

Enough speculation. Thankfully, God out of love for the world "spared not His own son, but delivered Him up for us all" (Romans 8:32) giving Him as a ramson for man's sin (1 Timothy 2:6). "Surely he [Jesus] hath borne our griefs, and carried our sorrows" (Isaiah 53:4). And that's man's eternal game-changer. God, in not sparing His only Son from the Cross, spared man from suffering the consequences of a life without grace. Hallelujahs to His name!

96   Strangeness of Grace

"When we were utterly helpless, with no way of escape, Christ came at just the right time and died for us sinners who had no use for him." "Now, most people would not be willing to die for an upright person, though someone might perhaps be willing to die for a person who is especially good" (Romans 5:6–7 TLB, NLT). Grace is a mystery. Its provision is a strange thing to understand and accept by some. Even Paul thought the concept quite amazing. He said (my paraphrase), "How is it that when it is highly unlikely that someone will die for a good person (might be willing to die for a really good person) that Jesus Christ was willing to die for the utterly sinful, helpless and hopeless."

To hear that the Son of God was willing to freely die at Calvary to atone for all man's sin—the immorality, drunken stupor, foul speech, bitter hostility, stubborn rebellion toward God, licentiousness, pornography obsession, thievery and every other sin—completely and freely is difficult to grasp. Why would He do something like that for "someone like me"? On the surface it just sounds so unlikely and strange.

It's strange that Christ would die to bestow grace upon all men without limitation.

It's strange that Christ would die for sin not His own.

It's strange that Christ would die for sin in this manner, for it runs contrary to human nature.

It's strange that Christ would die for people amid their imprecations (blasphemy) and ingratitude.

It's strange that Christ would die for His enemies. Vincent says, "Christ died for those who are at enmity with Him and who bitterly hate Him."[492] What man would do likewise for his enemy? Paul says in all likelihood, no one.

The basis for its "strangeness" is the unfamiliarity man has with the God of the Bible; His true identity, nature, and character. To know about God theologically and experientially intimately makes Jesus' death to atone for sin that was not His own more readily reasonable, believable, and acceptable.

Why did God provide grace in this "strange" manner? Out of demonstration of the greatness of His love for man. Paul says, "But God demonstrates His own love toward us, in that while we were still sinners, Christ died for us" (Romans 5:8 NKJV). Jesus Himself indicated the same, saying to Nicodemus, "For God so loved the world, that he gave his only begotten Son, that whosoever believeth in him should not perish, but have everlasting life" (John 3:16). The shedding of Christ's blood at Calvary was necessary to atone for man's sin (Hebrews 9:22; 1 Peter 1:18). And it was all prompted by God's great love for the world. "There is nothing man values so much as life. Friends, property, health, reputation, all are held cheap in comparison with life. To give life, therefore, is to give that which he feels to be of all the dearest things most dear. A man may express his affection by language, toil, gifts, but such expressions are weak compared with the sacrifice of life, which demonstrates powerfully both the intensity and the sincerity of that affection."[493] D. Thomas says, "The strength of love is proved by the sacrifice it makes. 'God...gave His only begotten Son.'"[494] "How it must have grieved the Father to think of His own holy, innocent Son being buffeted and scourged and crucified by the hands of wicked men, in the frenzy of their passion and hatred! What a sacrifice to make for our sakes, when God gave up His own Son to the death for us all! Herein is the proof of the reality of God's love."[495]

"Therefore being justified by faith, we have peace with God through our Lord Jesus Christ: *By whom also we have access by*

179

faith into this grace wherein we stand, and rejoice in hope of the glory of God" (Romans 5:1–2). Listen to the song "A Strange Way to Save the World," written by Mark Harris, David Clark [US] and Don Koch.

97 Settlement of Grace

A submarine off the Massachusetts coastline rammed by another vessel quickly sank. A diver sent down into the waters to evaluate the situation placed his helmet-covered head to the side of the vessel and heard someone tapping dots and dashes of Morse code. The transmission came slowly: "Is…there…any…hope?"

That was man's question prior to Calvary. Is there any hope for man's guilt, forgiveness of sin, reconciliation to God and eternal life in Heaven? Do we have a chance of escape from the baggage and guilt of sin? We look to God's Word for the answer. Paul writes, "Now may our Lord Jesus Christ himself, and God our Father, who loved us and gave us eternal comfort and good hope through grace, comfort your hearts and establish them in every good work and word" (2 Thessalonians 2:16–17 ESV). Paul reveals good news. God has provided "good hope" to resolve man's problem and dilemma of sin. And that good hope is through God's grace.

What is "good" about the hope God has provided?

It is a "good hope through grace," because it is the means of man's salvation, the solution to the problem with sin.

It's a "good hope," because God has done for man what none else could have done—make a way possible to reconciliation with Him and forgiveness of sin. See 2 Thessalonians 2:13–14.

It's a "good hope through grace," because of its invitation of divine mercy to every man. He says, "And the Spirit and the bride say, Come. And let him that heareth say, Come. And let him that is athirst come. And whosoever will, let him take the water of life freely" (Revelation 22:17).

It's a "good hope through grace," because the salvation it provides is absolutely free. It's a gift of love from God to you (Ephesians 2:8–9).

It's a "good hope through grace," for it provides an eternal relationship with God through His Son, the Lord Jesus Christ, and an eternal abode in Heaven at life's climax.

It's a "good hope through grace," for it is absolutely trustworthy and dependable. There's not the slightest shadow of doubt over its veracity. It's been tried and proven to be true by literally billions over the centuries.

It's a "good hope through grace," for it not only provides salvation but consolation. The "Father...hath loved us and hath given us everlasting consolation...Comfort your hearts" (2 Thessalonians 2:16b–17a). All the blessings and benefits grace affords follow the acceptance of the gospel message and its application to the heart by faith and repentance (Acts 20:21). Matthew Henry comments, "The outward call of God is by the Gospel; and this is rendered effectual by the inward operation of the Spirit. Note, Wherever the Gospel comes, it calls and invites men to the obtaining of glory; it is a call to honor and happiness, even the glory of our Lord Jesus Christ, the glory He has purchased, and the glory He is possessed of."[496]

> A message sweet is borne to me
>   On wings of joy divine;
> A wondrous message, glad and free,
>   That thrills this heart of mine.
>
> I'm saved by grace, by grace alone,
>   Through Christ, whose love I claim.
> No other could for sin atone;
>   Hosanna to His name!
>
> Oh, glorious song that all day long
>   With tuneful note is ringing,
> I'm saved by grace, amazing grace;
>   And that is why I'm singing!

I hear the message that I love
   When morning dawns anew;
I read it in the sun above
   That shines across the blue.

I hear it in the twilight still,
   And at the sunset hour—
I'm saved by grace! What words can thrill
   With such a magic power?

Oh, wondrous grace for all mankind,
   That spreads from sea to sea!
It heals the sick and leads the blind
   And sets the prisoner free;

The soul that seeks it cannot fail
   To see the Savior's face,
And Satan's power cannot prevail
   If we are saved by grace.

                ~ Fanny Crosby (1898)

Why are you downcast, O my soul, and why are you disquieted within me? Hope in God. For He hath provided a "good hope in grace" to cure the disease of sin and grant consolation and comfort through the trials and troubles of life. And this saving and sustaining grace is free. Believe it, receive it, rest in it, delight in it, and testify of it.

98 Strife of Grace

The moment sin entered the world, God's plan was pronounced that His own Son would embark on a mission to earth to save the world (Genesis 3:15). (It was however foreordained from the foundation of the world—Revelation 13:8). He would come to earth by a virgin birth through the seed of Abraham, the tribe of Judah and the house of David. Satan sought to prevent Christ's coming by attempts to obstruct that divine lineage. When that failed, Satan sought to undermine the virgin birth (incarnation) by having it counterfeited in other religions so it would be discounted as a myth, a mere hoax.[497]

Upon the birth of Christ, Satan sought to kill Him through implanting the devious thought in Herod's mind that He would usurp his kingship (Matthew 2:16–18). But that attempt to stop the mission of grace also was thwarted. But it was far from over. The Devil tried to use Peter to stop the crucifixion by his effort to keep Jesus from going to Jerusalem, where Jesus said He would be killed and rise again. Jesus rebuked him, saying, "Get thee behind me, Satan" (Matthew 16:23). Jesus was accused of possessing a "devil" for His claim to have had His beginning before Abraham, and an attempt was made to stone Him, but He successfully hid (John 8:59). Had God not intervened then and there, Jesus might have been stoned to death, preventing the crucifixion from happening.

Satan's effort to keep Christ from the Cross continued through the use of corrupt anti-Christian politicians, governmental officials, religious groups, traitors, kings, wicked and corrupt people, false witnesses, and slanderers. All the schemes and strategies that they manufactured could not succeed in keeping Christ from the Cross. Satan's final effort to keep Jesus from dying on the Cross to make grace possible for the forgiveness of sin was to tempt Him to save Himself by coming down off it (Matthew 27:40). That effort, too, failed.

The day Jesus died at Calvary, grace won, making atonement possible for the world. But grace yet is opposed and battled, not only verbally, religiously, and politically, but also through efforts by its antagonists to discredit it. But as was the case with Satan's initial effort to stop it, this endeavor also will fail. The weapons of a cross, nails, and a bloody crown of thorns and Jesus' resurrection three days later defeated Satan's effort to thwart the power of grace forever.

The strife is o'er, the battle done;
Now is the Victor's triumph won.
Oh, let the song of praise be sung.
Alleluya!

Death's mightiest powers have done their worst,
And Jesus hath his foes dispersed.
Let shouts of praise and joy outburst.
Alleluya!

On the third morn He rose again,
Glorious in majesty to reign.
Oh, let us swell the joyful strain.
Alleluya!

He brake the age-bound chains of Hell;
The bars from Heaven's high portals fell.
Let hymns of praise His triumph tell.
Alleluya!

Lord, by the stripes which wounded Thee,
From death's dread sting thy servants free,
That we may live and sing to thee,
Alleluya!

~ Francis Pott (1861)

99　Sweet Aroma of Grace

"Therefore be imitators of God, as beloved children; and walk in love, just as Christ also loved you and gave Himself up for us, an offering and a sacrifice to God as a fragrant aroma" (Ephesians 5:1–2 NASB). Jesus' sacrificial death at Calvary (torture of the nails riveted into His hands and feet, the sword thrust into His side, the crown of thorns pressed into His brow and ultimate death) ascended to the throne of God as a "sweet-smelling aroma," for it was met with God's eternal divine approval. "This is My Son, in whom I am well pleased," though unstated, nevertheless thundered throughout the realms of Heaven and the domain of earth the day Jesus died. "As He offered Himself," says Matthew Henry, "with a design to be accepted of God, so God did accept, was pleased with, and appeased by, that sacrifice. Note, as the sacrifice of Christ was efficacious with God, so His example should be prevailing with us, and we should carefully copy after it."[498]

More than 2,000 years have passed since that offering was presented. Skeptics, agnostics, and atheists all have assaulted it with their words of derision and disdain. Satan has attacked it through lies, falsities and deception. Liberal theologians have sought to undermine it and adulterate it. Saints that embrace "grace theology" have been persecuted in an effort to silence its teaching and spread. Yet the fragrancy of that supreme offering has not dissipated the slightest. Its sweet-smelling aroma envelops the life of every devout believer (the aroma of grace) and is forever irrepressible. It's nigh impossible to meet a born-again believer without "smelling" that aroma of a soul that's been set free by the supreme sacrificial offering of Christ.

But not only are believers fragrances of grace to the ungodly, but Paul says (2 Corinthians 2:15) "we are unto God a sweet savor of Christ." Adam Clarke explains, "We are a sweet savor to God—we have fulfilled His will in faithfully proclaiming the Gospel and fighting against sin."[499] John Gill adds that the believer is a sweet-smelling fragrance because of the doctrines of grace that adorn his life.[500]

Its fragrance is the "odor" of Heaven presently and will be forever.

> There is a green hill far away,
>   Without a city wall,
> Where the dear Lord was crucified,
>   Who died to save us all.
>
> We may not know, we cannot tell,
>   What pains he had to bear;
> But we believe it was for us
>   He hung and suffered there.
>
> He died that we might be forgiv'n,
>   He died to make us good,
> That we might go at last to heav'n,
>   Saved by his precious blood.

There was no other good enough
  To pay the price of sin;
He only could unlock the gate
  Of heav'n, and let us in.

Oh, dearly, dearly has he loved,
  And we must love him too,
And trust in his redeeming blood,
  And try his works to do.

~ Cecil Frances Alexander (1848)

100 Sublimity of Grace

The ultimate grandeur and utopia of grace is glory. "The LORD will give grace and glory" (Psalm 84:11). He that knows grace now, will know glory eternally. "God has married them, and none can divorce them."[501] Glory is but grace in perfection.[502] Spurgeon eloquently says, "Glory is nothing more than grace in its Sabbath dress, grace in full bloom, grace like autumn fruit, mellow and perfected. Glory, the glory of Heaven, the glory of eternity, the glory of Jesus, the glory of the Father, the Lord will surely give to His chosen."[503] To quote Spurgeon again, "What is glory? He that has been in Heaven five minutes can tell you better than the sagest divine that lives; and yet he could not tell you. Nay, the angels could not tell you; you could not understand them. What is glory? You must enjoy it to know it. Glory is not merely rest, happiness, wealth, safety; it is honor, victory, immortality, triumph."[504]

God promises that he that has been saved by grace through Him shall share glory with Him. We deserve Hell, but He will give us glory. We deserve eternal banishment from Him, but He will give us glory. We deserve anguishing torment, but He will give us glory. W. N. Richie says, "The kings of earth cause Daniel and Joseph to be clothed with royal robes, but God will clothe us with His own hands, with Heaven's best wardrobe out of the ivory palace."[505] What a royal gift sublime glory is to the believer. Hallelujah!

Two golden links of one celestial chain:
Who owneth grace shall surely glory gain.

~ Unknown.

101 Summation of Grace

God's grace is spectacular and wonderful. Paul, even with his great theological brilliance, said grace was an "indescribable gift" (2 Corinthians 9:15 NIV). It is a supreme gift. Grace (the loving-kindness, mercy and favor God freely dispenses to man) is the basis for salvation (1 Corinthians 15:10), conduct (2 Corinthians 1:12); holiness (Titus 2:12); service (1 Peter 1:10); strength (Hebrews 13:9); evangelism (Acts 20:24); future life in Heaven (1 Peter 1:13); help in sorrow, affliction and adversity, etc. (Hebrews 4:16); and the believer's standing, secure position (Romans 5:2). The whole of the Bible is a story of God's grace, and it fittingly ends with the benediction: "The grace of our Lord Jesus Christ be with you all" (Revelation 22:21).

Saith Spurgeon, "All that is good or ever will be good in us is preceded by the grace of God and is the effect of a Divine cause within."[506] Barclay says, "Whenever we mention the word *grace,* we must think of the sheer loveliness of the Christian life and the sheer undeserved generosity of the heart of God."[507] "There is grace to blot out your trespasses, though they be 'red like crimson.' There is grace to purify your hearts, though they be full of all uncleanness. There is grace to subdue your enemies, though they 'come upon you as a flood.' There is grace to console you amidst all your sorrows, though they be great and multiplied and protracted. There is grace to guide you through life, to cheer you at death, and to carry you to Heaven."[508]

Piper says, "'Treasuring all that God is' is a work of grace in my heart. I would not treasure God without a mighty work of grace in my life (Acts 18:27; Philippians 1:29; Ephesians 2:8f.; 2 Timothy 2:25). 'Loving all whom He loves' is a work of grace in my heart (1 Thessalonians 3:12; 4:9; Philippians 1:9; Galatians 5:22)."[509] George Swinnock said, "A desire to disgrace others never sprang from grace. It is ill to inquire into others' actions

187

that we might have matter to draw up a bill of indictment against them. Like those who, in reading books, mark only the faults, or such as take more pleasure in beholding a monster than a perfect man, such is a censorious person."[510]

Piper continues, "'Praying for all His purposes' is a work of grace in my heart (Philippians 2:13; Hebrews 13:21). And 'meditating on all His Word' is a work of grace (Psalm 119:36)."[511] "We must trust in His grace, for 'we cannot do any good thing without him.' It is from Him that we must obtain 'power either to do, or even to will' what is acceptable in His sight, and in every stage of our existence must we depend on Him for 'more grace' and receive from Him 'the grace that shall be sufficient for us.'"[512]

A concise "shorthand" of grace is found in Hebrews 4:16 in its answer to five questions. The text states, "Let us therefore come boldly unto the throne of grace, that we may obtain mercy, and find grace to help in time of need." Consider grace's four *W*s and one *H* (Who, When, Where, Why and How) that are revealed in the passage.

Who may come? "Let *us*," that is, the born-again believer is invited to come into Christ's holy presence to obtain mercy and grace.

How is the believer to come? "Come *boldly*," not cowardly or hesitantly but with "unstaggering confidence" that Jesus will grant the help sought. But at the same time don't come flippantly or irreverently.

> Come boldly to the throne of grace,
>   Ye wretched sinners, come
> And lay your load at Jesus' feet
>   And plead what He has done.
>
> "How can I come?" some soul may say.
>   "I'm lame and cannot walk;
> My guilt and sin have stopped my mouth;
>   I sigh but dare not talk."

Come boldly to the throne of grace,
    Though lost and blind and lame;
Jehovah is the sinner's Friend
    And ever was the same.

He makes the dead to hear His voice;
    He makes the blind to see.
The sinner lost He came to save
    And set the prisoner free.

Poor bankrupt souls, who feel and know
    The hell of sin within,
Come boldly to the throne of grace;
    The Lord will take you in.

~ Daniel Herbert (1838)

Where is the believer to come? Come "unto the *throne of grace*" (not the throne of judgment), the place where Jesus sits enthroned as King to dispense mercy and grace. It is the throne of spontaneous love.[513] See Hosea 14:4.

When is the believer to come? You are invited to come to "the throne of grace" in "time of *need*." That is, whenever there is a need for forgiveness, mercy, comfort, consolation, strength, healing, peace, rest or help of any kind, you may freely come.

Why is the believer to come? We ought to come to "the throne of grace" in order to "obtain [not simply request] *mercy*" (cleansing and pardon of sin, a constantly ongoing need) and the benefits of grace (the supernatural power of God to supply the believer's need, whatever it may be, if in accordance with His divine will).

His grace is enough for me, for me;
His grace is enough for me.
    Through sorrow and pain,
    Through loss or gain,
His grace is enough for me.

Just when I am disheartened,
    Just when with cares oppressed,
Just when my way is darkest,
    Just when I am distressed,

Then is my Savior near me;
    He knows my every care.
Jesus will never leave me;
    He helps my burdens bear.

Just when my hopes are vanished,
    Just when my friends forsake,
Just when the fight is thickest,
    Just when with fear I shake,

Then comes a still small whisper,
    "Fear not, My child, I'm near."
Jesus brings peace and comfort;
    I love His voice to hear.

Just when my tears are flowing,
    Just when with anguish bent,
Just when temptation's hardest,
    Just when with sadness rent,

Then comes a thought of comfort,
    I know my Father knows.
Jesus has grace sufficient
    To conquer all my foes.

~ J. Bruce Evans (1906)

Although mercy and grace are abundantly available, they must be requested. Maclaren states that the reference to "obtaining mercy" and "finding grace to help" suggests a metaphor. "The one expresses the heart of God (obtaining mercy); the other expresses the hand of God (finding grace to help)."[514] Graciousness is an attribute of God. God provides us grace because He is gracious. "The LORD, the LORD, the

190

compassionate and gracious God, slow to anger, abounding in love and faithfulness" (Exodus 34:6 NIV).

Be assured that the believer will get the right grace. There are "no blunders in the equipment with which He supplies us," says Maclaren. "He does not give me the parcel that was meant for you; there is no error in the delivery. He does not send His soldiers to the North Pole equipped for warfare in Africa. He does not give this man a blessing that the man's circumstances would not require. No, no; blessed be God, He cannot err."[515] The all-sufficient and limitless grace of Jesus (coping grace and helping grace) is dispersed based upon the believer's need when it is warranted (not before).

> Rejoicing in hope and patient in grief,
> To Thee I look up for certain relief.
> I fear no denial; no danger I fear,
> Nor start from the trial if Jesus is near.
>
> ~ Charles Wesley (1708)

Join Spurgeon in saying loudly and steadfastly, "Let the whole earth, and even God's professing people, cast out my name as evil; my Lord and my Master, He will not. I glory in the distinguishing grace of God and will not, by the grace of God, step one inch from my principles or think of adhering to the present fashionable sort of religion."[516]

> May the grace of Christ our Savior
>   And the Father's boundless love
> With the Holy Spirit's favor
>   Rest upon us from above.
>
> Thus may we abide in union
>   With each other and the Lord
> And possess, in sweet communion,
>   Joys which earth cannot afford.
>
> ~ John Newton (1779)

This is the true grace of God. Stand firm in it.

~ 1 Peter 5:12 ESV

ENDNOTES

[1] Needham, George C. *The Life and Labors of Charles H. Spurgeon.* (Boston: D. L. Guernsey, 1887), 7.

[2] Spurgeon, C. H. "God's Goodness Leading to Repentance" (Sermon No. 2857), delivered November 18, 1877.

[3] *MacLaren's Expositions,* 1 Corinthians 15:10.

[4] Murray, Andrew. *The Ministry of Intercession.* (Springdale, PA: Whitaker House, 1982), 73.

[5] Machen, John Gresham. *What Is Faith?* (Carlisle, PA: Banner of Truth, 1996).

[6] Achtemeier, P. J., *Harper's Bible Dictionary* (1st ed.). (San Francisco: Harpercollins, 1985), 357.

[7] MacArthur, John. *None Other.* (Orlando, Florida: Reformation Trust, 2017), 2.

[8] Hiebert, D. Edmond. *The Expositor's Bible Commentary,* (ed. by Frank Gaebelein). (Zondervan), 11:439

[9] Warren, Rick. "Living Under Grace" (part 16), https://sermons.faithlife.com/sermons/41818-16-living-under-grace-(part-16), accessed August 20, 2021.

[10] Vine, W. E. *Expository Dictionary of NT Words,* 509–510.

[11] Zodhiates, S. *The Complete Word Study Dictionary: New Testament* (electronic ed.). (Chattanooga, TN: AMG Publishers, 2000).

[12] Westminster Confession of Faith, Chapter IX, "Of Free Will."

[13] Yancey, Phillip. *What's So Amazing About Grace: Leader's Guide.* (Grand Rapids, Michigan: Zondervan Publishing House, 2000), from Yancey's letter to group leaders at first of book.

[14] Henry, M., and T. Scott. *Matthew Henry's Concise Commentary.* (Oak Harbor, WA: Logos Research Systems, 1997), Galatians 1:5.

[15] Morgan, Richard, Howard, and John. "G. Campbell Morgan: Preaching in the Shadow of Grace." https://www.preaching.com/articles/past-masters/g-campbell-morgan-preaching-in-the-shadow-of-grace/, accessed August 11, 2021.

[16] *Barnes Notes on the Bible,* Acts 13:43.

[17] Sproul, R. C. "Grace and Gratitude," November 20, 2020. www.ligonier.org/blog/grace-and-gratitude/, accessed June 11, 2021.

[18] Yancey, Phillip. *What's So Amazing About Grace: Participant's Guide.* (Grand Rapids: Zondervan, 2021). Session One.

[19] Murray, Andrew. *The Ministry of Intercession.* (Springdale, PA: Whitaker House, 1982), 73.

[20] Wiersbe, W. W. *The Bible Exposition Commentary* (Vol. 2). (Wheaton, IL: Victor Books, 1996), 436.

[21] *Maclaren Expositions,* 1 Corinthians 15:10.

[22] Spurgeon, Charles. *Faith's Checkbook,* March 19.

[23] Spence-Jones, H. D. M. (Ed.). *Acts of the Apostles* (Vol. 1). (London; New York: Funk & Wagnalls Company, 1909), 441.

[24] Zodhiates, S. *The Complete Word Study Dictionary: New Testament* (electronic ed.). (Chattanooga, TN: AMG Publishers, 2000).

[25] https://www.wisesayings.com/grace-quotes/, accessed June 4, 2021.

[26] Ibid.

[27] Ibid.

[28] Plumer, W. S. *Studies in the Book of Psalms: Being a Critical and Expository Commentary, with Doctrinal and Practical Remarks on the Entire Psalter.* (Philadelphia; Edinburgh: J. B. Lippincott Company; A & C Black, 1872), 1040.

[29] Newman, Randy. "Amazing Graces: How Complex the Sound!," from the spring 2018 issue of *Knowing & Doing,* https://www.cslewisinstitute.org/Amazing_Graces_How_Complex_the_Sound_FullArticle, accessed July 9, 2021.

[30] Exell, J. S. *The Biblical Illustrator: St. John* (Vol. 1). (London: James Nisbet & Co.), 70.

[31] Vincent, M. R. *Word Studies in the New Testament* (Vol. 4) (New York: Charles Scribner's Sons, 1887), 431.

[32] Exell, J. S. *The Biblical Illustrator: 1 Peter.* (London: James Nisbet & Co.), 439.

[33] Wuest, K. S. *Wuest's Word Studies from the Greek New Testament for the English Reader* (Vol. 11). (Grand Rapids: Eerdmans, 1997), 130. 130.

[34] Arichea, D. C. and E. A. Nida, *A Handbook on the First Letter from Peter.* (New York: United Bible Societies, 1980), 70.

[35] Spurgeon, C. H. Grace Abounding (Sermon delivered May 23, 1863). https://www.studylight.org/commentary/hosea/14-4.html, accessed September 1, 2021.

[36] Simeon, C. *Horae Homileticae: James to Jude* (Vol. 20). (London: Holdsworth and Ball, 1833), 281.

[37] Wiersbe, W. W. *The Bible Exposition Commentary* (Vol. 2). (Wheaton, IL: Victor Books, 1996), 290.

[38] Ibid.

[39] A. C. Dixon. Through Night to Morning (Greenville, SC: The Gospel Hour, Inc., no copyright date), Chpt 18.

[40] Louw, J. P. and E. A. Nida. *Greek-English Lexicon of the New Testament: Based on Semantic Domains* (electronic ed. of the 2nd edition., Vol. 1). (New York: United Bible Societies, 1996), 479–480.

[41] Lane, W. L. *Hebrews 1–8* (Vol. 47a). (Dallas: Word, Incorporated, 1991), 115.

[42] MacArthur, J., Jr. (Ed.). *The MacArthur Study Bible* (electronic ed.). (Nashville, TN: Word Pub, 1997), 1903.

[43] Henry, M. *Matthew Henry's Commentary on the Whole Bible: Complete and Unabridged in One Volume.* (Peabody: Hendrickson, 1994), 2387.

[44] Jamieson, R.; A. R. Fausset; and D. Brown. *Commentary Critical and Explanatory on the Whole Bible* (Vol. 2) (Oak Harbor, WA: Logos Research Systems, Inc., 1997), 450.

[45] Henry, M. *Matthew Henry's Commentary on the Whole Bible: Complete and Unabridged in One Volume.* (Peabody: Hendrickson, 1994), 2200.

[46] Ferguson, Sinclair. *The Whole Christ: Legalism, Antinomianism, and Gospel Assurance—Why the Marrow Controversy Still Matters.* (Crossway, 2016), 110.

[47] Geisler, N. L. Colossians. In J. F. Walvoord and R. B. Zuck (Eds.). *The Bible Knowledge Commentary: An Exposition of the Scriptures* (Vol. 2). (Wheaton, IL: Victor Books, 1985), 677

[48] www.whosoever.org/v2i3/pit.html. Accessed May 14, 2010. Adapted.

[49] Allibone, S. Austin, comp. "Prose Quotations from Socrates to Macaulay," 1880. https://www.bartleby.com/349/authors/94.html, accessed June 4, 2021.

[50] *The Pulpit Commentary,* Ephesians 1:6 (Homiletics).

[51] Reinke, Tony. "Amazing Grace for a New Year." January 2, 2017. https://www.desiringgod.org/articles/god-has-brought-me-safe-thus-far, accessed May 27, 2021.

[52] Hamilton, William W. *Sermons on the Books of the Bible* (Vol. II), 45.

[53] https://philipyancey.com/q-and-a-topics/grace, accessed June 2, 2021.

[54] https://www.azquotes.com/quote/868717, accessed June 3, 2021.

[55] Friberg, T., B. Friberg, and N. F. Miller. *Analytical Lexicon of the Greek New Testament* (Vol. 4). (Grand Rapids, MI: Baker Books, 2000), 318.

[56] Spurgeon, C. H. "The Treasure of Grace," delivered January 22, 1860. https://www.blueletterbible.org/Comm/spurgeon_charles/sermons/0295.cfm, accessed May 19, 2021.

[57] Barnes, Albert. *Notes on the Bible.* (1834), Romans 2:4.

[58] Spurgeon, C. H. "Grace for Grace" (Sermon #2087), delivered May 19, 1889.

ENDNOTES

59 Exell, J. S. *The Biblical Illustrator: Romans* (Vol. 1). (New York; Chicago; Toronto; London; Edinburgh: Fleming H. Revell Company), 434.

60 Tozer, A.W. *I Talk Back to the Devil,* 12–13.

61 Exell, J. S. *The Biblical Illustrator: Romans* (Vol. 1). (New York; Chicago; Toronto; London; Edinburgh: Fleming H. Revell Company), 434.

62 Spurgeon, C. H. *The Treasury of David,* Psalm 3:3.

63 Henry, M. *Matthew Henry's Commentary on the Whole Bible: Complete and Unabridged in One Volume.* (Peabody: Hendrickson, 1994), 946.

64 Ibid., 726.

65 Wiersbe, W. W. *With the Word Bible Commentary.* (Nashville: Thomas Nelson 1991), Matthew 14:1.

66 *Funeral Sermons and Outlines.* (Grand Rapids: Baker Book House, 1951), 11.

67 Spurgeon, C. H. *Morning and Evening.* (London: Passmore & Alabaster), March 3.

68 Plumer, W. S. *Studies in the Book of Psalms: Being a Critical and Expository Commentary, with Doctrinal and Practical Remarks on the Entire Psalter.* (Philadelphia; Edinburgh: J. B. Lippincott Company; A & C Black, 1872), 1006.

69 *Barnes Notes on the Bible,* 2 Corinthians 12:9.

70 https://quotefancy.com/quote/37756/Billy-Graham-The-will-of-God-will-not-take-us-where-the-grace-of-God-cannot-sustain-us, accessed December 4, 2021.

71 Henry, M., and T. Scott. *Matthew Henry's Concise Commentary.* (Oak Harbor, WA: Logos Research Systems, 1997), 2 Corinthians 12:9.

72 G. Campbell Morgan. "God's Sufficient Grace" (sermon). https://www.sermonindex.net/modules/articles/index.php?view=article&aid=4927, accessed August 11, 2021.

73 Spurgeon, C. H. *Morning and Evening,* January 27 (Morning).

74 Exell, J. S. *The Biblical Illustrator: Romans* (Vol. 1). (New York; Chicago; Toronto; London; Edinburgh: Fleming H. Revell Company), 440.

75 Hallock, G. B. F. *The Evangelistic Cyclopedia.* (New York: Richard R. Smith, Inc., 1930), 293.

76 Exell, J. S. *The Biblical Illustrator: James.* (Cincinnati; Chicago; Kansas City: Jennings & Graham), 367.

77 Ibid., 366.

78 Exell, J. S. *The Biblical Illustrator: I Corinthians 1:4,* "Life Enriched Through Christ," (Charles Gore).

[79] Henry, M. *Matthew Henry's Commentary on the Whole Bible: Complete and Unabridged in One Volume.* (Peabody: Hendrickson, 1994), 890.

[80] *The Spurgeon Study Bible,* 776.

[81] Needham, George C. *The Life and Labors of Charles H. Spurgeon.* (Boston: D. L. Guernsey, 1887), 38.

[82] Ibid. p. 39.

[83] Ibid.

[84] Exell, J. S. *The Biblical Illustrator: 1 Corinthians* (Vol. 2). (New York: Anson D. F. Randolph & Company), 405.

[85] Henry, M. *Matthew Henry's Commentary on the Whole Bible: Complete and Unabridged in One Volume.* (Peabody: Hendrickson, 1994), 2272.

[86] https://www.goodreads.com/quotes/17247-i-am-not-what-i-ought-to-be-i-am, accessed June 2, 2021.

[87] Vine, W. E., M. F. Unger, and W. White, Jr. *Vine's Complete Expository Dictionary of Old and New Testament Words* (Vol. 1). (Nashville, TN: T. Nelson, 1996), 142.

[88] Holladay, W. L., and L. Köhler. *A Concise Hebrew and Aramaic Lexicon of the Old Testament.* (2000), 187.

[89] Gesenius, W., and S. P. Tregelles. *Gesenius' Hebrew and Chaldee Lexicon to the Old Testament Scriptures.* (Bellingham, WA: Logos Bible Software, 2003), 765.

[90] Dixon, Francis. *Lansdowne Bible School and Postal Fellowship.* "Studies in the Epistle of James," No. 8. (Bournemouth, England, March 21, 1972.)

[91] Ibid.

[92] https://www.preceptaustin.org/the_attributes_of_god_-_spurgeon, accessed June 2, 2021

[93] McConkey, James. *The Threefold Secret of the Holy Spirit.* (Pittsburgh, PA: Silver Publishing Society, 1975), 98.

[94] Ibid., 100.

[95] Wuest, K. S. *Wuest's Word Studies from the Greek New Testament for the English Reader* (Vol. 10). (Grand Rapids: Eerdmans, 1997), 94.

[96] Ibid.

[97] Pink, A. W. *An Exposition of Hebrews.* (Swengel, PA: Bible Truth Depot, 1954), 210.

[98] Westcott, B. F. (Ed.). *The Epistle to the Hebrews: The Greek Text with Notes and Essays* (3rd ed.). (London: Macmillan, 1903), 110.

[99] Exell, J. S. *The Biblical Illustrator: Hebrews* (Vol. 1). (London: James Nisbet & Co.), 369.

[100] Chambers, Oswald. *My Utmost for His Highest.* "Drawing on the Grace of God—Now," June 26.

[101] https://www.azquotes.com/author/14750-Aiden_Wilson_Tozer, accessed August 25, 2021.

[102] Clarke, Adam. *Commentary on the Bible.* (1831), Hebrews 4:16.

[103] Pink, A. W. *An Exposition of Hebrews.* (Swengel, PA: Bible Truth Depot, 1954), 992.

[104] https://quotefancy.com/quote/1343595/John-Newton-Thou-art-coming-to-a-King-large-petitions-with-thee-bring-for-His-grace-and, accessed June 15, 2021.

[105] Exell, J. S. *The Biblical Illustrator: James.* (Cincinnati; Chicago; Kansas City: Jennings & Graham), 366.

[106] https://www.knowledgelove.com/quotes/john-wesley-quotes/, accessed June 3, 2021.

[107] Spurgeon, C. H. *Morning and Evening,* July 16 (Morning).

[108] Chambers, Oswald. *God's Workmanship.* (Grand Rapids: Daily Bread Publishing, 1953).

[109] Alexander Maclaren. Expositions Of Holy Scripture. The Measure of Grace, Ephesians 4:7.

[110] Westcott, B. F. (Ed.). *The Epistle to the Hebrews: The Greek Text with Notes and Essays* (3rd ed.). (London: Macmillan, 1903), 110.

[111] Pink, A. W. *An Exposition of Hebrews.* (Swengel, PA: Bible Truth Depot, 1954), 211.

[112] William Gurnall. https://www.brainyquote.com/quotes/william_gurnall_355100, accessed May 19, 2021.

[113] Clarke, Adam. *Commentary on the Bible.* (1831), Romans 3:4.

[114] Spence-Jones, H. D. M. (Ed.). *Galatians.* (London; New York: Funk & Wagnalls Company, 1909), 277.

[115] *Barnes Notes on the Bible,* Galatians 5:13.

[116] Spence-Jones, H. D. M. (Ed.). *Galatians.* (London; New York: Funk & Wagnalls Company, 1909), 271.

[117] MacArthur, J., Jr. (Ed.). *The MacArthur Study Bible* (electronic ed.). (Nashville, TN: Word Pub, 1997), 1798.

[118] MacDonald, W. *Believer's Bible Commentary: Old and New Testaments,* (A. Farstad, Ed.). (Nashville: Thomas Nelson, 1995), 1893.

[119] Henry, M., and T. Scott. *Matthew Henry's Concise Commentary.* (Oak Harbor, WA: Logos Research Systems, 1997), Galatians 5:13.

[120] McGee, J. V. *Thru the Bible Commentary: The Epistles (Galatians)* (electronic ed., Vol. 46). (Nashville: Thomas Nelson, 1991), 95.

[121] MacArthur, John. *Alone with God.* (Colorado Springs, Co: David C. Cook, 2011), 182.

ENDNOTES

[122] Robertson, A. T. *Word Pictures in the New Testament.* (Nashville, TN: Broadman Press, 1933), Hebrews 4:16.

[123] Exell, J. S. *The Biblical Illustrator: Matthew.* (Grand Rapids, MI: Baker Book House, 1952), 224.

[124] Ibid., 225.

[125] 20 Inspirational Bible Verses About Grace. https://www.whatchristianswanttoknow.com/20-inspirational-bible-verses-about-grace/, accessed June 17, 2021.

[126] Simeon, C. *Horae Homileticae: 2 Timothy to Hebrews* (Vol. 19). (London: Holdsworth and Ball, 1833), 216.

[127] Pink, A. W. *An Exposition of Hebrews.* (Swengel, PA: Bible Truth Depot, 1954), 210.

[128] Spurgeon, C. H. *Morning and Evening,* January 6 (Morning).

[129] Cowman, L. B. *Streams in the Desert.* (Grand Rapids: Zondervan, 1977), 108.

[130] Spence-Jones, H. D. M. (Ed.). *Psalms* (Vol. 1). (London; New York: Funk & Wagnalls Company, 1909), 280.

[131] Lea, T. D. *Hebrews, James,* (Vol. 10). (Nashville, TN: Broadman & Holman Publishers, 1999), 321.

[132] Ellsworth, R. *Opening Up James.* (Leominster: Day One Publications, 2009), 128.

[133] wisesayings.com/grace-quotes/https://, accessed June 4, 2021.

[134] https://www.quoteschristian.com/faith.html, accessed June 12, 2021.

[135] Spurgeon, C. H. *Morning and Evening,* June 17 (Evening).

[136] G. Campbell Morgan. Choice Gleanings Calendar.

[137] Simeon, C. *Horae Homileticae: 2 Timothy to Hebrews* (Vol. 19). (London: Holdsworth and Ball, 1833), 217.

[138] Henry, M. *Matthew Henry's Commentary on the Whole Bible: Complete and Unabridged in One Volume.* (Peabody: Hendrickson, 1994), 750.

[139] Spurgeon, C. H. *Morning and Evening,* September 19 (Morning).

[140] https://www.azquotes.com, accessed May 26, 2021.

[141] Murray, Andrew. *Humility: The Journey Toward Holiness,* 1896. Quote taken from its Ichthus Publication, 2014, 36.

[142] Murray, Andrew. *Humility: The Journey Toward Holiness,* 1896. Quote taken from its Ichthus Publication, 2014, 42.

[143] Spurgeon, C. H. *Morning and Evening,* April 5 (Evening).

[144] https://www.azquotes.com/quote/823997, accessed June 9, 2021.

[145] Vincent, M. R. *Word Studies in the New Testament* (Vol. 4) (New York: Charles Scribner's Sons, 1887), 431.

[146] Jamieson, R.; A. R. Fausset; and D. Brown. *Commentary Critical and Explanatory on the Whole Bible* (Vol. 2) (Oak Harbor, WA: Logos Research Systems, Inc., 1997), 450.

[147] https://everydaypower.com/grace-quotes-2/, accessed August 26, 2021.

[148] https://quoteflick.com/grace-quotes/, August 26, 2021.

[149] Ryle, J. C. "Growth in Grace," https://www.monergism.com/growth-grace, accessed August 26, 2021.

[150] Pink, A. W. *Regeneration or The New Birth.*

[151] Spurgeon, C. H. "Growth in Grace" (Sermon delivered October 17, 1858). https://www.spurgeon.org/resource-library/sermons/growth-in-grace/#flipbook/, accessed June 3, 2021.

[152] Spurgeon, "C. H. The Fullness of Christ the Treasury of the Saints" (Sermon). *The Metropolitan Tabernacle Pulpit,* Vol. 20, 1875, 229.

[153] Spurgeon, C. H. "Growth in Grace" (Sermon delivered October 17, 1858). https://www.spurgeon.org/resource-library/sermons/growth-in-grace/#flipbook/, accessed June 3, 2021.

[154] Henry, M. *Matthew Henry's Commentary on the Whole Bible: Complete and Unabridged in One Volume.* (Peabody: Hendrickson, 1994), 756.

[155] Spence-Jones, H. D. M. (Ed.). *Second Peter.* (London; New York: Funk & Wagnalls Company, 1909), 4.

[156] Zodhiates, S. *The Complete Word Study Dictionary: New Testament* (electronic ed.). (Chattanooga, TN: AMG Publishers, 2000).

[157] Spurgeon, C. H. "Growth in Grace" (Sermon delivered October 17, 1858). https://www.spurgeon.org/resource-library/sermons/growth-in-grace/#flipbook/, accessed June 3, 2021.

[158] Spurgeon, C. H. *Morning and Evening,* January 4 (Morning).

[159] https://biblehub.com › commentaries › homiletics › 2_peter › 1.htm, accessed June 3, 2021.

[160] Bridges, C. (1861). Exposition of Psalm 119: As Illustrative of the Character and Exercises of Christian Experience (Seventeenth Edition, p. 133). New York: Robert Carter & Brothers.

[161] Zodhiates, S. *The Complete Word Study Dictionary: New Testament* (electronic ed.). (Chattanooga, TN: AMG Publishers, 2000).

[162] Wuest, K. S. *Wuest's Word Studies from the Greek New Testament for the English Reader* (Vol. 12). (Grand Rapids: Eerdmans, 1997), 24.

[163] Spurgeon, C. H. *Morning and Evening,* April 16 (Morning).

[164] https://www.pinterest.com/pin/373798837814199789/, accessed June 17, 2021.

165 Plumer, W. S. *Studies in the Book of Psalms: Being a Critical and Expository Commentary, with Doctrinal and Practical Remarks on the Entire Psalter.* (Philadelphia; Edinburgh: J. B. Lippincott Company; A & C Black, 1872), 28.

166 Exell, J. S. *The Biblical Illustrator: 2 Peter.* (London: James Nisbet & Co.), 26.

167 Spurgeon, C. H. *Morning and Evening,* June 18 (Evening).

168 Spurgeon, Charles. "Ripe Fruit" in *The Metropolitan Tabernacle Pulpit,* Volume 16 (1870).

169 Ryle, J. C. "Grow in Grace." https://www.monergism.com/growth-grace, accessed August 25, 2021.

170 Jamieson, R.; A. R. Fausset; and D. Brown. *Commentary Critical and Explanatory on the Whole Bible* (Vol. 2) (Oak Harbor, WA: Logos Research Systems, Inc., 1997), 513.

171 Spurgeon, C. H. "Distinguishing Grace." Sermon delivered February 6, 1859. *New Park Street Pulpit Volume,* 5.

172 https://www.facebook.com/DesiringGod/posts/charles-hodge-the-doctrines-of-grace-humble-a-man-without-degrading-him-and-exal/10150319133319240/, accessed July 19, 2021.

173 Zodhiates, S. *The Complete Word Study Dictionary: New Testament* (electronic ed.). (Chattanooga, TN: AMG Publishers, 2000).

174 Liddell, H. G. *A Lexicon: Abridged from Liddell and Scott's Greek-English Lexicon.* (Oak Harbor, WA: Logos Research Systems, Inc. 1996), 741.

175 Jamieson, R.; A. R. Fausset; and D. Brown. *Commentary Critical and Explanatory on the Whole Bible* (Vol. 2) (Oak Harbor, WA: Logos Research Systems, Inc., 1997), 517.

176 Clarke, Adam. *Commentary on the Bible.* (1831), 2 Peter 3:18.

177 https://www.gracegems.org/30/short_pithy_gems_Spurgeon.htm, accessed June 3, 2021.

178 https://www.whatchristianswanttoknow.com/top-15-christian-quotes-about-pain-and-suffering/#ixzz6wiXrJjlz, accessed June 3, 2021.

179 Ryle, J. C. "Grow in Grace." https://www.monergism.com/growth-grace, accessed August 25, 2021.

180 Barnes, Albert. *Notes on the Bible.* (1834), Hebrews 4:16.

181 https://www.blueletterbible.org/Comm/mhc/1Pe/1Pe_005.cfm

182 Plumer, W. S. *Studies in the Book of Psalms: Being a Critical and Expository Commentary, with Doctrinal and Practical Remarks on the Entire Psalter.* (Philadelphia; Edinburgh: J. B. Lippincott Company; A & C Black, 1872), 484.

[183] Newman, B. M., Jr. *A Concise Greek-English Dictionary of the New Testament.* (Stuttgart, Germany: Deutsche Bibelgesellschaft; United Bible Societies, 1993), 48.

[184] *Vincent's Word Studies,* Ephesians 1:6.

[185] Spurgeon, C. H. *The Treasury of David*, Psalm 107:2.

[186] From the Album "Come Morning" (1994), Homeland Records.

[187] *Barnes Notes on the Bible,* Romans 1:7.

[188] Spurgeon, C. H. "The Great Assize" (Sermon delivered August 25, 1872). https://www.spurgeon.org/resource-library/sermons/the-great-assize/#flipbook/, accessed July 21, 2021.

[189] Knight, G. W. *The Pastoral Epistles: a Commentary on the Greek Text.* (Grand Rapids, MI; Carlisle, England: W.B. Eerdmans; Paternoster Press, 1992), 389.

[190] Ibid.

[191] Simeon, C. *Horae Homileticae: 2 Timothy to Hebrews* (Vol. 19). (London: Holdsworth and Ball, 1833), 18.

[192] https://www.wisesayings.com/grace-quotes/, accessed June 4, 2021.

[193] Wiersbe, W. W. *With the Word Bible Commentary.* (Nashville: Thomas Nelson 1991), 2 Timothy 2:1.

[194] Plumer, W. S. *Studies in the Book of Psalms: Being a Critical and Expository Commentary, with Doctrinal and Practical Remarks on the Entire Psalter.* (Philadelphia; Edinburgh: J. B. Lippincott Company; A & C Black, 1872), 1036.

[195] Spurgeon, C. H. "Strengthening Words from the Savior's Lips" (Sermon preached April 2, 1876). *Metropolitan Tabernacle Pulpit,* Volume 22.

[196] Dixon, A. C. "Through Night to Morning" (Sermon No. 12), 1913.

[197] *Barnes Notes on the Bible,* Acts 4:33.

[198] https://www.goodreads.com/author/quotes/394188.Alan_Redpath, accessed August 11, 2021.

[199] Hughes, R. K., and B. Chapell. *1 & 2 Timothy and Titus: To Guard the Deposit.* (Wheaton, IL: Crossway Books, 2000), 193.

[200] Simeon, C. *Horae Homileticae: 2 Timothy to Hebrews* (Vol. 19). (London: Holdsworth and Ball, 1833), 20.

[201] *Cambridge Bible for Schools and Colleges,* John 1:16.

[202] *Ellicott's Commentary for English Readers,* John 1:16.

[203] Chambers, Oswald. *God's Workmanship.* (Grand Rapids: Daily Bread Publishing, 1953).

[204] Gill, John. *Exposition of the Entire Bible.* (1746-63), Acts 11:23.

[205] *Matthew Henry's Commentary on the Bible,* Acts 11:23.

206 Newman, B. M., Jr. *A Concise Greek-English Dictionary of the New Testament.* (Stuttgart, Germany: Deutsche Bibelgesellschaft; United Bible Societies, 1993), 199.

207 MacArthur, J., Jr. (Ed.). *The MacArthur Study Bible* (electronic ed.). (Nashville, TN: Word Pub, 1997), 1694–1695.

208 Wuest, K. S. *Wuest's Word Studies from the Greek New Testament for the English Reader* (Vol. 2). (Grand Rapids: Eerdmans, 1997), 41.

209 Spurgeon, C. H. "God's Goodness Leading to Repentance" (Sermon No. 2857), delivered November 18, 1877.

210 Fitzmyer, J. A. *Romans: A New Translation with Introduction and Commentary,* (Vol. 33,). (New Haven; London: Yale University Press, 2008), 301.

211 Henry, M. *Matthew Henry's Commentary on the Whole Bible: Complete and Unabridged in One Volume.* (Peabody: Hendrickson, 1994), 2196.

212 Wiersbe, W. W. *Wiersbe's Expository Outlines on the New Testament.* (Wheaton, IL: Victor Books, 1992), 366.

213 Spurgeon, C. H. "God's Goodness Leading to Repentance" (Sermon No. 2857), delivered November 18, 1877.

214 Sproul, R. C. "Grace and Gratitude," November 20, 2020. www.ligonier.org/blog/grace-and-gratitude/, accessed June 11, 2021.

215 Pink, A. W. *The Attributes of God.* (Grand Rapids: Baker Books, 1975), 84.

216 Robertson, A. T. *Paul and the Intellectuals.* (Nashville: Broadman,1959), 98.

217 Packer, J. I. *Knowing God.* (Downes Grove, Ill: InterVarsity Press, 1973), 241–242.

218 Vine, W. E., M. F. Unger, and W. White, Jr. *Vine's Complete Expository Dictionary of Old and New Testament Words* (Vol. 1). (Nashville, TN: T. Nelson, 1996), 142.

219 Spurgeon, C. H. *Morning and Evening,* May 17 (Evening).

220 Henry, M. *Matthew Henry's Commentary on the Whole Bible: Complete and Unabridged in One Volume.* (Peabody: Hendrickson, 1994), 1918.

221 Watson, Thomas. *Biblical Illustrator.* "Grace, Power Of" (I Corinthians 15:10).

222 Gill, John. *Exposition of the Entire Bible.* (1746-63), I Corinthians 15:10.

223 Spurgeon, C. H. "An Immovable Foundation" (Sermon delivered May 13, 1866). https://www.ccel.org/ccel/spurgeon/sermons12.xxiv.html, accessed August 27, 2021.

[224] Henry, Matthew. *Complete Commentary on the Whole Bible.* (1706), 1 Corinthians 15:10.

[225] Spurgeon, C. H. "Five Links in a Golden Chain" (Sermon delivered November 6, 1887). https://www.spurgeongems.org/sermon/chs2439.pdf, accessed July 27, 2021.

[226] Spurgeon, C. H. "Distinguishing Grace" (sermon delivered February 6, 1859).

[227] azquotes.com, accessed July 29, 2021.

[228] *Vincent Word Studies,* Romans 1:14.

[229] Maclaren, Alexander. "Debtor to All Men," Romans 1:14.

[230] Spurgeon, C. H. *Morning and Evening,* July 18 (Morning).

[231] Henry, M., and T. Scott. *Matthew Henry's Concise Commentary.* (Oak Harbor, WA: Logos Research Systems, 1997), Romans 1:14.

[232] Spurgeon, C. H. "The Glory of Grace" (Sermon delivered in the Winter, 1869). https://www.ccel.org/ccel/spurgeon/sermons48.iv.html, accessed August 23, 2021.

[233] Exell, J. S. *The Biblical Illustrator,* Romans 1:14. "I Am a Debtor," W. Arnot.

[234] Spurgeon, C. H. "The Christian—A Debtor" (Sermon), delivered August 10, 1856.

[235] *Pulpit Commentary,* Ephesians 3:7 (Homiletics).

[236] *Jamieson-Fausset-Brown Bible Commentary,* Ephesians 3:7.

[237] Bruce, F. F. *The Epistle to the Galatians: A Commentary on the Greek Text.* (Grand Rapids, MI: W.B. Eerdmans Pub. Co., 1982), 92.

[238] *Barnes Notes on the Bible,* Ephesians 3:7.

[239] Gill, John. *Exposition of the Entire Bible.* (1746-63), Galatians 1:15.

[240] Spurgeon, C. H. "Prevenient Grace" (Sermon #656), 1865.

[241] Teacher's Outline and Study Bible Commentary—1 Timothy.

[242] Simeon, C. *Horae Homileticae: Galatians-Ephesians* (Vol. 17). (London: Holdsworth and Ball, 1833), 333.

[243] Exell, J. S. *The Biblical Illustrator: Ephesians.* (New York; Chicago; Toronto; London; Edinburgh: Fleming H. Revell Company), 357.

[244] Simeon, C. *Horae Homileticae: Galatians-Ephesians* (Vol. 17). (London: Holdsworth and Ball, 1833), 336.

[245] Exell, J. S. *The Biblical Illustrator: Hebrews* (Vol. 2). (London: James Nisbet & Co.), 523.

[246] Spurgeon, C. H. *Morning and Evening,* May 23 (Morning).

[247] Spurgeon, C. H. *Psalms.* (Wheaton, IL: Crossway Books, 1993), 11.

[248] Stott, John. Langham Partnership Daily Thought, 16 July 2021.

[249] Spurgeon, C. H. *Psalms.* (Wheaton, IL: Crossway Books, 1993), 3.

[250] Pink, A. W. *An Exposition of Hebrews.* (Swengel, PA: Bible Truth Depot, 1954), 988.

[251] Henry, M. *Matthew Henry's Commentary on the Whole Bible: Complete and Unabridged in One Volume.* (Peabody: Hendrickson, 1994), 744.

[252] Exell, J. S. *The Biblical Illustrator: Ephesians.* (New York; Chicago; Toronto; London; Edinburgh: Fleming H. Revell Company), 158.

[253] Spurgeon, Charles. *Faith's Checkbook,* November 16.

[254] Dunn, J. D. G. *The Epistles to the Colossians and to Philemon: A Commentary on the Greek Text.* (Grand Rapids, MI; Carlisle: William B. Eerdmans Publishing; Paternoster Press, 1996), 266.

[255] Piper, John. "Make Your Mouth a Means of Grace," October 12, 1986. https://www.desiringgod.org/messages/make-your-mouth-a-means-of-grace, accessed July 19, 2021.

[256] Criswell, W. A., P. Patterson, E. R. Clendenen, Akin, D. L., Chamberlin, M., Patterson, D. K., and Pogue, J. (Eds.). *Believer's Study Bible* (electronic ed.). (Nashville: Thomas Nelson, 1991), Col 4:5.

[257] Jamieson, R.; A. R. Fausset; and D. Brown. *Commentary Critical and Explanatory on the Whole Bible* (Vol. 2) (Oak Harbor, WA: Logos Research Systems, Inc., 1997), 382.

[258] Wuest, K. S. *Wuest's Word Studies from the Greek New Testament for the English Reader* (Vol. 6). (Grand Rapids: Eerdmans, 1997), 235.

[259] Dunn, J. D. G. *The Epistles to the Colossians and to Philemon: A Commentary on the Greek Text.* (Grand Rapids, MI; Carlisle: William B. Eerdmans Publishing; Paternoster Press, 1996), 267.

[260] Henry, M. *Matthew Henry's Commentary on the Whole Bible: Complete and Unabridged in One Volume.* (Peabody: Hendrickson, 1994), 2336.

[261] Exell, J. S. *The Biblical Illustrator: Philippians–Colossians* (Vol. 2). (New York; Chicago; Toronto; London; Edinburgh: Fleming H. Revell Company), 286.

[262] Ibid.

[263] Piper, John. "Make Your Mouth a Means of Grace," October 12, 1986. https://www.desiringgod.org/messages/make-your-mouth-a-means-of-grace, accessed July 19, 2021.

[264] Barnes, Albert. *Notes on the Bible* (1834), Ephesians 2:7.

[265] Garland, D. E. *2 Corinthians.* (Vol. 29). (Nashville: Broadman & Holman Publishers, 1999), 304.

[266] https://www.princeofpreachers.org/quotes/never-neglect-the-means-of-grace, accessed July 11, 2021.

[267] McGee, J. V. *Thru the Bible Commentary,* (electronic ed., Vol. 16). (Nashville: Thomas Nelson, 1991), Heb 12:15.
[268] Simeon, C. *Horae Homileticae: 1 and 2 Corinthians* (Vol. 16). (London: Holdsworth and Ball, 1833), 532.
[269] Morgan, Richard, Howard, and John. "G. Campbell Morgan: Preaching in the Shadow of Grace." https://www.preaching.com/articles/past-masters/g-campbell-morgan-preaching-in-the-shadow-of-grace/, accessed August 11, 2021.
[270] Ibid.
[271] Graves, Dan. "Alcoholic Mel Trotter Delivered from Drink," (adapted). https://www.christianity.com/church/church-history/timeline/1801-1900/alcoholic-mel-trotter-delivered-from-drink-11630650.html, accessed July 13, 2021.
[272] "Nicky Cruz: Salvation in the Jungles of New York," (adapted). https://www1.cbn.com/700club/nicky-cruz-salvation-jungles-new-york, accessed July 13, 2021.
[273] Swindoll, Chuck. *The Man of Heroic Endurance: Job.* (Nashville: W Publishing Group, 2004), 353.
[274] Quotation taken from *Devotions upon Emergent Occasions Together with Death's Duel.* (Ann Arbor, Michigan: 1959).
[275] Ibid.
[276] Ibid.
[277] Spurgeon, C. H. *Spurgeon's Sermons,* Vol. 17: 1871. (Woodstock, Ontario, Canada: Devoted Publishing, 2017), 200.
[278] Ulmer, Selah. "3 Things You Didn't Know About Spurgeon's Wife," October 17, 2017. https://www.spurgeon.org/resource-library/blog-entries/3-things-you-didnt-know-about-spurgeons-wife/, accessed July 7, 2020.
[279] https://www.goodreads.com/quotes/254564-there-is-no-pit-so-deep-that-god-s-love-is, accessed July 28, 2021.
[280] Spurgeon, C. H. "Grace Abounding over Abounding Sin," (Sermon delivered March 4, 1888). https://www.spurgeon.org/resource-library/sermons/grace-abounding-over-abounding-sin/#flipbook/, August 23, 2021.
[281] Clarke, Adam. *Commentary on the Bible.* (1831), John 6:44.
[282] Ibid.
[283] Criswell, W. A. "Changing Lives" (July 27), DailyWord@w.a.criswell.com, accessed July 27, 2021.
[284] *Barnes Notes on the Bible,* John 6:44.
[285] https://www.goodreads.com/quotes/566071-the-very-first-evidence-of-awakening-grace-is-dissatisfaction-with, accessed July 19, 2021.

---

[286] These quotes are from the sermon booklet, Predestined for Hell? Absolutely Not!, by Adrian Rogers, Love Worth Finding, P.O. Box 38800, Memphis, TN 38183-0300, (lwf.org); 1999; 2010. 901/382-7900.

[287] https://www.christianquotes.info/top-quotes/20-awesome-quotes-salvation/#ixzz50m1vi2ED, accessed December 9, 2017.

[288] Lee, R. G. *The Name Above Every Name.* Christ for the World Publishers; Revell, 1938.

[289] Lee, R. G. Lee, *God's Answer to Man's Question.* Zondervan, 1962.

[290] Rice, J. R. "Hyper-Calvinism: A False Doctrine." https://www.sermonindex.net/modules/articles/index.php?view=article&aid=10550, accessed July 19, 2021.

[291] Spurgeon, C. H. "The Silver Trumpet" (Sermon delivered March 24, 1861). Text, Isaiah 1:18.

[292] Ibid.

[293] Bunyan, John. *The Commemorative Edition of the Works of John Bunyan,* Volume 2. (London: The London Printing and Publishing Company, 1859), 1206.

[294] Spurgeon, Spurgeon, C. H. *Morning and Evening,* October 22 (Morning).

[295] Lucado, Max. "The Gospel of Second Chances," Maxlucado.com, accessed July 19, 2021.

[296] Ibid.

[297] https://www.christianquotes.info/quotes-by-topic/quotes-about-restoration/, accessed May 13, 2021.

[298] Spence-Jones, H. D. M. (Ed.). *First Peter.* (London; New York: Funk & Wagnalls Company, 1909), 222.

[299] Jeremiah, David. "Grace—Land of Opportunity." www.oneplace.com, accessed July 17, 2021.

[300] Chambers, Oswald. *My Utmost for His Highest.* February 18.

[301] https://www.christianquotes.info/quotes-by-topic/quotes-about-grace/, accessed July 20, 2021.

[302] Exell, J. S. *The Biblical Illustrator,* Matthew 5:7.

[303] *Barnes Notes on the Bible,* Matthew 5:7.

[304] Henry, M. *Matthew Henry's Commentary on the Whole Bible: Complete and Unabridged in One Volume.* (Peabody: Hendrickson, 1994), 975.

[305] Clarke, Adam. *Commentary on the Bible.* (1831), Matthew 5:7.

[306] Vincent, M. R. *Word Studies in the New Testament* (Vol. 3) (New York: Charles Scribner's Sons, 1887), 322.

[307] *Holy Bible: A Translation from the Latin Vulgate.*

308 Spence-Jones, H. D. M. (Ed.). *Second Corinthians.* (London; New York: Funk & Wagnalls Company, 1909), 144.

309 *Matthew Henry Commentary,* 2 Corinthians 6:1.

310 Plumer, W. S. *Studies in the Book of Psalms: Being a Critical and Expository Commentary, with Doctrinal and Practical Remarks on the Entire Psalter.* (Philadelphia; Edinburgh: J. B. Lippincott Company; A & C Black, 1872), 772.

311 Hindson, E. E., and W. M. Kroll (Eds.). *KJV Bible Commentary* (Nashville: Thomas Nelson, 1994), 2350.

312 *Matthew Henry Commentary,* 2 Corinthians 6:2.

313 Ironside, H. A. *Notes on the Book of Proverbs.* (Neptune, NJ: Loizeaux Bros., 1908), 24–25.

314 Spurgeon, C. H. "Fresh Grace Confidently Expected." (Sermon delivered July 20, 1873). https://www.ccel.org/ccel/spurgeon/sermons19.xxxiv.html, accessed July 23, 2021.

315 Ferguson, S. B. *By Grace Alone: How the Grace of God Amazes Me.* (Lake Mary, FL: Reformation Trust Publishing, 2010), xiv.

316 Henry, M. *Matthew Henry's Commentary on the Whole Bible: Complete and Unabridged in One Volume.* (Peabody: Hendrickson, 1994), 872.

317 Wuest, K. S. *Wuest's Word Studies from the Greek New Testament for the English Reader* (Vol. 4). (Grand Rapids: Eerdmans, 1997), 94.

318 Henry, M. *Matthew Henry's Commentary on the Whole Bible: Complete and Unabridged in One Volume.* (Peabody: Hendrickson, 1994), 2312.

319 Spurgeon, C. H. *Prayers from Metropolitan Pulpit: C. H. Spurgeon's Prayers,* 1906.

320 *Maclaren 's Expositions,* 1 Timothy 2:8.

321 Exell, J. S. *The Biblical Illustrator: St. John* (Vol. 1). (London: James Nisbet & Co.), 66.

322 Spence-Jones, H. D. M. (Ed.). *Acts of the Apostles* (Vol. 1). (London; New York: Funk & Wagnalls Company, 1909), 443.

323 Ibid., 440.

324 Ibid., 443.

325 Henry, M., and T. Scott. *Matthew Henry's Concise Commentary.* (Oak Harbor, WA: Logos Research Systems, 1997), Acts 14:3.

326 Morgan, Richard, Howard, and John. "G. Campbell Morgan: Preaching in the Shadow of Grace." https://www.preaching.com/articles/past-masters/g-campbell-morgan-preaching-in-the-shadow-of-grace/, accessed August 11, 2021.

327 Barnes, Albert. *Notes on the Bible.* (1834), 1 John 2:19.

[328] Swindoll, Chuck. "Claiming the Package." Today's Insight: February 9, 2013. https://www.oneplace.com/devotionals/todays-insight-from-chuck-swindoll/todays-insight-february-910-2013-11686823.html, accessed July 30, 2021.

[329] https://twitter.com/TheMoodyChurch/status/1276154361647947777, June 25, 2020, accessed July 30, 2021.

[330] Pink, A. W. The Attributes of God. (Grand Rapids: Baker Books, 1975), 85.

[331] www.azquotes.com, accessed July 30, 2021.

[332] Murray, Andrew. The Ministry of Intercession. (Springdale, PA: Whitaker House, 1982), 68.

[333] https://quotefancy.com/quote/73101/Max-Lucado-When-grace-moves-in-guilt-moves-out, accessed July 30, 2021.

[334] Dixon, Francis. "The Birth and Growth of a Child of God." (Bournemouth, England: Lansdowne Bible School and Postal Fellowship, April 25, 1967), Study #12, 2 Peter Series.

[335] Piper, John. "Grace Is Pardon—and Power!" (devotional). https://www.desiringgod.org/articles/grace-is-pardon-and-power, accessed July 30, 2021.

[336] Watson, Thomas. The Beatitudes, Or a Discourse Upon Part of Christ's Famous Sermon on the Mount. (London, 1671), 173.

[337] Spurgeon, C. H. 2,200 Quotations: From the Writings of Charles H. Spurgeon: Arranged Topically or Textually and Indexed by Subject, Scripture, and People. (T. Carter, Ed.). (Grand Rapids, MI: Baker Books, 1995), 87.

[338] Augustine. Confessions, 245.

[339] The Christian Treasury, (Contributions from Ministers and Members). (London: Groombridge and Son, 1868).

[340] MacArthur, John. Sufficient Grace from Our Sufficiency in Christ. (Wheaton, Illinois: Crossway Books, a division of Good News Publishers, 1991), 243. www.crosswaybooks.org.

[341] The New International Commentary on the New Testament, Paul's Second Epistle to the Corinthians. (Eerdmans, 1962), 451. www.eerdmans.com

[342] Calvin's New Testament Commentaries, The First Epistle of Paul to the Corinthians. (Eerdmans Publishing Co., 1960), 317–318.

[343] Ryle, J. C. Holiness. (Chicago: Moody Publishers, 2010), 54.

[344] Jones, Martyn Lloyd. The Cross. (Crossway, 1986), 75.

[345] Exell, J. S. The Biblical Illustrator: Romans (Vol. 1). (New York; Chicago; Toronto; London; Edinburgh: Fleming H. Revell Company), 607.

[346] MacArthur, J. 1, 2, 3 John. (Chicago, IL: Moody Publishers, 2007), 70.

[347] Maclaren, Alexander. *Exposition of Holy Scriptures,* 108.

[348] Spurgeon, C. H. "The Sweet Uses of Adversity," (Sermon delivered November 13, 1859).

[349] Wuest, K. S. *Wuest's Word Studies from the Greek New Testament for the English Reader* (Vol. 11). (Grand Rapids: Eerdmans, 1997), 131.

[350] *Barnes Notes on the Bible,* 1 Peter 5:10.

[351] Bengel, Johann. *Ellicott's Commentary for English Readers,* 1 Peter 5:10.

[352] Arichea, D. C. and E. A. Nida, *A Handbook on the First Letter from Peter.* (New York: United Bible Societies, 1980), 171.

[353] Barclay, W. (Ed.). *The Letters of James and Peter.* (Philadelphia: Westminster John Knox Press, 1976), 274.

[354] *Barnes Notes on the Bible,* 1 Peter 5:10.

[355] Clarke, Adam. *Commentary on the Bible.* (1831), 1 Peter 5:10.

[356] Barclay, W. (Ed.). *The Letters of James and Peter.* (Philadelphia: Westminster John Knox Press, 1976), 274.

[357] Wiersbe, W. W. *The Bible Exposition Commentary* (Vol. 2). (Wheaton, IL: Victor Books, 1996), 434.

[358] MacArthur, J., Jr. (Ed.). *The MacArthur Study Bible* (electronic ed.). (Nashville, TN: Word Pub, 1997), 1949.

[359] Wuest, K. S. *Wuest's Word Studies from the Greek New Testament for the English Reader* (Vol. 11). (Grand Rapids: Eerdmans, 1997), 132.

[360] Spurgeon, C. H. *Morning and Evening,* February 18 (Morning).

[361] Jamieson, R.; A. R. Fausset; and D. Brown. *Commentary Critical and Explanatory on the Whole Bible* (Vol. 2) (Oak Harbor, WA: Logos Research Systems, Inc., 1997), 312.

[362] Exell, J. S. *The Biblical Illustrator: 2 Corinthians.* (New York; Chicago; Toronto; London; Edinburgh: Fleming H. Revell Company), 374.

[363] Ibid, 376.

[364] Spence-Jones, H. D. M. (Ed.). *Second Corinthians.* (London; New York: Funk & Wagnalls Company, 1909), 200.

[365] Wiersbe, W. W. *The Bible Exposition Commentary* (Vol. 1). (Wheaton, IL: Victor Books, 1996), 655.

[366] Exell, J. S. *The Biblical Illustrator: 2 Corinthians.* (New York; Chicago; Toronto; London; Edinburgh: Fleming H. Revell Company), 374.

[367] Spence-Jones, H. D. M. (Ed.). *First Peter.* (London; New York: Funk & Wagnalls Company, 1909), 184.

[368] https://www.christianquotes.info/top-quotes/15-impactful-quotes-about-approval-and-fitting-in/, accessed August 3, 2021.

[369] Exell, J. S. *The Biblical Illustrator: Isaiah* (Vol. 3). (New York; Chicago; Toronto; London; Edinburgh: Fleming H. Revell Company), 18.

370 Ibid.

371 Simeon, C. *Horae Homileticae: Galatians-Ephesians* (Vol. 17). (London: Holdsworth and Ball, 1833), 298.

372 Spurgeon, C. H. "All of Grace" (Sermon #3479), published October 7, 1915. https://www.blueletterbible.org/Comm/spurgeon_charles/ sermons/3479.cfm, accessed June 19, 2021.

373 *Essential Works of Charles Spurgeon.* (Barbour Publishing, Inc., 2009), Chapter 7.

374 Spence-Jones, H. D. M. (Ed.). *Ephesians.* (London; New York: Funk & Wagnalls Company, 1909), 63.

375 Exell, J. S. *The Biblical Illustrator*, Romans 5:2.

376 Spurgeon, C. H. *Our Own Hymnbook,* (compilation). (Texas: Pilgrim Publications, 1866, 2nd Ed., 2002).

377 Tan, P. L. *Encyclopedia of 7700 Illustrations: Signs of the Times.* #5406.

378 Exell, J. S. *The Biblical Illustrator: 2 Kings.* (New York; Chicago; Toronto; London; Edinburgh: Fleming H. Revell Company), 89.

379 Ibid., 92.

380 J. C. Ryle. Calvary. Revival-Library, October 16, 2020. https://www. facebook.com/RevivalLibraryPage/posts/calvary-j-c-ryleyou-probably- know-that-calvary-was-a-place-close-to-jerusalem-wh/ 3419627141595234/, accessed August 5, 2021.

381 Spurgeon, C. H. "I Thought" (sermon delivered May 17, 1874), https://www.spurgeon.org/resource-library/sermons/i-thought/ #flipbook/, accessed August 5, 2021.

382 www.whatchristianswanttoknow.com/top-24-hudson-taylor-quotes/ #ixzz6vcV0DRbW, accessed May 22, 2021.

383 John Piper. What is Grace? (interview), https://www.desiringgod.org/ interviews/what-is-grace, accessed May 19, 2021.

384 https://www.azquotes.com/quote/773274, accessed December 4, 2021.

385 Westcott, B. F. (Ed.). *The Epistle to the Hebrews: The Greek Text with Notes and Essays* (3rd ed.). (London: Macmillan, 1903), 110.

386 C. H. Spurgeon. "Christ's Prayer for Peter" (Sermon delivered April 30, 1899). https://www.ccel.org/ccel/spurgeon/sermons45.xviii.html, accessed September 29, 2021.

387 Exell, J. S. *The Biblical Illustrator: 1 Corinthians* (Vol. 2). (New York: Anson D. F. Randolph & Company), 41.

388 Wiersbe, W. W. *Wiersbe's Expository Outlines on the New Testament.* (Wheaton, IL: Victor Books, 1992), 449.

389 Courson, J. (2003). Jon Courson's Application Commentary (p. 1058). Nashville, TN: Thomas Nelson.

390 George, T. *Galatians,* (Vol. 30). (Nashville: Broadman & Holman Publishers, 1994), 359.

391 *Criswell Study Bible,* Galatians 5:4.

392 MacArthur, J., Jr. (Ed.). *The MacArthur Study Bible* (electronic ed.). (Nashville, TN: Word Pub, 1997), 1797.

393 Jamieson, R.; A. R. Fausset; and D. Brown. *Commentary Critical and Explanatory on the Whole Bible* (Vol. 2) (Oak Harbor, WA: Logos Research Systems, Inc., 1997), 336.

394 Spurgeon, C. H. "A Seasonable Exhortation" (sermon delivered July 11, 1886). https://www.spurgeon.org/resource-library/sermons/a-seasonable-exhortation/, accessed August 11, 2021.

395 Ibid.

396 MacArthur, J., Jr. (Ed.). *The MacArthur Study Bible* (electronic ed.). (Nashville, TN: Word Pub, 1997), 1940.

397 Henry, M., and T. Scott. *Matthew Henry's Concise Commentary.* (Oak Harbor, WA: Logos Research Systems, 1997), 1 John 2:19.

398 *Barnes Notes on the Bible,* Ephesians 4:7.

399 Spurgeon, C. H. *Morning and Evening,* July 18 (Evening).

400 *Barnes Notes on the Bible,* 2 Corinthians 1:12.

401 Simeon, C. *Horae Homileticae: 1 and 2 Corinthians* (Vol. 16). (London: Holdsworth and Ball, 1833), 401.

402 Exell, J. S. *The Biblical Illustrator: 2 Corinthians.* (New York; Chicago; Toronto; London; Edinburgh: Fleming H. Revell Company), 24.

403 *Matthew Henry's Concise Bible Commentary,* 2 Corinthians 6:1–10.

404 Chambers, Oswald. *My Utmost for His Highest,* May 16.

405 Exell, J. S. *The Biblical Illustrator: Second Timothy, Titus, Philemon* (Vol. 2). (New York; Chicago; Toronto; London; Edinburgh: Fleming H. Revell Company), 93.

406 *Barnes Notes on the Bible,* Titus 2:11.

407 Clarke, Adam. *Commentary on the Bible.* (1831), Titus 2:12.

408 Henry, M. *Matthew Henry's Commentary on the Whole Bible: Complete and Unabridged in One Volume.* (Peabody: Hendrickson, 1994), Titus 2:12–3.

409 Exell, J. S. *The Biblical Illustrator,* 2 Thessalonians 2:16. "The Inspiration of Hope," Thomas Watson.

410 Exell, J. S. *The Biblical Illustrator: Thessalonians* (Vol. 2). (New York; Chicago; Toronto; London; Edinburgh: Fleming H. Revell Company), 69.

411 Exell, J. S. *The Biblical Illustrator,* 2 Thessalonians 2:16. "Good Hope Through Grace," J. C. Miller.

412 Barclay, W. (Ed.). *The Letter to the Romans.* (Philadelphia: The Westminster John Knox Press, 1975), 75.

[413] Henry, M. *Matthew Henry's Commentary on the Whole Bible: Complete and Unabridged in One Volume*. (Peabody: Hendrickson, 1994), 744.

[414] Ironside, H. A. *Studies in Book One of the Psalms*. (New York: Loizeaux Brothers, 1951), Psalm 1.

[415] Simeon, C. *Horae Homileticae: Romans* (Vol. 15). (London: Holdsworth and Ball, 1833), 117.

[416] Ironside, H. A. *Studies in Book One of the Psalms*. (New York: Loizeaux Brothers, 1951), Psalm 1.

[417] https://quotefancy.com/quote/863495/Martin-Luther-The-sin-underneath-all-our-sins-is-to-trust-the-lie-of-the-serpent-that-we, accessed August 30, 2021.

[418] https://www.christianquotes.info/quotes-by-topic/quotes-about-doubt/, accessed August 20, 2021.

[419] https://www.christianquotes.info/top-quotes/18-powerful-quotes-trust/#ixzz5Dj8gaFH7, accessed April 25, 2018.

[420] Spurgeon, C. H. *Morning and Evening,* May 23.

[421] *Barnes Notes on the Bible,* Psalm 20:7.

[422] Perowne, J. J. S. *The Book of Psalms: A New Translation, with Introductions and Notes, Explanatory and Critical,* (Fifth Edition, Revised, Vol. 1). (London; Cambridge: George Bell and Sons; Deighton Bell and Co., 1883), 239.

[423] Plumer, W. S. *Studies in the Book of Psalms: Being a Critical and Expository Commentary, with Doctrinal and Practical Remarks on the Entire Psalter*. (Philadelphia; Edinburgh: J. B. Lippincott Company; A & C Black, 1872), 273.

[424] https://www.christianquotes.info/top-quotes/18-powerful-quotes-trust/#axzz5Dj7VIZNh, accessed April 25, 2018.

[425] https://www.christianquotes.info/quotes-by-topic/quotes-about-doubt/, accessed August 20, 2021.

[426] https://www.brainyquote.com/quotes/saint_augustine_121380?src=t_faith, accessed December 4, 2021.

[427] Spurgeon, C. H. "Divine Love and Its Gifts" (Sermon delivered February 15, 1873). https://www.spurgeon.org/resource-library/sermons/divine-love-and-its-gifts/#flipbook/, accessed August 20, 2021.

[428] Being Trustworthy, APRIL 20, 2001. _https://www.ligonier.org/learn/devotionals/being-trustworthy, accessed August 19, 2021.

[429] Graham, Billy. *World Aflame*. (Doubleday, 1965).

[430] Hiebert, D. Edmond. *The Expositor's Bible Commentary,* Frank Gaebelein (ed.). (Zondervan), 11:439.

[431] Elliot, Elizabeth. *Shadow of the Almighty.* (New York: HarperCollins, 1979), 110.

[432] Bruce, F. F. *The Gospel and Epistles of John.* (Grand Rapids, MI: William B. Eerdmans Publishing Company, 1983), 43.

[433] Ibid.

[434] Henry, M. *Matthew Henry's Commentary on the Whole Bible: Complete and Unabridged in One Volume.* (Peabody: Hendrickson, 1994), 1918.

[435] Spurgeon, C. H. "Grace for Grace." (Sermon delivered May 19, 1889). https://www.spurgeongems.org/sermon/chs2087.pdf, accessed August 31, 2021.

[436] Exell, J. S. *The Biblical Illustrator: St. John* (Vol. 1). (London: James Nisbet & Co.), 66.

[437] Ibid.

[438] Simeon, C. *Horae Homileticae: Luke XVII to John XII* (Vol. 13). (London: Holdsworth and Ball, 1833), 209–210.

[439] Exell, J. S. *The Biblical Illustrator: Romans* (Vol. 1). (New York; Chicago; Toronto; London; Edinburgh: Fleming H. Revell Company), 434.

[440] Spurgeon, C. H. "The Perpetuity of the Law of God," (sermon #1660).

[441] Baptist Press. Junior Hill Cites Stats, Gives Counsel for Addressing "Itching-Ear Generation," November 03, 2000.

[442] Pink, Arthur W. Ed. *Studies in the Scriptures,* Volume 7. (York, PA: March, 1934), 69.

[443] Spurgeon, Charles. *Faith's Checkbook,* May 14.

[444] *Barnes Notes on the Bible,* Titus 3:5.

[445] Spurgeon, C. H. "It is Finished," (Sermon # 421, 1861). http://www.spurgeongems.org/vols7-9/chs421.pdf, accessed December 1, 2014.

[446] Hutson, Curtis. "Repentance: What Does the Bible Teach?," http://www.jesus-is-savior.com, accessed November 19, 2013.

[447] Spurgeon, C. H. *The Soul Winner.* (Whitaker House), 29.

[448] Gill, John. *Exposition of the Entire Bible.* (1746-63), Romans 7:18.

[449] Henry, M., and T. Scott. *Matthew Henry's Concise Commentary.* (Oak Harbor, WA: Logos Research Systems, 1997), Galatians 1:5.

[450] Spurgeon, C. H. *Morning and Evening,* February 3 (Evening).

[451] Spurgeon, C. H. "The Christ-Given Rest," (Sermon delivered March 5, 1893). https://www.spurgeon.org/resource-library/sermons/the-christ-given-rest/#flipbook/, accessed July 27, 2021.

[452] https://biblereasons.com/grace/, accessed July 28, 2021.

[453] Wiersbe, W. W. *The Bible Exposition Commentary* (Vol. 2). (Wheaton, IL: Victor Books, 1996), 433.

[454] *Cambridge Bible for Schools and Colleges,* Colossians 4:6.

[455] Clarke, Adam. *Commentary on the Bible.* (1831), 1 Peter 4:10.

[456] Spurgeon, C. H. "The Treasure of Grace," (Sermon delivered January 22, 1866). https://www.gracegems.org/Spurgeon/treasure_of_grace.htm, accessed August 29, 2021.

[457] Criswell, W. A. *The Criswell Study Bible,* Mark 15: 15.

[458] Eusebius. *Ecclesiastical History, Book 4,* chap. 15.

[459] Morgan, R. J. Nelson's Annual Preacher's Sourcebook, (2004 Edition). (Nashville, TN: Thomas Nelson Publishers, 2004), 103.

[460] Spurgeon, C. H. "The Treasury of Grace," (Sermon delivered January 22, 1866). https://www.gracegems.org/Spurgeon/treasure_of_grace.htm, accessed August 29, 2021.

[461] Barnes, Albert. *Notes on the Bible.* (1834), Jude 1.

[462] Spurgeon, C. H. "The Treasury of Grace," (Sermon delivered January 22, 1866). https://www.gracegems.org/Spurgeon/treasure_of_grace.htm, accessed August 29, 2021.

[463] *Preaching Magazine,* July 9, 2018, "Illustrations." https://preaching.org/pm_illustrations/truth/, accessed May 7, 2021.

[464] Ironside, H. A. *Notes on the Book of Proverbs.* (Neptune, NJ: Loizeaux Bros., 1908), 414–415.

[465] Lawson, George. Proverbs 29:1.

[466] Bridges, Charles. *Proverbs,* 556.

[467] https://quotepark.com/quotes/1834603-john-webster-i-know-death-hath-ten-thousand-several-doors-for/, accessed December 4, 2021.

[468] Spurgeon, C. H. "Thoughts on the Last Battle," (Sermon No. 23). *New Park Street Pulpit,* Volume 1. May 13, 1855.

[469] Spurgeon, C. H. "Abounding Grace," (Sermon delivered March 22, 1863), accessed September 1, 2021.

[470] Henry, M. *Matthew Henry's Commentary on the Whole Bible: Complete and Unabridged in One Volume.* (Peabody: Hendrickson, 1994), Luke 19:10.

[471] Spurgeon, C. H. "Abounding Grace," (Sermon delivered March 22, 1863), accessed September 1, 2021.

[472] Exell, J. S. *The Biblical Illustrator: 2 Corinthians.* (New York; Chicago; Toronto; London; Edinburgh: Fleming H. Revell Company), 258.

[473] Ibid., 260.

[474] MacArthur, J., Jr. (Ed.). *The MacArthur Study Bible* (electronic ed.). (Nashville, TN: Word Pub, 1997), 1947.

[475] Wuest, K. S. *Wuest's Word Studies from the Greek New Testament for the English Reader* (Vol. 11). (Grand Rapids: Eerdmans, 1997), 116.

[476] MacDonald, W. *Believer's Bible Commentary: Old and New Testaments,* (A. Farstad, Ed.). (Nashville: Thomas Nelson, 1995), 2277.

477 Spence-Jones, H. D. M. (Ed.). *First Peter*. (London; New York: Funk & Wagnalls Company, 1909), 173.

478 Schreiner, T. R. *1, 2 Peter, Jude,* (Vol. 37,). (Nashville: Broadman & Holman Publishers, 2003). 214.

479 Smith, James. *Handfuls of Purpose,* Series Two. (Hendrickson Publications, 2004), 288.

480 MacArthur, John. "True Marks of Saving Faith," May 2, 1982. https://www.gty.org/library/sermons-library/45-32B/true-marks-of-saving-faith, accessed September 1, 2021.

481 Ibid.

482 https://gracequotes.org/author-quote/e-m-bounds/, accessed September 2, 2021.

483 Bounds, E. M. *Power Through Prayer*. (Chicago: Moody Press, 2009), 52.

484 Ibid, 39–40.

485 https://wmpl.org/quote/the-one-concern-of-the-devil/, accessed September 2, 2021.

486 *The Cambridge Bible for Schools and Colleges*, 1 Corinthians 1:4.

487 Thiselton, A. C. *The First Epistle to the Corinthians: A Commentary on the Greek Text*. (Grand Rapids, MI: W.B. Eerdmans, 2000), 90.

488 Gill, John. *Exposition of the Entire Bible*. (1746-63), I Corinthians 1:4.

489 Ibid.

490 MacArthur, J., Jr. (Ed.). *The MacArthur Study Bible* (electronic ed.). (Nashville, TN: Word Pub, 1997), 1709.

491 Spurgeon, C. H. "Christ's Death and Ours," (Sermon delivered February 14, 1869). https://www.spurgeongems.org/sermon/chs3024.pdf, accessed September 2, 2021.

492 Wuest, K. S. *Wuest's Word Studies from the Greek New Testament for the English Reader* (Vol. 2). (Grand Rapids: Eerdmans, 1997), 81.

493 Exell, J. S. *The Biblical Illustrator: Romans* (Vol. 1). (New York; Chicago; Toronto; London; Edinburgh: Fleming H. Revell Company), 369.

494 Ibid., 371.

495 Spence-Jones, H. D. M. (Ed.). *The Pulpit Commentary: Romans*. (London; New York: Funk & Wagnalls Company, 1909), 143.

496 Henry, M. *Matthew Henry's Commentary on the Whole Bible: Complete and Unabridged in One Volume*. (Peabody: Hendrickson, 1994), 2348.

497 Aldrich, Willard Maxwell. "Satan's Attempt to Keep Christ from the Cross," *Bibliotheca Sacra* (BSAC 102:408 (Oct 1945)). Excerpt from the introduction.

[498] Henry, M. *Matthew Henry's Commentary on the Whole Bible: Complete and Unabridged in One Volume.* (Peabody: Hendrickson, 1994), 2315.

[499] Clarke, Adam. *Commentary on the Bible.* (1831), 2 Corinthians 2:15.

[500] Gill, John. *Exposition of the Entire Bible.* (1746-63), 2 Corinthians 2:15.

[501] Spurgeon, C. H., Morning and Evening, October 1 (Evening).

[502] Lockyer, Herbert. *Seasons of the Lord: 365-Day Devotional.* (New Kensington, PA: Whitaker House, 1990), August 15.

[503] Spurgeon, C. H., Morning and Evening, October 1 (Evening).

[504] Spurgeon, C. H. "A Feast for the Upright," (Sermon delivered May 14, 1882). https://www.spurgeon.org/resource-library/sermons/a-feast-for-the-upright/#flipbook/, accessed October 2, 2021.

[505] Exell, J. S. *The Biblical Illustrator: The Psalms,* (Vol. 3,). (New York; Chicago; Toronto; London; Edinburgh: Fleming H. Revell Company; Francis Griffiths, 1909), 481.

[506] Spurgeon, C. H. "Sovereign Grace and Man's Responsibility," (Sermon delivered August 1, 1858. https://www.spurgeon.org/resource-library/sermons/sovereign-grace-and-mans-responsibility/#flipbook/, accessed July 11, 2021.

[507] Barclay, Wm. *The Letters to Ephesians and Galatians,* Ephesians 1:14.

[508] Exell, J. S. *The Biblical Illustrator: Romans* (Vol. 1). (New York; Chicago; Toronto; London; Edinburgh: Fleming H. Revell Company), 440.

[509] Piper, John. "Sustained by All His Grace: Unpacking the Master Planning Team Document," October 29, 1995.

[510] Ritzema, E., and E. Vince (Eds.). *300 Quotations for Preachers from the Puritans.* (Bellingham, WA: Lexham Press, 2013).

[511] Piper, John. "Sustained by All His Grace: Unpacking the Master Planning Team Document," October 29, 1995.

[512] Simeon, C. *Horae Homileticae: Psalms, LXXIII–CL* (Vol. 6). (London: Holdsworth and Ball, 1833), 270.

[513] Maclaren, Alexander. *Alexander Maclaren's Expositions of Holy Scripture,* "Commentary on Hebrews 4." https://www.studylight.org/commentaries/eng/mac/hebrews-4.html, accessed June 18, 2021.

[514] Ibid.

[515] Ibid.

[516] Needham, George C. *The Life and Labors of Charles H. Spurgeon.* (Boston: D. L. Guernsey, 1887), 7.

www.ingramcontent.com/pod-product-compliance
Lightning Source LLC
Chambersburg PA
CBHW022016090426
42739CB00006BA/164